gimp,

surviving your survival

gimp,

surviving your survival

a memoir

alisa christensen

to Joe

From Alisa

xoxox

iUniverse, Inc.
New York Bloomington Shanghai

gimp, surviving your survival
a memoir

iUniverse books may be ordered through booksellers or by contacting:

iUniverse
1663 Liberty Drive
Bloomington, IN 47403
www.iuniverse.com
1-800-Authors (1-800-288-4677)

Because of the dynamic nature of the Internet, any Web addresses or links contained in this book may have changed since publication and may no longer be valid.

The views expressed in this work are solely those of the author and do not necessarily reflect the views of the publisher, and the publisher hereby disclaims any responsibility for them.

ISBN: 978-0-595-51065-8 (pbk)
ISBN: 978-0-595-61753-1 (ebk)

Printed in the United States of America

July 2004 / Venice Beach, LA

Reading old standbys from Pop to keep from killing myself; Sartre, Camus and Nietzsche the trinity. With Nietzsche it's the Monarch Notes Pop used in the sixties because my brain can't handle straight philosophy anymore. I tried telling Velvet what I was feeling but it came out disjointed, fragile and weedy. Creeping insanity, madness might be better than this.

'…there is a pleasure in being mad
that none but madmen know…'

—Shakespeare I think

Velvet was determined to break my depression, if only for the afternoon. She picked up her friend Bunny and took us to a comfy old restaurant in the marina. Sat by the water and ordered appetizers. Velvet and Bunny had dirty martinis I nursed a glass of Cab. Sociable chitchat. I tried to make it seem as if I was paying attention but most of what I was hearing was 'murmur murmur murmur HAHA murmur…' Don't care about an ex friend hitting on your husband and his appropriate and hilarious response, don't care about the climate in Houston or how many ants are crawling on the windowsill behind us. I try to listen—I want to reconnect with the pack—I love Velvet and her friend is charming. But the mind wanders.

Nietzsche counter's the view that conscious thought is opposed to instinctive behavior. I wonder. Is every apparently logical conclusion simply influenced by the thinker's instincts? Instincts don't often change. What if the thought process has been damaged? Are my instincts intact? I don't think they are I used to be streetwise, now I'm a mark.

Bunny asks if I've seen any good movies. 'Yes. I went to the Nuart and saw the Bukowski documentary.' 'I worked on one last month,' said Velvet. They start talking about documentaries and I drift again.

Camus said since God does not exist and man dies, everything is permissible. One experience is as equal as the next; the only important thing is to acquire

1

them, as many as possible. I love Camus and although I'm not an atheist, he helps ease my perspective. Nothing is good or bad, it just is. I catch myself wandering. Bunny's husband and friend have joined us. They work together and have funny anecdotes about their day. Sunset turning the harbor lavender, sailboats coming in, pelicans parking on the docks. 'I used to live on a boat,' Bunny tells me. 'Mmm…I'd love that.' Peaceful, rocked to sleep by waves.

A twenty something boy came over to our table. I had noticed him earlier; cute, shaggy and stoned. 'I'm sorry to bother you, but what happened to your hand?' 'No bother—I was in a fire.' 'Oh, well, I cut these three fingers off and look at them now,' he held out his hand. You could see where three fingers had been sewed back on. His girlfriend came over, California beautiful and clear-eyed. 'What happened to your hand?' 'Fire, how did you cut you fingers off?' He had our attention. 'Circular saw.' He showed us the motion he was making. Easy to see how it could happen. 'Just wanted to tell you not to give up, I mean, look…' he waved his miracle paw like he didn't quite believe it himself.

That experience was interesting.

Eventually the sun dipped we got chilly and said goodbye. Velvet drove me home and I thanked her for fetching me. Had a puff of spotch and watched The Daily Show. So. I got through another day. No matter what I tell myself before going to sleep, how positive I am how many things will be done tomorrow, its rubbish in the am. I'm going to wake up for the seven hundred and fortieth time in pain. A sinister twisted Groundhog Day, over and over, never ending.

To cheer up I think of Weed Troll and my brother, Kevin. We used to email each other gibberish—nonsense words—one day he sent me…

'…bi-rickie nubbie,
torro torro shim sham
weed troll is sniffin',
the blackberry jam…'

I responded, '…weed troll be dancin' as fast as he can…'

2

The story line started in ninety-nine, a never ending email fish tale about a Weed Troll. Now… when I'm down and troubled and need a helping hand, Weed Troll be dancing as fast as he can! Was feeling doom but I'm smiling as I write this. Silly Weed Troll.

I was injured over two years ago, the week between Christmas and New Years. Tony and I took off for the desert. Moon Tribe was out there and we were going to catch up with them the following evening for New Years Eve, I wanted to dance it in. We drove to Mohave via Joshua Tree as the sun was setting, gold, pink, amber, orange, magic. Drove through a lost settlement, shanty shacks falling apart, forgotten. Stopped and scavenged wood for fire. Found an old homestead, complete with abandoned wind mill, a falling down stock pen and trough. It was getting dark even with a full moon—cloud cover. I climbed up the windmill and looked around. No lights, no other habitations, not even abandoned ones. We were alone. It was beautiful, I had to admit. We had compromised on the outing.

Tony preferred to be alone and it was easier to let him have his way. He was an ex for a lot of reasons but his inability to get along with my friends was always a problem. We had lived together seven years earlier. I wasn't trying to repeat that fiasco, we were relatively normal as buddies. (Harpies as lovers.) Tony had been staying in my guest room for the past month; he'd paid rent and was helping me pack. I was going to Australia for at least a year, leaving by February.

He was sleeping far away from me. He'd found an old box spring, just the rusty wires left, the stuffing long gone. Yuk, I thought. Don't sleep so close to the fire, he said as I was dropping off. Bossy as usual, I ignored him. The fire was long out, a few glowing coals deep in a pit surrounded by rocks.

On a barge with Cypress tree's billowing / I was lying back on Moroccan blankets and pillows. It was a lovely night, full moon, billions of stars, slowly moving down the river. A man was up front, easing his long pole into the water-sand and pulling us along. Quite clearly, I heard my voice say, Get up Right Now or you're going to die. For a split second I considered staying, it was so comfortable. I knew pain would be involved; but fuck it, I woke.

Don't remember much / shock / feet burning! I had to get this shit off my feet! Couldn't escape, twisted tied like rope. Don't remember yelling or even calling out to Tony—shock—didn't realize how hurt I was.

Tony wrapped his sleeping bag around me and put me in the truck. I dug the cell from my purse and hit 911. Far from tower range the call failed. Tony hurriedly packed our stuff and we took off. The sleeping bag had melted and the substance had melded with my skin. My right arm felt like plastic.

We'd driven up a wash at the end of the day, now it was inky black. If we got stuck in the sand, I'd die. Made it to the dirt road and I had him stop so I could go to the bathroom. Climbing back into the truck I noticed the flat part of my left foot separating from the instep. That couldn't be true. Flew to a freeway / speeding, hoping to capture a cop but we were the only car on the road / phone finally worked, I told the operator I had been badly burned and needed the nearest Emergency Room. It was Needles; we were on the California Arizona border.

'I have good insurance and I don't want to die.' My body was shaking wacky jerky movement scary. I told them I'd need air lifting to a hospital with a burn unit. When we pulled into the ER it looked like a double wide trailer. It was white inside too white. Eyes didn't want to be open; when closed I was on a platform in a huge Egyptian sepulcher, I made out walls far in the distance. Lit by sconces, covered in hieroglyphics, they were dark smoky orange, comforting, ancient. I opened my eyes trying to answer questions. 'Where is your Insurance card?' 'In my wallet…' closed my eyes…the platform was going down; I was answering questions from a deep subway. 'Date of birth… was I allergic to any medication?' I could hear Tony on the phone and knew he would get me to a hospital, descending faster those infinite hieroglyphics flying past—mind shutting down all external functions—getting ready for the big fight.

During the early am I was transferred by air to the LAC / USC burn unit. Mind and body disconnected. All I remember clearly the 1st week were the pre-ops. They would reduce my medication enough to wake me up, then have me sign and date waivers and releases with my left hand. 'Press hard, you're making copies.' Shivery old lady hand writing.

'...weed troll is not very short
in fact he's rather tall
weed troll can't go playing
with others at the mall...'

—Weed Troll

My family got there a week later. Everyone was out of the country for the holidays. Memories of them are hands touching and faces coming in out of the shadows for a kiss. Everything was dark, they tried to get me to eat, seemed foreign, couldn't have anything in my mouth. Mid January I was moved from the ICU to the regular ward. Friend was either white or Latin, sixteen or seventeen; a homecoming party / a bonfire / burned her legs. She was getting ready to leave, she was cheerful and it was contagious. She'd sit on the corner of my bed and talk. Friends started to show up—everyone asked what I was working on—freakishly ironic that I was hurt camping.

Dr Carol had graduated from USC a few years earlier. (Emergency Room Medicine.) She was a friend from trapeze. She'd been skiing in CO and showed up when my family did. She became a liaison; she knew most of my surgeons and made sure everyone knew I was her friend. (I wasn't anonymous it was personal.)

Hydro-Therapy was both the favorite and most hellish time of day. My nurses would load me up on pills and disconnect the morphine drip. Transfer me from bed to thin cot with wheels and cart me into a room that smelled like swimming pools and was filled with long metal coffins. Carefully they'd undress my wounds, roll me onto a table that had a winch and pick me up. It was loud, like a construction site, I'd swing over a coffin and get lowered in.

Bliss.

Ariel (the little mermaid) would swim around in the tub with Disney fishes. They'd sing chirping quietly and pastel notes floated around my head. I'd doze while flowers and water lilies would bloom and start crawling over the edge. I was in the Altered States tank floating up to my nose in soothing hallucinations. All too soon the nurses would winch me out and then the torture began—drying me off with soft towels—unbearable.

I had vivid hallucinations; going to party, halfway out of bed when two male orderlies came running in and stopped me. 'I have to go, I'm already late…' I was wearing a black cocktail dress and carrying a small leather pouch. There was something wrong with my shoes however, I couldn't stand up in them and my feet hurt. They put me back in bed. 'You're in the hospital, you're not going anywhere. What day is it? What's your name? You can't walk…you have IV's…' Slowly it dissipated, I was back in my gown, wrapped in miles of bandages and the small leather pouch was my poor right arm. It returned time after time, the incessant need to get out.

'…weed troll is eatin'
a bumble bee pie
weed troll say Elvis
a mighty fine guy…'

—Weed Troll

Friend put pages on his website to let people know what had happened and where I was. Kevin and Tony sent regular e-mail's to a growing list and then posted them online.

Website / January 16th 2002

Kevin here with an update. First of all, I can't begin to thank everyone enough for the support pouring in. You're an amazing group of people. Thank you, thank you, thank you!! I'll try to keep you updated on a regular basis. I know everyone is eager to hear the latest. It's been chaotic but I think we now have a fairly decent e-mail list to begin firing habitual updates.

She went through her 3rd surgery yesterday. Took about 3 hours, mostly additional cleaning with an emphasis on the arm / hand. That area is of big concern & the doctors haven't yet decided on the best method to proceed. After looking at her yesterday, they decided to bring in two additional specialists, a hand surgeon and a plastic surgeon. Today they will look at her hand together & decide the best path. Best-case scenario at this point seems to be they would transplant muscle & tissue from her back, and possibly other areas, to her forearm / hand & attempt to rebuild it. She has some feeling in her fingers & palm, no infection has set-in, and so far she's healing at a rapid pace. So it seems as if they are leaning toward this procedure.

After today, we'll have a pretty good idea of what options she has. A friend of Alisa's, Dr Carol, arrived & will be talking with the surgeons before & after they look at her. I'll pass along her comments next round. She woke up about 3 hours after the operation yesterday and was surprisingly lucid. The doctors were pleased with this, because after the previous operations, she would sleep / rest for several days. She has become increasingly more alert just over the last couple of days. They typically do procedures in the morning hours, and she's trying to sleep at night. I would suggest sometime between the hours of 2p–8p would be ideal.
She's at:

LA County Hospital / USC Burn Center
12th Floor, Room # 5 (room #12440 for mail)
1200 N. State Street Nurse Station: 323-226-7991

Register on the main floor when you arrive. You'll go through a metal detector & they won't allow any cameras. Sometimes there's not a nurse in her room to coach people on the correct clean room procedure. If you arrive on your own, be sure and wash your hands, put on a gown & wear gloves. Everyone has to wear a mask. All the supplies are just inside the door to her room. A maximum of two people should go inside at one time. Cards & whatever else are OK to send at this time as well. Please send to her PO Box & we'll bring them over when she's alert. Finally, we opened an account to take care of her finances. Thanks so much to those who have already made a contribution. If you would like to contribute, please make checks payable to me & send to Alisa's address in Studio City listed above.—Kev

Kevin and Tony to raised a lot of cash from the stunt community. We're a small incestuous group, if you don't know someone personally there's only one degree of separation. Kevin started a savings account in my name and handled my paper trails for a few years.

> listening to a sexy slow beat
> with a low masculine voice
> saying he's weak for his freak
> what is this?
> none of your business

Tricky is the sexiest musician alive
to me.

Ahhh Tricky. Maxinquale is my favorite CD of his and makes me think of Wayne. Camping at Agnes Point, starry night fire toasty low, car door open and Maxinquale playing over and over. I went down under after 911. What to do? What to do with the rest of my life. Stunts are fun and adrenaline is addictive but it's a young woman's game. You take heavy hits once in awhile. Recovery is easy in your twenties but I was thirty-seven. I always wrote and in 1995 I started directing and producing. I'd had small but confidence building successes. I wasn't going to give up stunts completely but I wanted it to become a secondary income.

No one was traveling the month after 911 and I could fly on my brothers buddy pass. (Ross is a pilot.) I hadn't been to the South Pacific since 1996 and I had never been to Australia. I went to Hawaii and Guam first. I love to spend time with my nephews. Kids grow so fast; suddenly the enchanted years are gone. I wanted to be good memories from childhood. Right before I left Guam we were all out on the boat snorkeling. I was stung on the back by a jelly fish. I felt the whip like sting then I started to foam at the mouth! We were all surprised it happened so fast. (If you've seen the Friends episode, pee doesn't work. We had little Nephew pee in a bottle—bless his heart, no performance anxiety—but felt no relief as it poured down my back.) Zoomed to Guam's joke ER and learned that there isn't much to do for jelly fish stings. Shot of steroids and a Benadryl Valium cocktail. Ride it out.

There was only one Continental flight to Cairns every other week, so I flew to OZ the next day. Spent a couple days lounging—trying to ditch the residual jelly hell yuk—then rented a car, bought myself a couple maps and took off for Sydney. I was going to travel over two thousand kilometers, driving a clutch left handed on the wrong side of the road. I had to laugh. I was either going to have fun or kill myself. Stopped at Mission Beach, a cute touristy village, there was a big sign, 'Beware of Jellyfish!' Thanks for the warning! I wasn't going through that again.

I loved OZ the minute I left customs but was beginning to think that maybe I'd be lonely. I'd just spent almost two weeks alone. (Ross and wife working, kids in school.) Long drive, maybe I'd miss having someone to talk to… maybe if I could pick up a hitch hiker… like that guy right there. I watched him jog over, it was hot and his T shirt was tucked in the back pocket of his baggy shorts. Six-pack, crew cut, pierced lip, tattoos. He was Made For Me. As if God looked over and said, oh yea, you two are perfect for each other.

He was heading home, Melbourne, the other side of the country. When we arrived at Airlie Beach nine hours later, we were captivated. While you don't have to have commonality with a lover, you do need it with a cross-country traveling companion. Wayne *was* perfect for me. We thought the same things were funny and tragic, agreed on religion and politics, his personality was open, honest. That he was a good lover was icing. He was a mechanic; he was taking six or seven months to hitch around the country. Things didn't work with his girl, they had a four year old, he was clearing his head. We camped outside, stopped in second hand shops for supplies, two coffee mugs, two forks, candelabra. I'd a learned a lesson from Burning Man years back, when camping, more is more fun. He thought it was cute.

> '...I'm not the smartest guy in the world
> but I'm not a thief
> you remind me
> of who I really am...'
>
> paraphrasing Nickelback

This was our song. It was a hit in heavy rotation when we arrived in Sydney and we both liked. My chest still hurts when I hear it. We took fotos with throwaway cameras and developed them at Hour Marts. Late one night we stayed in a 'Do It Yourself' motel. Slip a credit card into the front door and pick a room from the screen. We woke to Mr Sunshine bringing us a bright new day. Took a few snaps of the funny little room—no flash—and developed them later that week. They were Ominous. A thick white light cut into his head at a slant; down the right side of his face. His jaw. I tried shaking it off but I'd found premonitions in pictures before—I was worried. I left OZ in November and he continued toward Melbourne; hitched a ride from a guy who turned out to be drunk; Wayne ended up in the hospital with a broken Jaw. (Camera malfunction? Or camera prophecy?)

I was startled when he stopped answering email, becoming frantic until he called me from his parents a couple weeks later. Wayne was just as startled when I disappeared the following month. Love is a snuggly blanket / lover disappearing is getting tossed in ice water. My friend Alison sent an Email to Wayne's Yahoo account (the only way to reach him) and told him what had happened but I wasn't able to ask her to do it for months. I was overwhelmed by circumstance.

'...weed troll he like things be smooth
nadda troll like the big deep groove
weed troll like em short and sassy
weed in the weedy like em nisty / nasty...'

—Weed Troll

10

Website / January 20th—2002

Hi Everybody, Kev and Tony here with a quick update. Alisa's situation now is this: Monday she's going to have the 4th operation, starting at 7:30 am and scheduled for 8 hours. The procedure involves taking a long strip of muscle tissue from her back and attaching it microscopically to the blood vessels along her arm. (Flap graph) While the arm is the main focus, her ankles are still very problematic because the exposed tendons keep pushing up and out of the surrounding flesh. At the same time, she needs to keep her feet moving every so often or the Achilles tendons will shrink permanently and 'point' the feet, preventing walking altogether. The latest estimate for her hospital stay is 6–10 weeks, with physical therapy probably taking up the better part of the remainder of the year. Thanks to your support, we have been able to take care of all her obligations in a timely manner so far.

Cards & small items are good, please no flowers. We've had to rotate some items out to keep access clear for the nurses. Thanks again so much for all your continued support! Sorry that we haven't had a chance to speak with everyone directly. We will catch up eventually. As always, please call anytime for info. Thanks again, Tony—Kevin

Dr Carol wrote the following for the web site.

> I know both surgeons well and feel them to be excellent both technically and clinically. They will take her right sided latissimus dorsi and about three parts of her serratus muscle (from her back) and place them on her arm from her elbow to her knuckles on the extensor surface (back) of her arm. They have informed me that after three debridements in the O.R., they are down to the muscles and bones in her hand, her wrist bones are

exposed (radius and ulna) about 3 inches and her olec-ranon (elbow bone) is also exposed.

They will evaluate the possibility for tendon transfers to the thumb and first two fingers in the O.R. on Monday. At this time they do not know. Further scarring as time goes on may make this hand non-functional but she has retained the sensation in her palm and they feel it will be better than a clunky piece of wood hanging off her. If tendon transfers are possible, she will have some grasp possibilities in the future with extensive physical therapy.

They will not place skin over the muscle flap until they are sure it has taken well. Therefore, her back will have a single long incision. The muscles they take will also not cause any disability in the future from their standpoint.

The surgery took ten hours, then back to the ICU for continuous flap monitoring. Woke in wretched pain dying for a drink of water, I asked for it with sign language, I had a breathing tube and they had to refuse. Torture! I couldn't rip the tube out my left hand was tied down, right immovable. I fought until they drugged me submissive. Soldiers and Ninja's coming through the ceiling, rappelling down, crawling up through the floor. The nurses ignored them they must be hallucinations but they're knocking into me, they hurt, they're loud, yelling, firing their guns, the Ninja's whipping stars everywhere. The muscles they took out of my back looked unwieldy sitting on my arm. The nurses used their stethoscopes to make sure blood was still pumping through it. It never looked good.

Website / January 24th 2002

It's been a couple days since the surgery & looks like the flap procedure is not working as expected. Blood flow on the output / drainage side is not adequate & it appears the new tissue is slowly dying. They want to wait a little longer (24–48 hours more) to make any more definite determinations about the extent of flap viability. It's still hard to tell where this is going. There's a chance that only part of the new tissue will need to be removed, salvaging the procedure & allowing her to keep the hand... the doctors appear to be leaning toward a darker outcome however... only time will tell.

It's important for Alisa to maintain a positive attitude right now. She's aware of what's happening, currently fairly awake / alert & obviously frustrated & scared. So if you can, please stop by over the next couple of days with a positive outlook on your face & give support.

~Tony

What I remember most was pain. Until then I'd been able to handle it. The daily bath was excruciating but it was *so good* too, I was able to get past it. This was a different animal. As if all pain medication had been stopped. The room was indigo with horrid white flashes. The pain the soldiers were shooting around was sinister red. I wasn't lying flat but propped to one side, presumably to let my back drain properly, I couldn't stand it. I know my friends were around / someone was being taken out by a Ninja star. Alison told me later that I kept trying to get up, it was disconcerting, I was covered in IV's.

Website / January 25th—2002

Quick update on Alisa's condition. The situation with the muscle flap procedure continues to degrade, as there is not adequate blood flow to sustain the transplanted tissue & it is dying. Her body is starting to really struggle with this added strain & they feel it's time to take some action. Tomorrow (Fri) they're going to operate again, remove the damaged tissue & re-assess her situation. A possibility still exists that enough tissue has survived / started to regenerate, which may allow further steps in an effort to save her arm / hand. Still hard to know where this will end up... At this point, they need to do some exploring and see what they have to work with. She's on heavy narcotics again & in rough shape, so it's probably best to suspend visitation for a few days and let her recover from this next round.

'…I'm sorry it failed,
I've done this surgery hundreds of times.…'

—Doctor Setjermindtoit

He held my left hand in both of his and looked into my eyes. He looked like he was going to cry, he was so concerned about me. I loved him for that; for showing humanity and humility. Doctor Allritini (Plastic and Reconstructive Surgery) had assisted. He'd graduated with Dr Carol and I think having a mutual friend cemented us. He came to express regret as well and I told him the same thing I told Setjermindtoit, 'you did your best, I love you.' I did.

Website / January 27th 2002

She went in for surgery around 9:30am Fri. and it lasted about 3 hours. Upon examining her condition, it was determined the entire flap was not salvageable and they removed all tissue. Infections had started in three areas on the flap and her body was struggling to fight it off. Being immobile for more than 3 weeks now and heavy painkillers were slowly taking a toll as well. It all seems a little like catch 22—they need to give it time to heal, but were running out of time because of infection.

Saturday after surgery her fever broke and she was immediately on the mend. She was awake, alert & amazingly coherent most of the day. Her eyes were focused, crystal clear & she was right there with you. She was so alert; it was wonderful & staggering at the same time. Hands down, this is the best shape she's been in so far. The doctors want to give her a few days to recover. Her body just went through a tremendous shock & she needs to recoup. We're going to assemble with relevant staff on Tuesday & discuss all available options. This discussion will include remaining options for her arm, action still necessary on her feet / legs, as well as possible outpatient needs. She has a time slot scheduled on Thursday for any necessary surgery.

So, now's the time to visit! Thank you for holding off. She was in rough shape a few days back, but she's now ready for friendly faces. Alisa's very aware of her condition, what the future may hold, and the struggle ahead. She was very reflective & tranquil this weekend.... thinking about the transition ahead & how to cope. She needs to hear she'll be OK & that a support network exists for the long run. Please pay a visit & give some love. ~TX Kev

The Burn Unit ICU had the best nurses, RN's, specialists. They made me feel safe, cocooned. I was no longer getting bathed in the coffins, instead it was in bed. It took three hours and was done every day. I'd pick music; usually either Elvis Costello singing Burt Bacharach or Dido, CD's from Alison. They'd start with my feet, spraying them with saline so that the bandages wouldn't stick as they were removed. They'd talk about any yada yada to keep my mind off the endless droning pain. They kept poker about my injuries. I couldn't sit up without help and they never let me look at my wounds uncovered. My back had been 'harvested' for skin grafts, big squares and they itched like mad. When I was turned onto my side to have it washed, it was Heaven! Never did it long enough. Every two or three days they would wash my hair. The arm wasn't touched, fragile and susceptible to infection. They only worked on it under anesthesia. Anguish as my nurses removed the wet sheets and replaced them with dry. It took at least two people, three was preferable. I had IV's in my arm, groin and neck. I was rolled to one side; they'd bunch up the wet sheets, start the new ones and roll me back the other way. By the time I was re-bandaged I was exhausted and usually fell asleep.

County of Los Angeles **Department of Health Services**
GENERAL HOSPITAL

SURGEON DATE OF OPERATION
Dr John Smith January 29, 2002
Resident

ATTENDING
Dr Goodfella

PREOPERATIVE DIAGNOSIS:
Third and fourth degree burns to the right upper extremity; and partial full thickness burns to bilateral lower extremities and perineum.

POST OPERATIVE DIAGNOSIS:
Same as pre-op.

ANESTHESIA:
General endothracheal anesthesia.

INDICATIONS:
The patient is a 37 year old female who has had a complicated hospital course secondary to extensive burn injuries. She is most recently status post failed free tissue transfer to the right upper extremity to attempt wound coverage— the most recent examination reveals these wound beds to be free of active infection.

> (This surgery report is four pages of cutting, pasting and stapling Hideous Frankenstein back together.)

Patent tolerated the procedure well and had no intraoperative complications. She was kept intubated and transferred back to the burn ICU in stable condition.

> NAME: CHRISTIANSON, MELISSA crossed out and spelled correctly by hand.

My name was always a mystery. The first surgery report my name was spelled wrong: Christenson, Alisa

2nd surgery my name was spelled worse, Christenson, Melissa

3rd Alicia Christionson

4th NAME: CHRISTENSON, ELISSA—crossed out and 'Alisa D' written by hand.

'…smoke yo crack big mama
smoke it up so fast
Weed Troll mama feel so bad
her crack it never last…'

—Weed Troll

SAG Residual Checks—Mail Date: Spring 2004

Another day another mental breakdown. SAG stands for the Screen Actors Guild. Residuals used to be directly deposited into my Credit Union account, then they'd mail the check stubs. 'Over or Under $20,' was the game I played while opening them. (Only gross, net was max tax, 42%, not as fun.)

Mouse Hunt / Feature Motion Picture	Total Gross	26.22
Simone: DVD / Feature Motion Picture	Total Gross	70.17
Man On the Moon / Feature Motion Picture	Total Gross	30.23
Deep Cover / Feature Motion Picture	Total Gross	13.74

AFTRA (American Federation of Television and Radio Artists) Residual Check

Mad TV—yrs 1–6   95 / 01   Gross   26.71   (Net 16.06)

Four of the five are over twenty, still they depress. AFTRA / SAG reports them in my monthly bank statement but I hardly open those either. Hard to deal with mail. Alison opens it for me. I drive up to the valley once a week and we have lunch at Vivian's Café. My hut is a teeny Bachelor a block from the hoops in Venice. Daylight hours I go to the beach, have coffee and a smoothie, I'll drive around and do my errands, doctor appointments, hit the gym. But the minute the sun sets I'm done; watching television and smokin' weed.

This minute: 'The Next Action Star' is *great* super trashy 'reality.' Gerry Lively is the DP (the Director of Photography) Kurt Bryant is the stunt coordinator and Victoria Burroughs is the casting director. I know and like all three. Kurt is talented and fun; I loved working for him; safe and playful. He hired me a lot so I recommended / reunited him with a busy film producer I used to date. Work begets work, he was always loyal. Gerry Lively and I worked together in the Philippines and Victoria ran the dog charity I used to volunteer with. The Next Action Star is funny television in a mean vulture way; they take fledgling actors with fragile ego's that are easily swamp-able and have them doing long stunt sequences. Think of a play still in rehearsal—<u>nothing</u> like a real shoot, where a stunt sequence is done in pieces and can take days even months to film. The mean humor suits my mood but it's so bad it'll be gone tomorrow.

Law & Order SVU, I like the Mariska. I agree with my friend Georgene that a show dedicated to misogamy and pedophilia is disturbing on many levels but hey, I like the Mariska.

And The BBC World News, which is US news free of US propaganda. (The UK does more US news than CNN.)

> 'When you witness one of these epoch-making sessions in which nothing ever happens except more vetoes, more referenda, more adjournments, more protocol, more full-dress regalia, more banquets, more airplane trips, more threats, more preparedness, more panic, more hysteria, more stockpiles, more and better bombers, more and more battleships, cruisers, submarines, tanks, flame throwers, you know quite definitely that the millennium is not being ushered in. You know that two lascivious monkeys at the zoo, two monkeys picking fleas off one another's backside, are doing just as good a job.'

—Henry Miller
Big Sur and The Oranges of Hieronymus Bosch

He wrote that in the 50's, could have been yesterday.

More Residual Checks: Spring 2004

Diagnosis Murder / Mind Over Murder	26.10
Man on the Moon / Feature Motion Picture	30.57
The Doors / Feature Motion Picture	11.11
Dharma & Greg / Like Dharma's Totally Got	28.80
Wishmaster II: Evil Never Dies / Feature	12.96
Candyman: Day of The Dead / Feature	22.54
Mulholland Falls / Feature	4.27

I doubled Tracy Nelson once on Diagnosis Murder and again on a quirky dark film 'The Night Caller.' Cool girl, real / cancer survivor. I have good memories of work, it was usually fun and most actors are cool; Nick Nolte, Jim Carrey, George Clooney; all fun and funny. I think residuals are depressing me because there will never be new ones. Slowly depleting memories.

Speaking of actors, three women I've doubled have series right now. Dina Meyer on Point Pleasant, Kelly on The OC and Poppy Montgomery on Without A Trace. I don't miss work but I watch all three shows. Subconscious longing? OC fills my Melrose Placey soap need but I probably wouldn't be working on it, the movie I doubled Kelly on was Candyman 2, she was frosty. Point Pleasant I watch because it's on after The OC. Dina is a good actor and plays a weird psycho but it won't last—they have no production budget— you can see it on the screen. I like Dina even though I hardly ever saw her. (Second unit, the fun unit, miles from the 1st) I doubled her on a couple of films, Nowhere Land and Past Tense.

Without A Trace is the best written, money's being spent, sets are cool. I doubled Poppy on two films; the first one she was a teenager, a Sci-Fi flick called Cold Equation then years later a comedy, This Space Between Us. Without A Trace would be the show to work on, it'll be syndicated; it will pay residuals for a long time. I worked on Hunter for two episodes in 1989. Doubled the lead and played a prostitute, both stunt jobs. I just got two residuals for a buck a piece. (.56 after taxes). So I guess I do miss work, more for peace of mind than anything else.

'...when I was almost done for
because I was almost done for
I began to reflect on this fundamental irrationality of my life—idealism.
It was only sickness that brought me to reason.'

—Nietzsche

Kevin brought this laptop to our parent's home in the fall of 2002. He was worried about me, everyone was. Lost in a foggy quagmire of unreal and surreal, I stared at walls, could barely speak and only in a whisper. 'Try to write, honey...' It was hard to type left handed and depressing that it was so hard; my right arm bandaged and painful lying uselessly on a pillow next to me. (It didn't seem a part of me.) It took an hour or more to write a paragraph. (Thank you, spell check.) I couldn't read yet, so couldn't *re-read* what I'd just written. Some crossed wire in my cranium would put me to sleep within a few minutes. It lasted for a couple years and still turns on occasionally. Maybe since I used to read to make myself sleepy, that's what kicked this particular symptom on overdrive. I couldn't re-read what I'd just written for over a year; it took me a couple weeks to write the following:

September 2002—Smallville, MN

There's service in Smallville run by volunteers, most of them senior citizens, which take you back and forth from the hospital. Oscar was my driver today and he was an interesting 'ol cat. He joined the service in 1946, at seventeen. No combat, the war was over but he did go to the south pacific and saw the Philippines. I was in the Philippines in '96, fifty years after Oscar and we agreed that poor country was messed up.

I was hired to double Robin McKee on a monster movie called DNA. The company needed a jungle. The country side could have been Hawaii but it was covered in litter. If that's where you grew up, never knowing any thing different...who's to say? Maybe I'd throw trash in the street too, but the thought is so alien I can't imagine it. (Not every poor country I've been to is covered with garbage. I don't understand the difference between those that throw trash and those that don't.) The FX guy and I were taking a cab in Manila one day and our driver casually tossed his candy bar wrapper out the window. 'If you did that in LA it would be a thousand dollar fine,' FX said, disgusted. 'Not here, it's OK,' Cabbie assured us. I tried a different approach. 'Think of the Philippines as your home, you wouldn't throw trash in your home, would you?' He smiled in the rear view, 'I live miles away from here.' Silly girl.

While I was there, a smelting plant a few islands away churned its discharge directly into the ocean. There was nothing left alive for a dozen miles around it. The local fishermen were screwed; the government did nothing, collecting payoffs presumably. And the girls—horrifying child abuse—legal and abundant. The papers said one in ten would turn to prostitution but seemed worse. Dance Club's littered Manila, almost every corner was sporting one; girls so young they hadn't even started growing breasts stood around on a stage in bikini's or hooker shorts looking sad. A customer would pay the Mama-San a small fee for their company.

The Heritage Hotel is five stars, beautifully appointed suites with dirty rag covered beggars scratching at the car window before you enter the safety of their property. 'They're faking, tourists are suckers,' said my driver. I believed him; they looked like they came from Central Casting. In my room there was a note on the desk blotter. 'Please inquire as to your guest's age...' Warning their pedophile patrons to ask for an ID (fake of course) to avoid get popped by the police. It was Heartbreaking and it was Everywhere. Pagsanhan, too. (A village we stayed in.) Robin and I would see teenagers leaving our hotel pre-dawn. I don't have a problem with prostitution in theory. It's a victimless crime, in theory. But facts always blow theory. A fifteen year old girl shouldn't be worrying that the fat, fifty year old pig picking her up doesn't want to wear a condom. The young mother of two might tell you she's fine with it but her children won't eat tomorrow unless she sucks dick tonight. Poverty was everywhere but the American film crew was sheltered. We stayed in a refined mountain top resort next to a huge man made lake. An old Marcos retreat I was told. I had a lovely cabana over looking a well kept garden with a view of the lake. I could see a big stone Buddha from my balcony.

'The horror…'
—Apocalypse Now

Channeling Brando. We were on the same river Coppola used in 1979. Helicopters flying, slow motion, The Doors playing The End, Ka BOOM the hill explodes. We came back fifteen years later and blew up the same hill. Hawaii wouldn't let a film crew wreak environmental havoc but in the Philippines everything's for sale.

I made friends with the Visiting Team women on the crew immediately. There were seven of us. Number seven wasn't even on the shoot, Jurgen Procnow (our bad guy) had his girlfriend Birgit join him. We'd climb into the vans pre-dawn and watch beautiful sunrises during the hour long drive down the mountain, meet up with the Home Team at base camp and then take banca boats pushed by cute smiling teenagers up the river. (Robin and I dubbed them The Fabulous Banca Boys.) My actress was a sweetheart and I thanked Buddha for her more times than you could shake a fourteen year old hooker at. It's nice to be around someone who laughs. How could you not? Laugh or cry, cowboy.

There were stray cats around my cabana. Old One Eye and The Twins were the only ones that would come close at first but there were more hiding in the shadows. I started feeding them; cans of tuna from town and my lunches that were suspect. I wasn't vegan back then but I rarely ate meat in the third world, too sad to think it might be dog, cat or horse; I'd seen them skinned and hung in the markets. One afternoon as I was watching The Twins devour what may have been beef and rice, One Eye finally relaxed enough to let me pet her. A couple of guys from the crew were walking by. 'You're getting them fat enough to eat said one, and tame enough to catch!' said Tweedle Dum. They laughed. They were probably right but I fed them anyway. They're hungry now so I'm feeding them now—the future is in flux and will deal with itself.

Our star was Mark Dacascos. (Martial artist and Iron Chef aficionado.) One morning, I had just showered and was waiting around the office for a call from the states. Mark walked past me to go up to accounting—then turned quickly—grabbed me by the shoulders and pulled me to him. Putting his face in the damp hair by my ear he breathed deep and growled softly, 'Mmmm, Woman!' Laughing he apologized and continued up the stairs, saying he was going crazy waiting for his girlfriend. 'No problem,' I had a chuckle; he was a sexy boy and it was nice to see a man not partaking in the flesh fest. The 7 were having breakfast one morning, some of the crew were seated a table over. They were talking about the prostitution and how could the guys who were married with children bla bla… speaking a little too loud seemed contrived. Our set designer swung around and yelled at them, her British accent sounding so cute; 'why don't you shut up and wipe the lipstick off your dicks!'

Radiohead fit my melancholia perfectly

'…the crunch of pigskin
the grime and the screeching
the capitalist occupation
the terror the vomit
the horror the strangulation
God loves his offspring
God loves us…'

paraphrasing Radiohead

Website / January 30th 2002

Hi Everybody, Tony here w / a quick update. Alisa was in surgery once again today, partly because the doctors felt that they hadn't exhausted all avenues yet. During the 7 hours of this surgery (the 6th), they covered the elbow and the ankles w / some sort of temporary, artificial skin, that they hope will promote some more growth of her own tissue.

It is supposed to stay on for 3–5 weeks before being removed and covered w / her own skin. Some areas around her legs have been fixed as well but the main problem is the advanced deterioration of her Achilles tendons. The left one is severed already from being burnt and exposed for 4 weeks now, although they're trying to keep the ankle from 'freezing' by moving it as much as possible. The bottom line is that they want Alisa out of bed as soon as possible but before that they need to cover more of her open wounds. It's OK to go and see her for the rest of the week unless something else un-foreseeable happens. As before, please no flowers and make sure you wash your hands before going in and don't forget the face mask. We have been able to keep any major infections away and would like to keep it that way.

It looks like we are moving along on the apartment front, let us know if you have some spare time and can help out a bit. We would really need somebody who could do some PA work (phones, running some errands etc.) for a few hours a day. Please let us know. Thank you all a million, for your continued support. p&l ~Tony

    NAME: CHRISTENSEN, ELISA

With the E crossed out, replaced with a handwritten A and my middle initial D.

When I woke from this operation, Kevin was sitting by my bedside. Heartbroken. 'They said that your Achilles tendon was split.' He looked like he'd been crying. I was sad for him but I simply didn't believe it. I was used to my doctors being the harbingers of doom. Whatever, I knew my feet would be all right. (Woman's intuition, my Achilles tendons both work.) They had told Kev that my left hoof would be frozen at a ninety degree angle and he pictured me stumping around The Hunch Back of Studio City.

Website / February 4th, 2002

Hi everyone, The doctors are pleased with the way the artificial skin has been taking since the surgery last Thursday. They basically covered all open areas on her ankles, elbow, forearm, and some spots on her legs with [Integra].

There was one small problematic area on the elbow that needed to be redone Friday, but overall it's turning out better than expected. This procedure was somewhat experimental, as they have never grafted such large areas with this new material before. The general ideas is that her body will fill-in & heal up to the bottom surface of this layer, then the artificial layer will be removed in 3–5 weeks and replaced with her own skin.

The ankles are healing fairly well after last Thursday's procedure. The main problem is the continued deterioration of her Achilles tendons. The left one is beyond repair. The right Achilles and other surrounding tendons (on both feet) are critical but could still recover. If she continues to mend without complications she is expected to keep her feet, although it's still an extremely unfavorable situation and much recovery time remains. If the new grafts continue to heal OK, then surgery on her feet is complete for now. Her left foot will heal, fixed around 90 degrees, without mobility. Once she completely heals, it is possible to go back and try to reconstruct the left tendon. This would be down the road however, 1–2 years.

The hand continues to degrade. All surgeons are in agreement that everything possible has been done to save it over the last month, and they are now recommending amputation. Alisa has been discussing this outcome with staff, family and friends for a couple of weeks now and has decided this is the best course. The procedure is scheduled for later in the week—Thurs or Fri. It's becoming increasingly more urgent for her to get out of the hospital. We're praying this agonizing decision to amputate will support a more rapid recovery, as well as sustain the best possible quality of life for her long-term. Alisa is generally awake now but still in / out as expected due to the morphine routine. Visitation over the next couple of days to keep her spirits up would be advantageous. Thanks everyone. ~Kevin

'...I was weary and bitter
with a restless wandering soul
and when I had almost crumbled to dust
you appeared like an angel
and saved me...'

paraphrasing the Thompson Twins

My friends came, tons of them, over and over. An ICU nurse said she'd never seen so many visitors for one person. All big religions weighed in: Buddhist, Jewish, Hindu, Muslim and every kind of Christian. Methodist, Protestant, Born Again, Catholic, Baptist, I can't think of them all, topped off with Agnostics (like me) who pick bits and pieces and toss the hate. All praying for me. Pray away and thank you for doing it too.

Neighbor Friends came to chant. They're Buddhist; Friend started to explain the prayer, noticed me constantly clicking the morphine button and said, 'I'll just tell you where to come in.' She gave me a little book. They did verses and I joined for the chorus. It was long, long, long soothing. I slept when they were done. Even a pack of Evangelicals no one knew started visiting—my wacky Auntie had sent them. She was anxious; if I died, I was going to hell unless I converted to her specific sect. She called a church in Riverside; she was in Phoenix and didn't know how far Riverside was from LA. (Hours down Hwy 10, traffic hell.) I let them Save me whenever they stopped by. Driving in from Riverside and didn't know me from Adam? That's Christian and I appreciated it.

Everyone pray dammit, there's no crying in baseball! I was loved it was tangible tactile. I could see love; teal, pink and lavender waves, a sunset of ocean rolling over me.

Friend Charlene brought her daughter to pray for my arm, Cherish had insisted. I watched her grow up. Charlene Tilton and I met on a pilot called 'White Trash' we played sisters, it was a comedy and it was funny but snaggled up in legal mumble jumble (who owned what) and never got made. Sad, sad but shit like that happens all the time. Charlene and I became friends; we lived six blocks from each other and hung out a lot. (I have to laugh at myself name-dropping. We agreed it was gauche and embarrassing, done by wanna-be's and tourists.)

The doctors at USC had given up on my arm. Just waiting for my fever to break then chop chop. 'Can I stand? Or…' Cherish was looking at my nurses through the glass. 'Whatever you want, they're cool.' They were. She started softly, tenderly but once she got rolling it was evident they had a personal relationship. At one point she was yelling, 'You are not taking This Arm! Do you hear me? No!' She put her hands on me and they were hot, she was fully engaged. I think teenage women can be psychic / powerful when they focus. Maybe that was the last hum of energy that kept my arm from going to the trash as medical waste.

Website—February 6th, 2002

Hi All, Tony here w / a little update. The doctors were all present for a dressing change today and were very enthusiastic about Alisa's condition. The artificial skin (Integra) seems to be doing much better than expected.

The outcome of today's checkup was the decision to wait a little longer (at least until Monday) with any more surgery. I'm naturally all for that, if only to give whatever the healing power is, that seems to be kicking into gear, some time for a chance to do something. Her spirits are very good today; she feels more peaceful and looks very clear. The progress in the last few days has been remarkable (and this comes from the usually very pessimistic doc-s) so while the amputation still seems unavoidable, everything else is so far going very well.

Alisa is very lucid and knows about everything that's going on and is ready to do anything to get out of there. She's happy to see anybody that can make it down there for a visit. Just as a reminder, visiting hours are from 1pm to 8pm in general but they have been very good about letting people stay or come later as well. If you want to bring something she'll enjoy, movies would be it. She watches quite a few these days and if you can leave them for a few days and pick them up your next time there, that would be awesome. The latest estimate for her remaining hospital stay is a minimum of 4–6 weeks, with around 3 surgeries still to come.

[Tony did a few thick paragraphs on the apartment hunt.] We still haven't found a nice place for her once she gets out of the hospital, so we'll put her stuff in storage for now until we find a place. Saturday morning at 11am, we got a truck at the apartment but would definitely appreciate a few people helping w / loading the truck. Please let us know if you can come by for a couple of hours. Thanks to all of you for everything. p&l, Tony

It was hard to get used to being out of control. I told Kevin, Alison, Husband and anyone who else would listen *I didn't want another apartment!* I knew it would be too hard to live alone. Everyone said, 'yes, that's fine honey, whatever...' and continued looking. I thought Tony was pushing it because he was still homeless and planning to force himself into my life again. There was a lot of drama backstage. Everyone was careful not to burden me with bullshit. (Greatly appreciated.) I got confirmation months later that Tony was a big bloated nightmare. No surprise. Mean to my friends, yelling, bullying, going as far as *throwing furniture* at Husband; he was completely ensconced and wasn't going anywhere.

On the one hand, he was there every day, that's huge George don't complain. On the other hand, *he was there every day* the controlling prick, chasing away people that really knew and loved me. Tony had moved out of my place seven years earlier and we did not keep in touch. I let him stay with me that December because I was in love with Wayne—everyone is nicer when they're in love. I could use a little rent and he was helping me move. We were bringing boxes to my friend Moe's pool house.

Tony was a trapeze catcher with a thick German accent when we met. Cut to 1 Year Later: He spoke *almost* flawless English and told people he was born in NYC. He wasn't the man I fell in love with. And his temper, boiling under the façade, was hell to live with. I knew I wanted out of that relationship for months but Tony was ensconced then as well and not leaving easily. I was the idiot paying the bills. I paid his SAG initiation fee, not cheap. He saw how much I was making and wanted to do stunts too. (Christ on a stick.) But he seemed like a natural, I thought if he worked, he'd chip in and pay a few bills. I even bought him a car just to keep him out of mine. He was a prick, it had nothing to do with me, it was his nature. It was my lowest point with a man. I wasn't a victim. Ever. I'd never had a lover scare or scream at me. (He didn't hit but he punched walls and threw things around.) I didn't have a boyfriend anymore, I had surly teenager with expensive tastes. Wasn't sure how it happened but it was a definite turn off. I got a job out of town and slept with an old friend for a few weeks, a Man with a shoulder to lean on. Told Tony about it when I returned. He surprised me and cried real tears. It was a chicken shit way to end a relationship. After he'd been gone for a few years, I started remembering the good things about Tony, his dark sense of humor, his body. Given enough time, I can forgive anyone anything.

When he called looking for a place to stay that December I said yes. It was good to have closure. After spending a month with Tony, I knew I'd made the right decision. His negativity was exhausting and cemented my love for Wayne. I missed Wayne, upbeat, self sufficient Wayne. I couldn't wait to return to lovely, beautiful Wayne. I had a job to do in January that would pay off my bloated credit cards and then I was gone—off to OZ and a new experience. A general rule of life: Learn from mistakes (your and others) and Don't Look Back.

'Weed Troll starts his drinkin'
during breakfast time with mama
'Pass the crack you big fat ho!'
is what he likes to holla...'

—Weed Troll

In the summer of 2002, Mom was care taking The King and I. His eyesight has been bad for years and he lost most of it that winter. No reading, no driving, no flying. Dad was as depressed as I was and, like me, trying to make the best of it. 'Make the Best of It' is a Midwestern mantra. It's one of the reasons we're so fucked up.

I had the same initial reaction many near death survivors have. Pure love for everyone and everything—incomparable—but nine months later my new reality was sinking in. I had gone from 'smart, attractive, athlete' to 'stupid, scarred, gimp.' I was falling apart.

Miller Dwan Hospital has a burn unit and Dr Phukup is a plastic surgeon there. I had webbing along the top of my fingers caused by multiple skin grafts. Dr Allritini said it was common and easily repaired. The procedure would require a skin graft and would leave a five inch scar. I didn't anticipate brilliance but I expected competence. Phukup told me I could choose the graft site. I picked my left thigh.

My stomach was nearly scar free. I have one donor site on my lower belly and it's fading. I called Phuckup and asked more questions. How long has he been in practice, how many times had he done this surgery? 'Ten years and more times than I can count.' Attitude. Red Flag! If a doctor won't behave with basic queries, hire someone else. I should have waited to get back to LA, but not thinking clearly, I made an appointment for surgery. I was wheeled into the operating room and put onto the table, I checked with Phuckup one last time before going out. 'Here…' I pointed to the spot on my left thigh. 'That's going to work just fine.' I woke in recovery with bandaging taped to the middle of my stomach, *above and below* the belly button. Devastated, I couldn't speak.

To control disastrous depression I'd been telling myself 'you're not done healing.' My arm truly frightened Friends children, legs were a train wreck, brain damage had disfigured my face and harvest sites had scarred my back— but my stomach still looked good—I'm curvy, have an innie, my tummy is cute and fashion this minute shows belly. *I was clinging to that diaphanous idea.* I couldn't articulate, couldn't grasp what that idiot had done to me. Like Nancy Kerigan I was reduced to sobbing WHY! WHY!

Crying in front of Mom is waving a red cape. 'You have so many scars; I can't believe you're making a big deal out of this one!' It got worse from there but I expected sympathy from Pop. Instead he was yelling bizarre things like '…maybe he was protecting your ovaries!' Huh? 'I don't believe he would do anything to hurt you! Doctors NEVER hurt their patients! The Hippocratic Oath is sacred!' It seemed like temporarily insanity. (Of course doctors hurt patients, it happens hourly.) Now I can look at the incident with time tempered judgment; poor Pop had been 'Making the Best of It' for six months. How do you get over loosing your eyesight? Make the Best of It doesn't work forever. I think he snapped and I was collateral damage. Desperate for a hug and the 'everything will be all right' speech, I shut down when they both attacked. In 2002, having my body react *physically* to emotions freaked me, it was raw and uncontrollable. I had been in four hospitals in three states in ten months; not one of my therapists warned me—or even mentioned—stroke related emotional madness.

Stress causes a strong metal taste (think of sucking dirty change) then either the inability to speak or slow weird stuttering. I don't s-s-stutter typically, instead there are long gaps between words. I think of what I'm trying to say but can't spit it out. Or the word I'm about to use disappears or I think I'm making sense when I'm using the wrong words. Or I hear myself saying one thing when I meant the opposite. (Like take a left turn.) Chest hurts, panic attack, scary. The first couple years it was almost always narcoleptic as well.

Mom can't handle negative emotions she was an abused child. My sweet, kindly grandfather beat his kids. Almost everyone did, it was considered normal. It took years to see Mom objectively and stop thinking her temper was about me. (The all-important Me.) In college, psychiatric interns were available to students. I talked my head off to a girl a few years older than me. She offered coping skills, Mother / Daughter we had the same temper. You can do nothing about hers so stop trying. Change yourself. When Mom was mean, I'd picture a scared baby girl. I'd check my ego and try to defer, not engage. Took a few years but when I reached my late twenties and finally stopped fighting with her, surprise! I really liked her. We were happy to see each other and had fun together. We'd go to the cabin, out to lunch, in for videos, I'm sure we would have continued down that path if I hadn't been injured. Mom will always be difficult to understand. And that's fine; I had no requirement to change her. And I lived 1,500 miles away. Things distorted with brain damage, stripping away years of built up armor. I was fragile and they were frazzled.

I slept most of the week, waking long enough to piss and change bandaging but finally made it in to hand therapy. Then started sobbing uncontrollably. Sweet Hand Therapist was so empathetic she was crying with me.

In the surgery report Phukup wrote: 'The size of the skin graft was then transferred to the lower abdomen where a skin graft was harvested with a scalpel…presents now with concerns about the position of the donor site. No other complaints at this time.'

October 2002—Smallville

Was in the gym for two hours today. (Not as impressive as it sounds, it takes 10–20 minutes to change machines and I'm using the lightest weight.) At one point, a Shakira song comes on. A year ago I worked on her music video at Universal. Husband got me that job. He was the FX coordinator and told the producers, 'you need a stunt coordinator for all this flying stuff and I know just who you should hire.' I practiced the rigging with the FX boys, making it smooth and safe before we hooked her up. Shakira jumped off a mountain, flew out of water onto a spongy surface and dove into a big glass tank that they could shoot through. Sony was going to push this album—her US cross over—we shot everything in Spanish and English. It was a good video, good director, fun to be part of. Over two G's for two days work wasn't bad either. Quick think of something else! Bjork starts singing 'This wasn't supposed to happen…' My eyes welled up. Bjork is right. Fortunately the next song was Cher and it broke the spell. I like her attitude but that music is boring to me.

'…when I'm focused
and positive
I can see the light

but quarrel and strife
make me lose my sight...'

paraphrasing Baby Fox

Spent the weekend with Rag, going to miss sweet baby Rag, he kept me from suicide this summer. The first time we slept together was fifteen years ago but we didn't do it often. He was a friend of my brothers, it was unseemly. Rag told me back then he'd been fantasizing about me for years. Time Flies: Rag got married, had a couple kids, then his wife left him. I told him a few weeks ago that he made me feel human again. 'You make me feel the same way.' What I got from Rag was the realization that I still like sex and love and life. To give myself over to that brief moment that goes on infinitely. The little death. (Who said that? Bronte? DH Laurence? Seuss?)

Friend came up from Minneapolis for the weekend. Saturday night Monk came over with his kids. Helped them decorate for Halloween, watched Mad TV and Saturday Night Live. I worked on Mad TV a couple of times. First time, I doubled Nicole Sullivan, she was playing a pediatrician and Stuart the Baby kicked her (me) out the window. The second time I was a bride in a skit.

Camera in front, looking through the windshield, the scene starts: Nicole is giving driving lessons to a nervous student. The car was up on blocks with long two by four's under it so it could be bounced around by the grips. 'OK, we're going to turn right at the light... signal, good....' A siren starts up—cop lights begin to swirl. 'Oh no, should I pull over?' 'Step on it!' She was a bank robber (or something like that) and they go careening off. FX had a wind machine behind the camera and began throwing stuff into it. They started small. Leaves, little branches... then squirrels, raccoons... 'Go through the Confetti Factory!' She yells. A wall of confetti hits the windshield. They go through a fish cannery, a wildlife park, FX is furiously throwing stuff. 'Watch out for that circus...' BAM! A Little Person hits the windshield. 'Cut through the church parking lot!' BAM! The Bride (me) smacks the hood of the car and rolls up and off. 'Sorry! You looked nice...' 'Go through the Gap...' Tons of Gap clothing and a sales clerk smack the hood of the car. (Stunt coordinator, Friend) 'Oh no! A bicycle race!' Bing Bang Boom! The sketch went on and on and on. Funny. Mad TV rehearses for a week then films with a live audience.

October 2002, Smallville MN

I have been waking in the middle of the night all summer in excruciating pain. Molded into the fetal position, I can't straighten my knees and have horrid cramps. I have to get out of bed and stand to get them to normalize. I stand there in pain, stretching my legs back out. Takes five to ten minutes before I can stand up straight. The burns, I guess, since it's affecting both legs. That's the way I tell the difference, if my whole body hurts, burns. Right side only, CVA.

My mother gave me a little bell to ring if I needed help during the night and put it on the night stand next to the bed. Freakish fetal leg curl wakes me; I crawl out of the covers and slowly ease up to standing. And stand there. I'm awake now, maybe a little music? I can barely hobble—I'm missing the tips of toes on the left foot and the right is in a sleeping cast—I get to the stereo fine but on return I start falling in slow motion. Frozen.

I landed on my sleeping cat's bladder. Meouch! She pissed herself and bit Hard into my bicep! My poor Scrub! It still makes me laugh. What a way to wake up. We were both stuck for a minute. She didn't bite again just scrambled to free herself. I was half on half off the bed and did a controlled crash to the floor. Heart pounding, I remembered a physical therapists advice. 'When you fall, don't try and get up right away. Sit still, catch your breath and calm down. Then check for injuries.' My knees really hurt, crumbling to the floor had forced them to bend and my right bicep had vampire punctures, but over all, could be worse. Scrubby poked me in the head with her paw. 'Meow?' The Bell! Thanks for the reminder! I swung it and the clapper flew across the room. 'Meow?' She poked my head again. I laughed, it was all too stupid. I pulled myself up on the bed then used my cane into the kitchen. Washed my bicep with soap and water. Came back, pulled off the sheets and crawled back under the blankets. Surreal. In the morning I wasn't sure, was it Real? Oh yea, vampire bite, pee sheets.

'...live to the point of tears...'

—Albert Camus

Leaving Smallville, I could finally get up from the floor with nothing to lean on! My occupational therapist and I were laughing little kids. She was into her job and came up with good ideas. I missed my life, I mentioned yoga once and she found some easy poses to hold at our next session. She was never finished, we'd climb stairs, kick balls, she'd put on a harness (hang for safety) so I could walk fast on the treadmill.

Arm Therapist gave me a last massage. We've been trying to get my right arm over my head 180 degree's all summer. Started with 40, left at 165. Thank God my therapists were positive and good at their professions, because the doctors in Smallville were so negative, so completely effed that they're hard to describe. Compared to the doctors in LA (who are no great prize) I can't even say they're 'Black and White' because they're both colors, still in the same family. The difference is Black and Potato.

2007

Dr Stupidio was my physiatrist at the clinic. [A doctor that co-ordinates all of the specialists and therapists working on your various parts.] I hated him (arrogant ass) and he knew it. His egotism was unwarranted. He called one afternoon and gave me an unwanted, unasked for opinion on a recent elbow X-ray. Nasty and gleeful, he told me 'your elbow is fused, there's no way to fix it and I wouldn't even try!' Not an orthopedic surgeon but an expert on hurting his patients. I said nothing just hung up covered in stress and narcolepsy'd to bed.

One of Smallville's finest Plastic Surgeons, Doctor Beast, WENT OFF when I dared to complain about the scar on my stomach. Doctor Phukup was perfect and I should have my arm amputated! It's stupid to keep it! You're a stupid idiot! It Looks Awful! There's no way it can ever be fixed! He was chasing my mother and me down the hospital hall like a ghoul. 'Cut it off! Cut it off!!!'

'…stop fighting stop fighting
stop fighting stop fighting
I want to reason with you
be diplomatic
sensible & levelheaded
can't you try?
just try…'

paraphrasing Burning Spear

I couldn't stay in Smallville any longer. My internal thermometer has been reset—I'm cold in temperate weather—and CVA symptoms get worse in cold. I flew back to the land of traffic, smog and 21st Century doctors. Home Scrub flew to Portland to stay with K & Y.

October 2002 / Sherman Oaks, CA / PaulDDB's

Alison took me back to USC, it was bitter sweet. The way the place smelled— especially hydro therapy—came rushing back. I was glad to see them and they were happy to see me smiling, walking, talking, limbs in tact.

Dr Goodfella was just out of surgery and I gave him a hug. Surprisingly shy and short. Happy to see me. We went into my old room—empty and being used for storage—to see how my skin grafts were healing. 'They look great!' He looked happy, ICU Nurse came in and oohed and ahhed. 'They really look good!' I had to laugh.' You are the only people that could look at these legs and think they look good.' But to them they *really did look good* and that made me feel better. I felt at home there, how lucky I am. How lucky to have survived.

But there was one incredibly sad note, Latham just died! ICU Nurse came and told me as Alison and I were waiting for the elevator. 'We didn't want to tell you right as you walked in the door, she said, I know you were friends…' He had died the previous morning over breakfast. Heart attack, quick, not much pain and into the skull farm. Super unexpected, he was only fifty something. Latham was one of my night ICU nurses and a fellow burner. I didn't recognize him (morphine hallucinations) but he recognized me from our camp, 'Debbie's Petting Zoo.'

High Tech Pagan: That's how I describe Burning Man, it's a weeklong party in the Black Rock Desert outside of Reno. A gang of us went for a few years at the end of the '90's. Latham and I had that 'small home town love,' he came to see me when I was released to Rancho and sent me email all summer.

'...one day sperm, blink of an eye, dust....'

—Unknown

Rest in Peace Latham.

2007

His death was my fault, I was sure of it. I couldn't tell anyone, really didn't understand it, but I was so guilt riddled I couldn't eat. A year before my injury I had read 'The Seduction of Madness' by Dr Edward Podvoll. An interesting and empathetic look at insanity; a lot of Podvoll's insight seemed to parallel my thoughts. I felt at the center of a huge destructive energy—everyone who loved me was in peril—I created doom.

Latham had told me he was quitting nursing, he wanted to teach, even had a particular collage in mind. Less money but fun is priceless, a secret Latham knew. (Not everyone does.) Being an ICU nurse in a burn unit was hard, it had burned him out but he wasn't sniveling, he was looking forward to the next chapter. Latham and I became friends and it killed him. Right before his escape. (Like I was nearly killed before my escape to OZ.)

Everything is quite possibly intertwined with everything else; madness is thinking it revolves around you.

'Peace be with the dead! Regret cannot wake them.
With a sigh to the departed

let us resume the dull business of life,
in the certainty that we also shall have our repose.'

—Byron

County of Los Angeles   **Department of Health Services**
GENERAL HOSPITAL

SURGEON   DEPARTMENT   DATE OF OPERATION
Dr Girlnaboysclub   Plastic Surgery   2 / 12 / 02
Attending

ASSISTANT
Dr Dianetics

PREOPERATIVE DIAGNOSIS: same as the
POST OPERATIVE DIAGNOSIS:
Open wound to the right wrist

PRIMARY PROCEDURE:
Right external fixation placement to the wrist by Orthopedic Surgery. Debridment
of right hand and forearm; excision of the right middle phalanx; removal of pin
fixation; and placement of VAC wound dressing.

ANESTHESIA: General endotracheal anesthesia.

ESTIMATED BLOOD LOSS: 50 cc
FLUIDS: 2 liters
URINE OUTPUT: 625 cc
SPECIMENS: Right fifth middle phalanx
COMPLICATIONS: None

INDICATIONS:
An attempt will be made at debriedment as well as placement of the VAC
wound system in an attempt to promote granulation tissue and healing to her
right upper extremity.

PROCEDURE:
The wound was initially debrieded and the orthopedic team placed an external fixater device to the right wrist. Please refer to the orthopedic operative note for details of their procedure.

We continued to debried the right hand and forearm using both a tongue blade and a scalpel. After this copious irrigation was performed to the right hand and VAC sponges were placed. It should be noted that all five pins were removed from the patient's hand, as well the fifth middle phalanx. After placement of the VAC sponges, including around the external fixator device, the seal was placed on the VAC dressing and suction was then applied.

The patient tolerated the procedure well and was extubated in the operating room and transferred to the floor in satisfactory condition.

NAME: Christensen, Alisa

The first time my name was spelled right!

The wound VAC saved my arm. All of my many Doctors had given up except Girlinaboysclub. She told me she had an idea—it was experimental—did I want to go for it? Yes. It involved fixing my wrist in a useable position (my hand was pointed down, she wanted to straighten it out) and then apply a vacuum device over the open bones. It consisted of sponges, black and shrink wrapped. The VAC sucked away the fluid that would form around the bones on my hand and forearm; tubs of the pink stuff. There was a big metal fixater holding my wrist in place. The entire device looked something like The Borg from Star Trek.

I loved Girlinaboysclub and not just because her first name was Debbie. Deb never acted too busy to talk to me. She was leaving in March—off to Okalahoma City or Kansas City some flyover state—to run their burn unit. She was tired of California's expensive medical malpractice and the rampant poverty that came with working at the County Hospital. Deb told me she couldn't stand leaving and have me lose the arm if she didn't try everything she could think of.

'...forty years went by
or four thousand days
we felt them all in a slow rush
of withering wind
and woke surprised to find
only one night had passed...'

~Al Christ

USC's burn unit is on the twelfth floor of General Hospital, on the east side of downtown. It was built in <u>1930,</u> it's old and used. Its hallways are cavernous, decrepit deco, its emergency room dirty and over crowded. It's the only place to go in LA if you're uninsured.

USC is a teaching hospital and wealthy students learn on the insolvent. USC is building new hospitals like Lego Land, blocks of them. They have tons of money and *none of it* is wasted on the broken, working poor. Student doctors should be learning compassion. Instead the poor are kept in archaic conditions, in a building that should have been leveled years ago. It keeps Ugly Poverty away from Real People with Money and Insurance. Real People get the Real Hospital. It teaches wealthy students that the poor are disposable.

Dr Carol used to work the jail ward during her internship. It's on the 11th floor of General Hospital. We'd sit in the hot shade at trapeze, taking turns flying and she'd amuse us with stories of the inmates; the crazy shit they'd do. Homeless, HIV and Hep C positive, untreated diabetes and schizophrenia, drunk, funny, tragic and sad—the jail ward is psychiatric by default.

Website / February 13th, 2002

A quick update... Some good news and more good news...The surgeons did not find any problem areas during inspection today, and are extremely positive about the results so far. Her feet / ankles are still a big concern, but for now there appears to be no further degradation and her condition is stable.

In general, she's doing OK. Her spirits are up / down and she's climbing the walls to get out, as you would expect now hitting the 42-day Right Now. She moved out of ICU back into the ward tonight (same room as before.) Latest estimates have her in the hospital for at least six more weeks. Videos are like gold to pass the time, please continue to bring them by if you can.

Extra special thanks to everyone who participated in the apartment search as well as the move. All of her belongings are now out of the apartment & in storage. We have a lot of candidates thanks to your efforts and hope to finalize a place soon. Heartfelt thanks to everyone.

~Kevin

November 2002, Sherman Oaks, PaulDDB's.

Back from San Jose, Baja. Friend Catherine took me to Mexico for a long Halloween weekend. Air fare is so cheap its crazee. (Halloween is the wedding anniversary with her ex she wanted to get OOT.) Alley and her husband have a B & B. Spent a lot of time in a hammock reading Henry Miller—Big Sur and The Oranges of Hieronymus Bosch—and falling asleep. Lovely.

Alley had changed for the better. I'd never seen her sober. Clear eyed and beautiful, she was fun and funny. She hadn't stopped drinking completely, still had the occasional beer but her self destruct bomb had been defused. She'd found a good therapist and was ready to change. Alley also had a near death experience, rolled her jeep a mile from home (ironically, sober) and whacked her back. We clicked.

Things with Cat weren't as smooth. She'd be complaining about some shit and I'd catch myself drifting off. I don't care. The same thing for years, nothing changes. Wondered if I was being overly critical, then I'd catch Alley's eye, she'd smile, shake her head a tiny bit.

One afternoon at the neighbors Cat almost slammed my good hand in the car door. Jesus Luis! I snatched it away at the last possible nano second. 'Oh my God, I'm sorry!' she said, realizing what almost happened. I'm sure she was but to think of my remaining hand being smashed to broken finger pulp in Mexico shook me up for hours. It shakes me now. I'm still really hurt—Cat weirdly refuses to acknowledge it—she doesn't want today's Alisa, she insists on last year's model.

Alley and her husband have a couple of Upstairs / Downstairs cabañas, an open air Bar & Restaurant and a separate building with bathrooms and showers. They're rustic—bamboo doors and thatched roofs. Cute but no. I stopped using a shower seat when I left Smallville (just because it was hard to travel with, not that I still didn't need it.) I need something to hang onto. It takes a long time to shower, everything is left handed slow. When I re-wrap my affected paw I need a comfortable seat, it takes over an hour. Open wounds need to be kept sterile. I use many different lotions potions and voodoo to keep infections away. Put thick vitamin E cream on all of my skin grafts and then wrap everything up again with pressure garments. There was no way I could do it outside. Their private home is separate. I was embarrassed but had to ask if I could use their private shower. And I needed to be driven; it was too far for me to walk. 'No problem, I had no idea how hurt you still were, Catherine told me you were great. I thought you were recovered.' 'Well, I am recovering, but…' I faltered. 'It will probably take years,' Alley finished for me. 'Yes,' relieved to be understood.

Had a Lance Armstrong minute. Sister In Law had given me a water color set. It was Japanese, sweet little bowls, palates, brushes. To make a gold fish…brush, swish, swish, brush. To make a panda…brusha, brusha, swoop and swirl. Landscapes, pagodas, fish and flowers were perfectly illustrated with step by steps. I'd had it for months but only looked at it. Losing my right hand is harsh. Thinking of anything artistic, drawing, doodling, painting my walls, breaks my heart. OK, shut up, I can do this left handed. That's part of the fun, mocking of the perfect illustrations. I was painting orange and black panda's. Cat put down her book and came over. 'This is fun!' she approved. She took a fresh piece of rice paper. Brush, swish, swish, brush. Perfect goldfish. Brush, swish, swish, brush. Another one.

In It's Not About the Bike, Armstrong was just starting to get his strength back. Members of his team were riding with him, giving encouragement. I can do this he was thinking and was passed going up hill by an over weight, middle aged woman. Reality hit him like a ton of lost endorsements. Alley hung our pictures behind the bar. Cats refined painting of several goldfish swimming in a glass bowl and my splotchy, supposed to be panda bears but more like fat ghosts, standing in a puddle. I had to laugh, it was funny in a sad your hand is fucked kind of way but I didn't want to paint anymore. I gave the set to Alley.

We went into town the last night and got a room at a nice hotel. It had a winding staircase to a bedroom that looked 'Fabulous!' according to Cat. I took her word for it. I could barely make the scary stairs to the bathroom, steep with no railing. 'I have to have fun *at least once* while I'm here,' she told me, smiling a dog smile. 'Go out, I feel like watching a movie.' I was tired of feeling guilty for being hurt. I had house keeping bring me a blow up mattress and bedding to put on the floor of the living room. Turned on HBO, ordered room service and was asleep by ten. (I woke at six to a handsome young man sheepishly leaving. That was funny; Cat always finds the cutest pet around.)

We got stoned on the way to the airport. Reasonable, airports are boring and we weren't going to fly with weed. I got a wheel chair; Cat was pushing me along, chattering away and drove me *into an elevator door.* 'Sorry, she laughed, I guess I can't be trusted.' We found ourselves on top of a steep, glass lined walk way to the tarmac. Looked formidable. 'Maybe I should pull you backwards…?' 'No way! You're fired! Hey you!' I yelled to a security guard, 'will you take me down, por favor?' I could see myself crashing through the glass like a stunt from the Naked Gun movies. She was huffy, I cajoled her, 'honey, when you said I can't be trusted I believed you.' Cat has always needed skyscraper maintenance. I used do it without thinking. '…baby it will be OK, you'll be fine…' What we all need to hear occasionally, she just needs it all the time. I realized I just wasn't able right now. Neither of us were prepared. I miss my old life so much it causes physical pain.

2007

The one thing I didn't complain about is the most interesting. I was in Alley's bedroom using the shower, an oversized walk-in with an open entryway. There was a quick KnockKnockKnock then Cat Burst into the room / no eye contact / staring at my naked body / no eye contact / up and down up and down / look at those legs oh god look at that arm / no eye contact / my burn scars were at their worst, red and purple, Freddy Kruger. I was in Shock unable to move, a grotesque statue. She finally looked into my eyes and stammered, 'I uh, I came in for…lotion!' She grabbed a bottle of whatever and took one last peek at the monster body before scurrying out. Hideous Frankenstein! She was a little girl scaring herself by looking at the sideshow freak. The experience was too painful to acknowledge, I couldn't think about it, I tucked it away in the nebulous netherworld.

November 2002, Encino—Velvets

Last night I dreamed of smoking, realistic, woke glad it was only a dream. Velvet told me once in a while she dreams of doing lines even though it's been twenty years. I met Velvet producing my friend Moe's short, 'Guido Takes A Hike.' When making a low budget film you work around the clock and become close, fast. Velvet has been a friend ever since and she really came through for me this past winter. She helped pack my house, came repeatedly to the hospital and she dealt with Tony's irrational mood swings with equanimity.

Her son is twenty one and in the Marines, stationed in Korea. She's worried about war. I can't get started on Bush, I'll lose it. This administration has decided to go fortune hunting in Iraq, the worst kind of profiteering. War for revenue has been waged for thousands of years, nothing changes. The good can't believe how evil the bad are and let themselves be used; the bad can't resist the pull of the dark, money and power money and power.

'…it's the year of the dragon
and men are going to disappear

no word is ever heard
and they won't be back next year…'

paraphrasing Wycleff

Velvet and I were at the farmers market in Sherman Oaks the other night; she was selling wreaths and I was keeping her company. I called Mr Right Now, he stopped by. Broken nose again from boxing; dark, sarcastic, funny. We dated for awhile but in the end in, were better off as friends. He was a little too… can't come up with a word. But Mr Right Now is also brainy, witty, masculine / back to his place / foreplay, foreplay, nada. He told me he was afraid of hurting me, I looked fragile. He didn't have to say it. I'm Hideous Frankenstein.

Slept and dreamt of falling ashes. One night Wayne and I drove through burning fields. Miles and miles of fire with news paper sized ashes lazily floating around. Intentional burns before the new crop is planted. It was crazee beautiful.

Right Now and I went to Matador Beach in the morning and watched dolphins. Matador is my favorite, it's small and mostly deserted, at the end of Malibu, you have to climb thousands of stairs. I love those stairs, they keep most people out.

2007

Of course Right Now was telling the truth. We'd been friends for years. He had come to Rancho, sent emails during the summer, was supportive and worried. Right Now wanted to hug and protect me, he was sweet. Trying to get through a day at a time, I couldn't see reality through other people's eyes. I couldn't escape the immediate Me.

County of Los Angeles   **Department of Health Services**
GENERAL HOSPITAL

SURGEON   DEPARTMENT   DATE OF OPERATION
Dr Dianetics   General Surgery   2 / 15 / 02

ATTENDING
Dr Girlnaboysclub

PREOPERATIVE DIAGNOSIS:
POST OPERATIVE DIAGNOSIS:
PRIMARY PROCEDURE:
ANESTHESIA: [all left blank]

INDICATIONS:
The patient is a 37-year-old female with extensive soft tissue injury to her right upper extremity after a 37% total body surface area burn. The patient was recently taken to the operating room on 2 / 12 / 02, where she underwent placement of a right upper extremity back dressing system.

On 2 / 18 / 02, because of the patients inability to tolerate back dressing change at the bedside, the decision was made to take the patient to the operating room to undergo back dressing change under conscious sedation.

DESCRIPTION OF PROCEDURE:
The back dressing was removed and a new dressing was applied after irrigation of the wound. At the end of the case, the patient had a left internal jugular triple lumen catheter, which was removed by Anesthesia. There were no complications during the procedure. The patient tolerated the procedure well and was transferred from the operating room back to the Intensive Care Unit.

        NAME: Christensen, Alisa

This is the procedure that gave me the CVA (stroke). A fucking dressing change. There were TWO equally short and suspicious surgery reports about the CVA. (I couldn't tolerate a dressing change on the 18th so they reversed time and did this procedure on the 15th?) The cover up makes me sick.

When I woke up with my cerebral vascular accident, everyone was speaking differently; slowly, as if talking to a two year old. No one was sure how brain damaged I was, how much I would recover or if I would recover, strokes kill people all the time. I would open my mouth to try and talk and a load of jumbley goo would spill out, 'blee ma nana bobba...' slow, like a drunk. I could hear rubbish but couldn't stop it from happening. For the most part they ignored me and spoke normally to each other, which made me think I was going insane.

One of the nurses finally figured it out. 'Do you understand what we're saying?' I nodded yes. 'You can't find the words?' I started crying, frustrated, freaking out. 'It will come back, give it time...' Guessing. A few days later someone gave me a children's book. Picture's and words; dog, cat, ball, etc. For ages two to four. I couldn't make sense of it; I knew they were commonplace things but, what were they? I couldn't say. I couldn't read three letter words! Horrified. No speech therapy, no explanations.

I thought the CVA was my fault *for a year* because I couldn't tolerate dressing changes awake. Doctor Goodfella and a pack of students had looked at my arm as I HOWLED in agony a few days before. They had to strap me down. It was crazee cool to see red muscle around white bone but I told my nurses I couldn't take that again.

Dr Girlinaboysclub, who'd been friendly and informal, suddenly wouldn't make eye contact and referred to me as 'The Patient' when she had to come in the ICU. It scared me! I was so effed up she couldn't even talk to me? Girlinaboysclub and I had developed an easy banter over the past 6 weeks. It was replaced by a cold sterile wall. She felt guilty and she was a coward. She could have looked at me, talked to me, tried to calm my fears. Instead she tucked her tail between her legs and ran away, a sniveling little bitch. She was already in cow town dreaming sweet dreams about running a burn unit so she let a couple of Interns stick a catheter in my jugular. (C U next Tuesday, Debbie.)

> '...I'm shameless when talking of my conquests
> but modesty hits when asked to describe the tortures I suffer
> once I fall in love
> love breaks me in two...'

paraphrasing Jean Cocteau, Diary of an Unknown

I was twenty-five when I met Ken Russell. He's a British director and the film was Cheap Date. I was hired during pre-production as a photo double for Theresa Russell, (camera tests, different lenses) then played a dancer / hooker once principal photography started. (Theresa and Ken haven't been married, just a coincidence about names. Theresa used to be married to another British director, Nicholas Roeg.)

Ken was heartbroken when he heard about my injury. He always thought I'd be hurt at work and would FAX me scary premonitions whenever I got a big job. Maybe he foresaw This and assumed it was from a stunt. When I was strong enough for a ten hour flight, I went to visit for a couple weeks. Married to wife # 4, she's cool and went to NYC and let us be. After everything I went through that year, visiting Ken was a slushy fruit drink with a tiny umbrella in it. He's one of my oldest friends and the only person I knew who'd had a stroke.

November 2002—New Forrest, UK—Old Tinsley's

In England, sitting in the solarium of Ken's cozy cottage. Wild pony's ramble outside, with the space heater on the sun gives the impression of a warm summer morning though it's late November and chilly.

Distracted—Ken walked in and turned off the heater, opened a window. I should be able to write, but what?

...sitting on a carousel of paint chipped ponies
growing ever slower, older, colder...

Distracted. Ken asks about the next installment of 'Pirate Story.' I wanted to create the most despicable character I could imagine and kill him off in some spectacular way. But my characters quickly took over their own lives and they didn't want to die, it turned from novella to soap. Started in 1990, I only have new stuff on this machine.

Distracted. By the minutia around me, birds singing, the way the [beugonvel-lia—spell?] goes perfectly with the light and the back drop of the old Skipton grandfather clock. A truck driving by, Nipper's gentle snoring. I'm dropping off, a little nap, to sleep, perchance to dream.

When I was at Rancho [live in therapy] my days were filled; breakfast, therapy, lunch, therapy, visitors, dinner, more visitors, bed. I wasn't left alone for long. Didn't have much time to think, thinking was bad. Everything I lost would come flooding in—it was too much. Always unbidden, the thought that would annihilate me. Piano (seven years of classical) drawing, trapeze, skiing, biking up the canyon, yoga, stunts. I became good at living a day at a time. When that was too hard—often was—I lived for the hour. 'You can get through this hour...' I would read the little Buddha book I got from Friend. 'Healing Meditations, by Tulku Thondup, how to deal with serious illness or injury.' I would read the same passages like a mantra.

Ken asked me if I ever thought about the dirt nap. Yes n No. I know what I lost will be replaced by something else. Dostoyevsky said 'If you're unhappy, and you are unhappy...' Funny, no avoiding it. I had embraced existentialism as a teen. Here and now is all there is and when we die, we're dust. The end. Why kill yourself? Why bother? Camus died in car crash at forty six. When I think of my life, it's never been boring, so nothing has really changed.

'...the fuzz break into Weed Troll's hut
and fill his closets with cocaine
they gonna make a fancy bust
and then they on the gravy train...'

—Weed Troll

Ken is making us a late lunch, the sun has set and it's 4:20. Nipper's sleeping beside me. Listening to a sexy Brazilian girl singing old seventies disco. Amusing. I just need to dig out my pain killers—my arm is being stabbed over and over in the same place. Nothing I'm not used to but it wears me out.

I love the New Forrest. (Called 'New' because it was planted by Henry VIII.) Life seems easier, (I realize it's an illusion). Thatched roof cottages hundreds of year's old dot the countryside, ponies meander their way into the little shops and pubs and though we stay connected through the news, it's far enough away to make it seem innocuous.

Pre dawn I skritch-scrabbled the sleeping brace from my right leg—ripped my pressure garments off—I couldn't stand it! Achy and electrocuted from the stroke, the burns, I couldn't move. Eleven months ago I didn't sleep with anything on but my radio boys, just my radio. (Channeling Monroe) Now I wake being strangled and electrocuted. Horrid..

Ken brought me tea and meds at eight. I had three tabs of Neurontin and ten mgs of Baclofen and was finally able to get up at nine. Sitting in the solarium looking at blue sky, I have to get up walk and stretch to get rid of the residual effects. My right side is still seizing. Arm is the worst.

Disturbing dreams. With a bunch of other women on a work team; we were replacing toilets in a run down lavatory. High ceilings, dirty stained walls. A girl pointed out a toilet she just installed; she was proud of her accomplishment. It looked ridiculous to have a new commode in this horrid, run down place. I think we changed three or four out of twenty. Ken said, 'you can finish them tonight…' Ha-ha, I hope not.

Bathtub Heaven. Had a dry practice in and out with tennis shoes and then went for it naked. Do it or don't bathe for two weeks, Old Tinsley's doesn't have a shower. Lovely to sink into a giant tub of hot water, put a mask on my face, conditioner in my hair and drift away. Haven't taken a bath in a year.

'…but Mama Hoover down the sniff
before the feds can even blink
Weed Troll have a big fat laugh
and wash his kitten in the sink…'

—Weed Troll

Ken is writing about Elgar in the living room. I'm in the observatory with the candlestick.

We went to the latest James Bond but I missed the last five minutes; I couldn't keep my eyes open. The theatre was cold and my faux fur so cozy that I dropped off. Lee Tamahori directed it; I worked with him. The first time he blipped my radar was a low budget film he did in his home world, New Zealand. The kid at my video store recommended it. 'It's hard core.' High praise, he watched films all day long. It was 'Once Were Warriors,' brilliant in a tragic, short life kind of way. When I heard he was in town doing pre-production for Mulholland Falls I knew I wanted on that film.

I was working on Jade, doubling Linda Fiorintino. She was great—sarcastic and intellectual—my favorite combo. 'I'm on the cover of three magazines and I still can't get laid,' she quipped the morning I met her. She was cool and likeable but Jade was a stress factory. Our director was a screamer and was always cutting out someone's liver. The environment was charged with his short fuse.

A film set isn't a democracy; more of a monarchy (sometimes a pirate ship). If you have a magnanimous ruler who knows what he wants and can communicate effectively, the empire is happy. We must please our King! Nothing is too much. The camera broke? No problem. We lost a location? No problem. The lights aren't set right, something's wrong with accounting, need a script change, wardrobe ripped, actor had a meltdown, the every day disasters that go with film making piling up as usual. No problem your Highness, we can fix it, replace it, re-write, re-stitch, we can fashion gold out of mud, make cake from sand, get the actor a valium, anything for you boss and have it done yesterday.

However, if your King is a snarling bitch, the serfs get surly. Nothing's smooth. You fall behind schedule, the show goes over budget and camaraderie turns into bickering. Not intentionally, no ones guilty of sabotage but something is lost. Maybe it's the sense of pride you get when *you* make something. If the boss doesn't give you respect, you're just working for a paycheck and no matter how good it is, fifteen hour days get long. Poor Jade. Everything that could go wrong did and our commander in chief was a spoiled child. Sometimes (only alone) I would start laughing. He was such a cartoon.

Jade and Mulholland Falls were both Paramount pictures. Some of Jade's actors were going from one to the other and a lot of the crew as well. As our end date came and went, the saying 'Who do I have to screw to get off this film?' was the tired joke. We wrapped Jade after midnight on Saturday and started Mulholland Falls pre-dawn the following Monday. It was like the scene from 'Who Framed Roger Rabbit;' when they drove into Toon Town. The world is brighter, squirrels playing, bunnies scampering... Ahh... Lee Tamahori. Benevolent Ruler.

'The strength of thy own arm is thy salvation.
Above thy head through rifted clouds, there shines
A glorious star. Be patient. Trust thy star!'

—Longfellow

Ken and I went to the Beaulieu Auto Museum, it was kitschy. (I love.) It's on the grounds of a medieval monastery. Elegant cars, crazee cars and a little train ride through the life span of cars, like a ride at Disneyland. Outside, we rode the sky tram around the park, foggy but not cold and I made the stairway up to the tram! Farthest I've climbed, four flights. Went into Lymington and had acupuncture from Dr Natural. She's Chinese—I trusted her—needles from my head to my toes and a great massage after. Marvelous. 'You can come twice a week?' No. But I can look for an acupuncturist when I get home. We bought her herbs and potions and laughed at how we were both suckers for slick product packaging.

Ken and I discussed stroke's, how crazee and unpredictable, the weird new pain—brain damage pain. The horrid electrocution-esque mornings, the frustrating language loss. His stroke was no where as severe as mine and he didn't feel normal for five years. Hang on, sweetie. He let me cry, empathized, offered encouragement and insight. He helped me laugh, told me to keep writing, to write a book. I felt safe enough to talk about my broken heart. He gave me hope. Buoyed with good will I leave for the states with a debt of thanks to Wife # 4. Ken tells me she's his favorite.

2007

Ken's a comrade in satire, a mentor a champion a wise guy who never lost his sense of humor. We had similar temperaments and had some big fights but we both found it impossible to stay angry for long. At times it felt like he was the only other person who realized we were playing Absurdist Theatre. Absurdity was the initial intrigue. We were having a loungy lunch at Ken's rented house during pre-production of Cheap Date. A couple actors, the producers, the DP, the production manager, we were talking about Ken's current book, A British Picture. It was going to be released in America and his publisher wanted to change the name. 'How about A British Bastard,' I said. Shooop! All noise suddenly sucked from the room. The producers had a fight or flee dilemma, the actors waited to see what would happen. I looked at Ken quizzically, he looked amused. 'Of course you know I'm kidding,' I said to the table, laughing at them. Relieved, they all laughed with me.

That was absurd.

For me, Hollywood had long exceeded all expectations of toady flatterers, infantile idiots, yesterdays baby models, self propelled Rambo dolls, we had an enormous surplus of ass kissing sycophants, afraid to say or do anything of their own mind. A bad idea becomes GREAT if it's uttered by an A lister. When you think, 'I've just seen the creepiest behavior ever, the day changes. And the reverence with which some people are held is bizarre. The top echelon get away with so much shit it's unreal. (From petty theft to murder.) Sometimes Ken would ask for outlandish perks just to see how far he could push it and we were often surprised how long the yeses kept coming. He was provocative, super fun and always surprising. This is a journal entry after I'd been to the UK a few times.

January 7 1992

Home from London yesterday, still jet lagged. I drank so much I'm detoxing on brown rice and grapes.

Went down to Stone Henge and New Forrest and scouted locations for his next film. Lovely Cathedrals. Met some of his friends, loved them all, super fun New Years Eve. Our relationship keeps getting stranger. We made the gossip columns, the silly cow kept misspelling my name. It kills me that I found the perfect man for me and he was born 20 years too early. He's older than my father, how long could it last? A year? We'd end up hating each other.

Maybe I'm just afraid of commitment…

I had started to convince myself to just do it, get married and forget the May / December cliché's. [The 2nd line told me what I needed to think about, I drank too much.] I sent him a Valentines Day card. Few weeks later I got a response.

March 7 '92

Big news today / a letter from Ken saying he's getting married to a girl he met last month on 'Bax.' I can't believe it—so sudden. He sent me a picture of her. Curly blonde, pursed lips, looks like a bitch.

Couple years go by: The Directors Guild was doing a retrospective of Nicholas Roeg and the British Consulate was throwing a garden party for him. Ken called me out of the blue with an invite and the sad story of Wife #3. Their marriage was short and disastrous. Marrying a man older than my father wouldn't have been smart or nice. We never fooled around again and had a running joke: 'Sex, baby?' 'No thanks sweetie.' The Bitch took a bullet for me.

August 1998

…with Ken I am absolutely sure, without a doubt, that he love's me for my shit as well as my shine.

'…friendship isn't an instinct, it's an art
art that's enchanted and mysterious and it requires TLC
deceitful cynics will invent reasons, motives
being analogous to their own petty sexual or monetary interests…'

paraphrasing Jean Cocteau, Diary of an Unknown

December 2002, Los Angeles—Catherine's

Jet lagged. I liked the people I was sitting between: Larry was a pilot but on a break, traveling around Europe since 911 and Missamo was from Pasadena via Tanzania and had been visiting her family.

Larry was talkative. He used to work for a charter airline that would occasionally fly celebrities. He was star struck. Mentioned a dozen or more people that he'd buzzed around, hinting that in that short amount of time, flying the plane, he'd made a connection, they were pals. I'd worked with some them for months and I don't know them at all. (I didn't tell Larry, I liked him.) I'm not crazee for actors—they tend to be narcissistic which gets boring fast—but I was star struck in 1989. I got a call from Central Casting about photo doubling Madonna for Dick Tracy. I loved her and was happy to get hired. Dick Tracy was a show everyone wanted to work on. Big budget for the time (I think fifty mil) and Madonna was hot; twenty nine-ish and about to go super nova.

They had three units going. I was sent to the Third, we spent the day doing inserts. Not all of it was photo doubling her; I was a catch all double. Someone's hand holding a cocktail glass, Madonna's shoulder as a door closes, cockroaches—Madagascar hissing ones—crawling out of a gangsters pants leg; bits of this and that.

It was fun, at the end of the day I was asked if I wanted to come back to be Madonna's stand in, the last one had left for a better job. Yes. Stand In's are part of the camera / lighting crew. The director will have the actors (First Team) come in and rehearse the scene to be shot, then when he's satisfied with the action, Second Team is called in to light. It can take 30 minutes or all day. Actors, stunts, photo doubles, stand in's and extras start overtime after eight (with an hour break for lunch) we were shooting fifteen hour days, so I was making rent.

Most of the actors wore cartoon makeup and looking that wacky every day combined with sleep deprivation causes silliness. I remember rolling laughter with Henry Silva and Ed O'Ross, Pacino cracking jokes, I also remember meeting Beatty and thinking, OK I can see it now. He was charismatic in person, held eye contact, easy smile and remembered my name. (Pays attention.) You couldn't swing a dead cat without hitting a woman who'd had him. Not kidding, I knew <u>three</u>. The village bicycle, he got good reviews. Madonna was a smitten kitten, adorable with Warren but snappish with the peons. There was a rule on the set: 'Don't speak to Madonna unless spoken to.' Reasonable request and easy to follow, she was bitchy. I only broke it once. I had been standing on marks for over an hour. (Colored tape put on the floor to specify the different actors.) First Team was called. She was sewn into impossibly tight dresses and wore platform heels. (I was hired because I was her height in tennis shoes.) I went to sit where I could see the set; an hour goes by, still fiddling around with the lights. Did she look uncomfortable? I walked over. 'I can stand here if you'd like to sit down.' She looked at me slightly amused and said, 'honey, when I'm here nobody wants you... no offense.' 'OK,' I said feeling a bit stupid and strangely satisfied. I was officially in the club. She got everyone. Makeup and Hair dubbed her The Bitch. I could hear chattering on the walkies in the mornings and it always cracked me up. 'Got an ETA on The Bitch? ... The Bitch arrives at 7:30.'

One late night, we were shooting a scene where Al is yelling at her. Camera was on her close-up, Warren was shooting take after take, endless. Suddenly Al improvises, 'you think you think you're a star? You're nothing! No talent, you can't sing, you can't dance...' Something off script, unexpectedly mean. She looked hurt. CUT! Usually when the director calls Cut, bells go off and work starts up again but the whole stage was quiet, waiting to see her reaction. She was capricious but also witty, she just laughed and said, 'stand up straight Al, I like my men erect.' I was never star struck again. She was the 1st in a long line of divas I found myself laughing at over the years, men and women. I think I understand that behavior (insecurities) and it's not that bad—there are far worse things than being mercurial—it just doesn't impress. Poor behavior from an actor is like dealing with a spoiled child; you can't discipline someone else's kid, put up with it or get fired.

Website / February 16^{tt}, 2002

Kev and Tony here with an update... Alisa has gone into surgery as planned on Tuesday and everything with the surgery itself went well. It only lasted for about an hour and involved putting an airtight dressing over a layer of sponge that has been put on the open areas on her wrist and hand.

Everything is then hooked up to a sort of pump that keeps a constant, slow suction on the arm, promoting growth of her own cells in the right areas and hopefully regenerating enough tissue to cover the bare spots of her bones in the arm and hand. As mentioned, everything went well with that part of it.

The first small problem began to appear a few hours after surgery when she should have woken up but still hadn't. Since her breathing had become labored as well and just to be on the safe side she was moved back into the ICU at around 5pm, after being changed to 'Ward-status' just the night before. The nurses unsuccessfully tried throughout the evening to wake her up and were busy trying to ease her breathing. They finally seemed to be getting her lungs cleared up (she really has very knowledgeable and caring ICU-nurses) and it was only discovered the next morning, when she fully awoke, that Alisa had suffered a multiple stroke at some time during the previous night or day.

They are now running a ton of tests to discover the cause of the stroke. It happened in the left side of her brain, pretty deep inside near the spine. The right side of her body is paralyzed at the moment and her speech is very slurred. Her mind was wide awake but when trying to say something only the left side of her face moved and she couldn't say anything that could be understood by anybody.

They're not allowing visitors except family. Please wait w / coming down to the hospital for a couple of days or so, we'll keep the e-mail updates current. Kevin is in town over the weekend as well; please feel free to call us for the latest news. If we're not up in the ICU (no cell phones allowed), we'll be answering calls. More info should be available as well on the website, probably by the weekend. We realize that this is not great news and we're still dealing with it as well as trying to be there for Alisa as much as we can. Thank you all for your support and help in these tough days. More soon... p&l Tony

I still don't know what to say about the CVA. I listen to talk radio in my car and there are always adverts saying, '...at the first sign of a stroke get to a hospital!' I was in a hospital and didn't get treatment until a day and a half later? mutherphuckersmutherphukers

> Aside: Mom had a pulmonary embolism (blood clot in the lung) in February of '02, the same week as my CVA (blood clot in the brain.) Creepy coincidence?

December 2002, LA—The Biltmore Hotel

Hard to get up. Bad 'tone.' The tame medical term for electrocution, I get every am. I'm staying with Kevin who's working at the Convention Center; I've been torturing myself by looking at my body in the full length mirror. Something from Hellraiser. I'm not this mess, I'm somewhere else.

Had a shower that I actually enjoyed yesterday at my old neighbor's. I spent a couple days in his spare room wandering in and out of memories. He lived across the hall from me at 'We Ho Manor.' An oasis to come home to after a hectic, creepy, obtuse, annoying, cloying, typical tinsel town day. I would walk into my secret garden and shed the thick skin that kept me safe. BBQ's, swimming pools, movie stars—ya'll come back now, ya hear? I miss my old neighbors. We were in Avalon or the lost city of Atlantis, or maybe one of Grimm's Fairy tales because there was a troll we had to occasionally do battle with in the form of an ancient, bitter manager. It wouldn't last forever. I remember floating in the pool one halcyon afternoon thinking exactly that; watching my friends interacting with the home team, stereo speakers out the first floor window, turkey burgers grilling, sound of the blender mixing up margaritas. Some lazing in the sun, some jumping off Friends balcony into the pool, some cooking, some getting baked, everyone laughing, enjoying themselves, made sweeter by the knowledge that it was fleeting. I always tried to be aware of the moment, easy to do when life is interesting and fun. Trapeze was great for brain drain, everything goes everything slows. I would stand up on the platform between tricks and think, I'm so lucky. I have so much. One day sperm, blink of an eye, dust.

Walking is harsh. The burn scars on my left hip aren't healed and feel achy and tight under the skin. Right hip hurts in the joint / the CVA. Left foot is killing me, burns. The Biltmore has a little gym and I've been doing their Stairmaster. Not sure if it's helping or hurting but the masseuse here is great! I took his card. Cheryl and Boop (girlfriends from trapeze) came to see me. We sat in the opulent lobby and had iced tea and a few laughs. 'You look better honey.' They meant it. I have to keep reminding myself of that.

2007

I was in a lot of pain that winter. I couldn't get my pain medication or anti-spasmodic filled before I left for the UK. I was Very Under Medicated. Saw my pre-injury physician, Dr Coolchick when I returned to Los Angeles. 'Did it happen at work?' The question everyone asks. I filled her in on my year and made another appointment to see her in February when I returned from Portland. (I needed a Pain Specialist but wasn't thinking clearly.) Coolchick wrote another batch of prescriptions properly.

Methadone and Oxycodone for pain.
Neurontin and Baclofen for stroke symptoms.
Celexa to keep me from killing myself.
Ambien to let me sleep.

Finally right, I thought. No. I went to the burn unit's Christmas party. It was nice to see my nurses again and I saw Friend (the 17 year old who'd been bonfire'd.) She was healing great, could bend her knees into a squat and stand up easily. Gave me hope, I still wasn't there. I had taken my last methadone pill the night before but was certain I could fill Coolchick's prescriptions at the County Hospital; they had enough narcotics to kill a field of elephants, but the pharmacy wouldn't fill them. 'It's a new rule,' Goodfella said. A lot of pharmacies don't carry narcotics anymore. The DEA *must win* the war on drugs, now take your pain and get out! The sickest part of this story is that if I went to any corner of that shitty neighborhood I could get Anything I asked for. The Drug War is over, Drugs won. The government just makes it difficult for truly hurt people to get medication. Kevin and I caught a flight to Oregon that afternoon and I had my prescriptions filled in Lake Oswego.

'Man can live with any 'how' as long as he has a 'why.'

—Nietzsche

Website / February 18th 2002

Hi Everybody, Kev & Tony here w / another update. The main priority today was to find out where the shower of blood clots came from but so far all the tests have been negative. That's good in one way but still leaves us with the uncertainty of the cause. Some major lab test-results are due back in a day or two but it looks doubtful at best, as to whether they'll ever be able to pinpoint the exact cause of the stroke.

So, we sit and wait anxiously once again, hoping Alisa's spirit will be strong enough to take this latest hit as well. Everyone, including the doctors and nurses, is understandably upset by this latest turn of events and everything possible is being done for her. She had a pretty hectic day yesterday with all kinds of departments coming / going and doing one or another kind of test.

According to the doctors, these next two to three days will show how much actual damage has been done to her brain and how much functionality will be restored when the swelling reduces and the clots break up. Unfortunately the blood-thinning medication that is required to treat the stroke is eventually working to the disadvantage of the wound on the hand. Now is a very good time to put some intent into chants and prayers, moonlight dances and sweat lodges, circles and ceremonies... anything else you think might help.

Thanks to all that supplied videos for Alisa to watch, it's been great for her to have such a variety to choose from. If you brought over some videos and can't find them once you're going back to visit; please let us know they're in Tony's truck. We have to take them out once viewed. The no visitors rule is still in effect, so please stay in a holding pattern. We always take all get well cards and good wishes to the hospital for her and she really enjoys reading them. We can see how much it means to her. Thank you! We'll keep you posted. ~ Kev & Tony

I watched movies all day. For the Oscar push, the studios send academy members' films they hope will be nominated and Friend brought tons of them. Lord of The Rings won that year; it was one of the best for delusions. Little ring wraith horses jumped through the TV screen (staying the same size) and ran around my bed. The ICU was a dark cavernous room; mahogany bedroom furniture in my corner of it, my bed was king size, four posts with canopy, plenty of room for a tiny horse run.

Website / February 21st 2002

Hi All, Just a quick update from the hospital; Alisa is again doing much better and was moved out to the ward today as expected, which means she can have visitors. She's up to it as well, said she'd love to see some people. If you make it down there, she's in room #5 on the 12th floor. She told me again to say thank you for all the cards and wishes and gifts and help... So, looks as good as it can be expected, and then some. The hand is doing well at the moment and with the up-trend continuing, she'll be better every day. More soon... p&l, Tony

'...On 03 / 01 / 02 anesthesia pain management consulted and reviewed the current medications which were MS Contin, 45 mg q. 8h, Neurontin 300 mg t.i.d., Paxil 20 mg p.o. q.d.

Their notes indicate that patient is probably developing neuropathic pain, which will be tolerant to optiods like morphine. The patient also seems under dosed since she had dilated pupils. Recommendations to increase the Neurontin to 600 mg t.i.d. discontinue the MS Contin, and start methadone 20 p.o. q. 6h. If the patient is too sedated, decrease it to q. 8h.

Use the methadone 10 mg p.o. on a p.r.n. basis for breakthrough pain and adjust around the clock. Base pain dose on the frequent requests for breakthrough pain. Continue to use intravenous optoids or Demerol for painful maneuvers such as dressing changes. Methadone is recommended because it is an NMDA receptor blocker and can reverse optoid tolerance, which occurs in neuropathic pain, and therefore enhances its own optoid effect. Medications like morphine, Dilauted and Fentanyl lower this effect. The patient did have a decrease in pain with the use of methadone...'

I was in a fresh new hell. The hydrotropic ossification in my elbow had started. (HO for short.) My brain was busy, sending information to heal—bones, skin, nerves, ligaments, veins, arteries—doing a great job until the CVA. Deep inside my skull, mixed signals were wrecking my right elbow—extra bone was growing over the joint—excruciating. HO is caused by a brain-trauma-bone-trauma cocktail and develops in an unlucky 20% of us. (Car accidents are the most common way to get it.) I was told it could be a *year* before it would stop. It had to stop growing on its own. Tony didn't mention it.

'...with the up-trend continuing, she'll be better every day.

Sans reality, he was writing stories for his friends on the list. I was sinking into the vile oozing swamp of despair. I couldn't talk, couldn't read, make sense of a magazine or a movie. No speech therapy, no massage, no stretching or acupuncture. No one showing me pictures, flash cards, anything to try and wake up, get some recognition. No one touching me, brushing my hair, rubbing my neck, talking and getting me to talk back. I was Lonely and left to Vegetate. (The worst thing possible.)

One hour a day I'd have physical therapy. The physical therapists at USC were a couple of young woman. Sheri and Berry. They were focused on my right arm and growing HO. They seemed to work well together but personality wise, they were polar opposites. Sheri had the patience and kindness of a water buffalo. Berry was easy and loveable. When they were in the room together it was OK, funny in a weird way. But usually it was one or the other who would come by mid morning and having Sheri roll her eyes and snipe at me was torturous. My right side was affected by 'tone' seizures all day. New brain damage pain. My jaw would lock and the strong taste of metal would hit so strong sometimes it would gag me—lasting up to a minute—about 20 times an hour. All tentative plans for the future were shattered against the rocks, dirty foam and rubble left behind as the tide went out.

'...so he grabs his piece and baggy pants,
and heads on down to Popeye's
he starts a flippin' chicken
and servin' toast and hot pies
he sees 'ol Poncho stagger in and make eyes at his 'ol lady
so he pops a cap in Poncho's ass
and claims he is Slim Shady...'

—Weed Troll

USC memories: I would float like a ghost for of Out of Body experiences. Looking down at the doctors operating on me, naked partially covered by a sheet, spinning counter clockwise, watching them debride my feet.

A wash of reality being in the operating room looking at my right hand. The room is yellow and green with an orangey wash hazing over my eyesight. Dr's preparing to operate. My fingers are held together with thick black wire twisting around each one. I want to ask / can't talk / a swirling mash real and surreal. I was looking at the photos Ken and I shot in New Forrest and came up with an analogy; CVA was like fotos shot with a throw away camera. The Beaulieu museum was light and cheery but when the pictures came back they looked dark and menacing, the headlights of an old Rolls coming out of the murky night.

> '...how do you know what I'm going through
> when you haven't been where I've been?
> seen what I've seen?
> stop thinking you comprehend my state of mind...'
>
> paraphrasing Cypress Hill

The winter of 02–03 Kevin, Y and I went to the gym three times a week. I couldn't move fast enough to work up a sweat but I did a half hour walk on the treadmill then weights. Mostly legs with little or no weight. Thinking of Friends progress, I worked on a squat. I would hold my balance on a bar and bend my knee's as far as they would go. Took months, when I finally did it I felt proud of myself! For a minute. I wrote the following...

> Two women came up to me. 'You are an inspiration! What happened to you? I'm *so sorry*! You gonna be OK? They looked at me with pity and made ugly faces. 'Well, just keep up the good work, you poor thing, TRY to stay strong!' They clucked away.

> It's the worst. How do you react when somebody says shit like that to you? No choice, you must be polite. The more frightening your injuries are to sheep, the more over the top their reactions. Expressing horror and pity, making the Shocked & Pained face, (the ugly mug) shows you they know

how you feel. It makes them feel better about themselves. (Thank God I'm not her!) It happens all the time.

My new reality was I have to deal with chicken clucking fools for the rest of my life. Extremely depressing. Thinking of Wayne all day wasn't helping either; what might have been might have been good. I called his parents house the summer of 2002 and he was there. We talked and talked, I was so sad I was crying. It was night and I was lying on the fold out sofa bed in my parent's library. I tried to explain my situation but had a hard time talking. I listened to his voice telling me what he'd been up to. He missed me. We should have been together. He told me it didn't matter what I looked like and I know he meant it. It broke my heart to be so far apart. I couldn't fly to OZ (too hurt) and he couldn't afford to fly here. (Ross's Buddy passes don't work out of the country for anyone but family.)

> '...better to remember falling in love with the magic hour glow that time provides than to have him see what I've been reduced to...'

Phone calling was excruciating; numbers on the phone would scramble and my stutter would get worse. Mom gave me a phone card with twenty tiny numbers you had to get right the first time, no do-over's AND THEN *dial ten more*. It was a cruel joke, there's no way I could do it. I tried dialing Wayne's parents (normally) three times before I got it correct. When Mom got the phone bill a week later with my long cathartic call to OZ she went Bengal. I was not allowed to use their phone for long distance calls! Write a check immediately for the two hour call to Australia and <u>never do it again!</u> Hands on hips, she watched me write. Now I would say, 'don't worry, I can pay the phone bill,' but in 2002 I couldn't think clearly. When we heard Wayne's voice saying, 'call me back, babe...' on the answering machine a few days later she gave me a hard stare, *don't you dare*! I didn't. I couldn't forgive myself *for years*. $75 bucks an hour to talk to a man who loved me, was worried about me and wanted to connect <u>was worth it</u>. Why couldn't I stand up for myself? It's madness, looking back now. *I was scared to death of her.* Childhood terror—she could do whatever she wanted—I was helpless / hopeless.

'Gloom despair
and agony on me
deep dark depression
excessive misery
if it weren't fer bad luck
I'd have no luck at all
gloom despair
and agony on me…'

—Hee Haw

In January 2003 I found an Acupuncturist in Portland, Dr Beijing. In the 80's, Dr Beijing was a <u>Burn Surgeon</u> in China. He was sent by Buddha. He and his wife wanted to have more than one child so they applied for political asylum and ended up in Portland. He didn't want more med school so learned his grandfathers' art, acupuncture. I saw him twice a week and it usually made me sleepy. I'd nap on the comfy sofa in the living room.

We went to the anti-war rallies. There were a lot of them; it was good to see so many people protesting. Too painful to walk, we watched and took pictures as the marchers went by. Rag and Monk came to Oregon for a week and we went downstairs to Kevin's studio and made music. It was super hard singing with a CVA—my voice was slow and whispery—but super fun. It gave me an idea of what I was up against. Trying to sing and keep the beat was great speech therapy. Another analogy, brain damage is being at the beach in thick fog, waves wash away the sound of voices and you can't see anyone clearly. The brain damage dance also changes your personality. My politics were suddenly black and white, like a teenager. Good vs. Bad simplistic.

(I see All politicians in varying shades of depraved gray, suspect by their choice of profession Democan, Republicrat they're the same. They're both rickets riddled, rheumy eyed, pus filled and festering; ripping flesh off the elderly and poor.)

My television like's / dislikes changed drastically as well. Suddenly I watched Lizzie McGuire, 7th Heaven and Everyone Loves Raymond. Sweet Teenager,

Unitarian Christianity and Romano's traditional borderline boring sit-com. I had never watched more than a minute of any of them, now I was addicted. The near death / brain damage combo scrambled up a temporary childlike persona while the real me was hibernating and healing. I was occasionally waking up filled with anger however, I had to do something about it or my head would explode. I got a reputable firm to represent me and filed suit against the Sleeping Bag Co.

February 2003—Lake Oswego, Oregon

News this morning is sad. The space shuttle was coming in for a landing and was lost. Long white streaks of debris, no contact for an hour; that's the way to go. (I'd rather burn up in space than a sleeping bag.) Astronauts are the last of the Magellan's. RIP.

Joe Millionaire was on last night. I like this stupid show. The big dumb oaf, the sneaky girls and the ridiculous situations the producers dream up. This one chick has done fetish videos. Feet stuff, apparently. 'Very tame,' she says and she did it for money. (The men worshiping your toes will be heartbroken, they thought you did it for love.)

Reminded me of this silly gent trying to get me to produce fetish videos. His particular kink was food throwing. I told him I'd meet him at the corner. It was too funny; I had to hear this pitch. I lived a couple blocks up the hill from Ventura Boulevard and my usual haunt served a great brunch. I had doubts that I could be talked into it but I'd have a few laughs and see. I went with an open mind anyway. Producing a little fetish video might be good for a couple grand and if memory serves, I was broke. He brought all these magazines to show me and I was unable to control the occasional guffaw as I looked through them. Oatmeal, baked beans, honey, ketchup, eggs… girls with an occasional dude thrown in, rolling around, having food fights and being covered in the stuff.

Nothing pornographic either (porn, yuk) the models were wearing string bikinis. Chocolate cake, mustard, all kinds of dairy products, often times mixed together with bizarre outcomes. Imagine gooey peaches and teriyaki sauce or canned spaghetti with gloppy brown gravy.

The talent wasn't top shelf. 'I would get better looking girls.' I knew models that looked great in bikinis and friends with gorgeous back yards and good senses of humor. Digital camera, late afternoon sun / wouldn't take long to edit. Give it a funky back beat sound track, go for silly and fun, slow motion once in awhile, sexy models laughing as they throw pies. I started to warm up. 'Pre-production for a couple weeks, shoot it in a day and post for a week. We'd have to get some good looking food too, none of this pea soup and canned corn business, some nice big fluffy pies to throw; maybe whipped cream in spray cans…'

He didn't want to spend five hundred a day on swimsuit models and he was working hard to get me to come down on my (quite reasonable) fee for producing / directing / editing this feat of cinematic beauty. 'How about we do a test shoot first? He said, we could use …hmmm I don't know… how about me?' Ahh. He was harmless, even endearing in the way truly homely men are but I wasn't going to fulfill a whack fantasy for a stranger. 'Sweetie, I'm not into this fetish, it's not my bucket of tea.' He was crestfallen as I left; it was a hilarious meeting and brunch at The Bistro was always nice.

2007

War bound that winter, I wrote pages and pages, obsessed. Much was prophetic but anyone with common sense could see this train wreck coming. I don't find any satisfaction in 'I told you so.' The country had lost its collective mind and seemed to *be begging* for fascism. (The Patriot Act?) It was insane that NO ONE would challenge the embarrassing junk yard dog masquerading as president. Afghanistan and Bin Laden were forgotten as the Iraqi Bad Guy was trotted out for viewing pleasure. Hey sheep, look over here. *And they did.*

'…with a heart of furious fancies
whereof I am commander
with a burning spear and a horse of air
to the wilderness I wander…'

—Tom O' Bedlam's Song

Website / March 5ᵗʰ, 2002

Hi Everybody, Kev and Tony here with some good news. The doctors present for the dressing change today said everything was healing better than expected and Alisa is supposed to be released from the hospital into inpatient physical therapy in about a week from now, realistically probably toward the end of next week.

The consent seems to be that it would be good for her to start therapy as soon as possible, especially the neurological and speech rehab. There are two different places in discussion right now where she would get both, burn- and neurological-rehab in one place. At any rate, it's definitely a big change in the right direction and it's pretty safe to assume that Alisa will welcome the finishing of the first big cycle and taking the next step toward recovery. The plan is to let her heal a little more while getting her used to being in a wheelchair. She has one minor surgery left and leaves with an even ten within ten weeks. Visiting is OK right now; just remember that she's still in isolation because of the wound-infection. So, things are moving along it seems. Springtime should be the best time for healing anyway and will hopefully shorten her stay in permanent care. Both parents will arrive later this week as well and be here through the transition period. Thanks to all of you again that helped in one way or another with everything that was done.—Tony

'On 03 / 06 / 02 there was a change in mental status, increased slurred speech over the last few days. The patient was receiving treatment for muscle spasm on the right side, especially in the right lower extremity.

Neurology followed up; mental status and memory should improve when analgesics are tapered. Recommend an MRI scan, MRA scan brain when metallic hardware is removed. The length of time for Lovenox use, possibly three months.

Neurology indicated that they would start the patient on Baclofen for mytonic spasms. Thoughts were to place the patient on Coumadin.

Pharmacy consulted and indicated Warfarin interferes with hepatic synthesis of vitamin K, and concurrent use of anabolic steroids of oxandralone, SSRI, quinolones, may result in an increase in anticoagulation activity. Interaction between Warfarin and anabolic steroids are potentially severe.'

'...potentially severe...' Lucky I'm alive.

February 2003—Back in So Cal, Silver Lake—Husband's

Need to sleep, mind racing. Three doctors and my dentist in the last three days, seeing a neurologist tomorrow (Dr Average) trying to get myself as far back to normal as possible. Thinking positively on the road to success. (I'm Hallmark.) Alison drove me to Dr Allritini's in Santa Monica. He told me my hand 'looks good.' Made me laugh. Only to you, babe. It resembles a hand abstractly. Something Salvador Dali dreamt up. But he makes me feel better. When I was leaving he hugged me and I felt the 'almost kiss.' (He looks in your eyes and holds you a just a few seconds past appropriate...crazee.)

> '...life is but a dream to me
> different from anything you know
> you wouldn't believe where I go
> I've disappeared somewhere
> vanished in the atmosphere...'
>
> paraphrasing Delerium

Cat threw a Valentines party and Tricky was at her studio. It's best to be introduced to a stranger by a mutual friend and it was too hard to find one. I'm a too slow, stuttering, cane using, no-makeup wearing, Frankenstein idiot to meet Tricky (but someday I'll thank him for Maxinquale.) Cat had rented the theatre next door and had a Little Tiki Bar set on stage. A Little

Person bartender, low straw ceiling, children's chairs, kitschy decorations, silly fun—and centrally located—so I didn't have to walk or dodge drunks. (Canes are drunk magnets.) Eventually everyone came by to get a drink. Friend and Friend picked me up, stayed til three.

February 2003—Melinda's, Sherman Oaks

Met Dr Specialisto, an orthopedic surgeon at USC. He was positive he could make my elbow work again. Told me what the surgery would entail, he would saw off the HO. Bones bleed, he wanted to start supplementing vitamins and iron. Said he'd try for a 100% range of motion but I may have to settle for a little less. Specialisto wanted a CT scan so we could see the HO exactly, his assistant made the appointment. He's confident of *his* abilities but not arrogant. He wants a plastic surgeon to make the incision to see that the skin grafts are OK and the nerve doesn't get damaged. 'That's the only thing that concerns me. We'll get a plastic surgeon you like. Everything is going to be OK.' I love him, I've had a useless flipper for a year.

Had a 2nd opinion already scheduled with another orthopedist yesterday am with the CT scan at noon. Alison picked me up in the morning. To get from the valley to Dr Baby's office downtown by ten, we'd leave by nine. He's a children's orthopedist but also an elbow specialist who used to work with burn patients. (Accidental serendipity?) Showering took longer than I'd planned (surprise) and cell wasn't charged so Alison couldn't tell me she didn't have Melinda's address. Eventually I called her (Melinda and Alison live 10 minutes apart) then couldn't find my cane when she arrived. I felt like Shmeagle from The Lord of the Rings, goluming around.

We were finally on the 101 by 9:30, not too bad for Shmeagle. Alison said she also felt Shmeagle-ish and we were off. All day precious this and precious that. 'Shssshmeagle sees a doctor, precious little doctor…' Dr Baby was a gentle cat with an eastern European accent, easy to picture him with kids. He took more X-rays. My arm has changed so much. Three fingered hand pock marked with holes and an elbow that resembles a squashed tennis ball. I've been doing isometric exercise but my muscles are wasting. Baby sympathized and agreed surgery would work.

By the time we arrived at USC for the CT scan we were beyond stupid. Drunken sailors, the forms were endless and all in different locations. Every time we got sent to another floor we'd be dying. 'Ssssmmmeagle likes the fills out forms, precious precious forms...' Name? 'Alissssssmeagle.' Sex? 'Yes please.' Took over an hour, laughing the whole time. We eventually were led outside to a double wide trailer in a parking lot. The machine looks like a big doughnut. You lie in a thin little tray and slowly move through the pastry cooker. The technician and I tried several ways to isolate my elbow. Can't trust myself not to get vertigo and fall off. (I had a bad fall at Melinda's the other night, black and blue knees.) He finally had me lie flat on my back with my elbow at my side. Every 'slice' of the CT scan went through my internal organs. (CT's equal 200 regular Xrays.)

'Weed Troll kissin' all the ass
Weed Troll hopin' it will pass
Weed Troll slippin' on a mite
Weed Troll feelin' so uptight...'

—Weed Troll

Website / March 7th 2002

Hi All, Hope you enjoyed hearing about Alisa's pending release from the hospital as much as I did. She was wheeling around in a wheelchair again today and actually got to sneak outside for a few minutes. The news about her release caught us a little off guard as well, to tell you the truth, but it seems that just during last week her wound-healing progress has tripled and quadrupled. So, we don't really mind those kinds of surprises.

That brings me to another point, speaking of surprises; one was presented to me today as well. When I came back to the truck, somebody had smashed in the window and took a few things, amongst them my cell phone. Right in front of the hospital. My number will stay the same but of course, I lost all the numbers I had saved in the phone. Please call me in a couple of days, if you know I had your number, so I can get you back in the new phone. Or e-mail your number. Sorry about that, I should have backed up more. :) Talk to you soon, p&l, Tony

My arm was back on the chopping block. Goodfella wanted to give it six months and since he was in charge, they grudgingly accepted. But: Surgeons I didn't know would come in with interns and yakkedy yak as if I wasn't there. My hand would never work again; I'd lost too many tendons, veins, arteries bla bla… Dr Hacksaw wanted to chop it off so badly he was salivating. 'Just say the word my dear, I can take it off before breakfast.' Snidely Whiplash with a bad haircut. He came in after the Oscars, waltzing around in a cape and top hat. 'I went to Puccini, I never watch the Oscars, so classless, so nouveau riche, so can I cut it off? Can I? Can I cut it off yet?' Tony almost punched him and Hack Saw sidled away, a wistful look in his beady eyes.

The nurses tried to keep my spirits up. They had started to wheel me around what looked like an antique electric chair. It was difficult transferring from my bed—sometimes it hurt too much—but what a relief to get out of my room. Had an adventure with an orderly, Jerry. I was propped up in the wacky contraption, sitting on pillows, back supported by pillows, legs encased in more pillows and my tender right arm gingerly set upon one last pillow. Puffy the Dough Boy.

Through cavernous dusty unused unlit corridors to the smoking area on the 12th floor. It was the only place to get outside. Felt like a prison yard. High walls you couldn't see over, the loud hum of industrial air conditioning and the smell of old butts. 'Let's go outside, no one will know,' Puffy the begging puppy. Please please please… he thought about it. 'We have about 20 minutes.' We snuck into Cardiac and took their elevator to the ground. He wheeled me outside and I got a breath of fresh spring air for the first time in three months.

HEAVEN!

Jerry thought we could sneak back up through the jail. We took a regular elevator to the 11th floor where he knew a guard, then the freight elevator to the 12th. We started to congratulate ourselves / rounded a corner were confronted by a pack of snarling wolves. Taking me off the floor was a big deal, threat of infection. Kevin had stopped by during the escape and asked where his sister was. Half an hour later they'd searched the floor. Jerry took a lot of shit but at the end of the day didn't lose his job. Thank God Buddha Shiva! I never would have forgiven myself. Jerry took me to heaven and gave me hope.

> Aside: I was still trying eat vegan, (impossible if you have no control.) One day the family wanted to order a pizza, I wanted it without cheese but kept asking for pizza without tomato sauce. 'No, that's not what I meant, I don't want tomato sauce. No! I mean the stuff on top, the tomato sauce…'

Website / March 14th 2002

Hi everyone, well, the roller coaster ride continues… I think last we left off, everything was progressing at an above-average rate & they were targeting her release from USC this week. Since then, it's been down & back up again. (!?!)

Almost a week ago her consciousness & coherency plummeted. This was initially thought to be the result of over-medication, but her condition worsened; even after dramatically reducing her intake (main cocktail is currently methadone.) It became impossible for her to stay awake for more than brief periods, and communication nearly stopped.

They started the barrage of scans again, looking for a second stroke or other probable causes to no avail…medication was adjusted…. specialists called in… heads were being scratched…. nothing was ascertained… transfer out of USC was halted. This continued for several days, but recently she started showing signs of improvement. It's still a mystery what happened, but an adverse reaction to the myriad of drugs is highly suspect. So, for now the roller coaster goes up! She's awake again, eating, talking, moving... getting better.

On the burn-side, things are still gradually improving. Ankles / feet are healing & doing OK.... No infection or anything to worry about I'm told... final skin grafts seem to be taking fine & there's not a lot of new activity happening down there, except for physical therapy & dressing changes. PT was halted during this last week, but they're now getting back on track. Regarding the hand, the doctors say "you couldn't beg us to amputate at this point," which is quite a relief since that discussion has still been coming up, even recently. She still has an outside support rod from wrist to forearm & they're planning to remove it next Tuesday. A few open wounds still remain on the back of the hand & across the tops of her fingers, so they'll probably attempt skin grafts Tues as well. They might do the back of the hand in two stages—artificial skin, and then replace with her own later on.

It's definitely not a pretty picture with the arm yet & lots of recoup time remains, but she's improving. Also, her right shoulder is tightening up from lack of movement & she needs to get it moving soon.

'...a few open wounds on the back of the hand...' were all five metacarpals and forearm open to the elbow.

The entire 5th metacarpal was open. Girlinaboysclub had 'saved' half of my little finger to be used as a flap. She had wanted to remove the little finger bone and flip the skin and muscle backward to cover the metacarpal. That was pre CVA. Now she was a bad memory and no one else would touch it. Sweet Kevin was in town and wanted to watch a dressing change. He wanted to see what I was going through and stay in the room for the daily nightmare. I wouldn't, *couldn't* let him stay. (Why they chose to listen to me *then* I find annoying, I was usually ignored.) I begged him to leave—changed my mind 5 minutes later—and my nurse wouldn't call him. (Mean bitch. Surreal.) I was *ashamed* of the hideous hand. Swollen and white, it wasn't part of me, it was part of a monster. I was Hideous Frankenstein, put together poorly. Mortified, irrational fear caused by the CVA. I wish Kevin would have seen my paw; his descriptions would have been more realistic. I always wanted someone who *loved me, with me.* No one explained that irregular groundless fears were <u>common</u> after a stroke. No one spoke of the CVA at all. Dot.

SO.... they're now planning to release her from USC in about two weeks (Provided we don't get ambushed again!) She'll then move to another 24 / 7 facility where she can continue to receive medical attention, but more importantly begin a rigorous neurological / speech & physical / occupational therapy program.

We've all pretty much decided it's best for her to stay in LA for now, so it seems the preeminent facility there is Rancho Los Amigos in Downey. They're a hospital / burn center with a great neuro & physical rehab program. She'll stay in Rancho for 1–2 months. After that...???... hopefully Alisa can better participate in the decision at that time.

So, up & down, up & frickin' down.... she's doing good now, still in the same room, visiting hours are the same 1p to 8p every day (if you get in before 8 you can stay longer). If you stop by, the perfect thing to bring is a snack of good (vegetarian) food. She needs to consume mass quantities, but the hospital food is defective at best & pretty rough. She positively appreciates anything yummy. Thanks all, hope to have good news to report after Tuesday's session!! Fyi, Tony's not on-line but will be in a few days.... He asked, please call if you've been e-mailing him with no response. Thanks, as always.—Kevin

'Defective at best...' Kevin's too nice.

With the exception of plain white rice, I couldn't tell what the slop was. Nothing could make me eat the compost the county was calling food. My nurses tried coaxing me and when that didn't work they tried threats. 'We'll put the tube back in…' The food tube went into my stomach through my nose; I'd been 'feeding' off it for months. 'Fine. I miss it.' I reached a compromise with Goodfella, if I'd drink five cans of Boost Protein a day they would let me ignore the swill. A year later—when I could read labels again—I saw with disgust that his precious Boost was <u>half sugar</u>! Horrible to feed the healthy!

Burn patients should eat protein and try to gain weight eating Healthy, not sugar and empty carbs. I should have been eating every two or three hours. I was covered by Producers Health Plan (SAG's insurance) one of the best in the city but I wasn't in a private facility, I was in the County Hospital receiving sub-human handling. Seeing from a patient's POV how wretchedly the poor are mistreated. There's no excuse for inedible swill in LA, California fruits and vegetables grow year round.

Alison cornered Allritini and asked him why I wasn't getting speech rehab; no one could understand what I was trying to say. 'There's one speech therapist for the whole building.' She couldn't believe what she was hearing. 'You'd better make sure they get up here!' An intern showed up a few days later with a paper showing how to do facial exercises. 'Do these three times a day.' Never saw her again.

I should have been moved, Cedars Sinai was just a few miles away and they have great stroke rehab. The USC doctors would have complained like sniveling little bitches but I could have and should have been moved to a private hospital. I needed real doctors and therapists, not overworked students. I needed someone who had my back who was truly looking out for my best interests. Tony is *the last* person I would have chosen for the job.

February, 2003—Sherman Oaks, Melinda's

Spent the day with Friend. He had funny stories about the ICU. I flew all over. I said, 'I've been flying above a field of wild horses.' Sounds nice. (I told Alison, 'I cant go to Mars today, I'm too tired, it's too far to fly…' 'It's OK she told me, you don't have to go.') Also, 'let's go outside and smoke,'

Friend would explain I was hospitalized and I'd respond, 'just push my bed outside for a minute, they won't notice...

Friend said it was a relief I didn't know how hurt I was, I looked five minutes from dead. He said if it had been up to him, he would have let them take off my arm. It caused agony; was infected, putting my life in jeopardy. Kevin said the same thing a few months ago; if it wasn't for the Pit Bull he would have given them the OK. There was just no getting around him, Tony was there every day. He hated amputation talk (so did my father he had backup.) He wouldn't let anyone discuss it in my room. Doctors, nurses, anyone, they would leave, Tony was threatening. He acted like he was still my boyfriend and <u>everyone else did too</u>. Maddening. Pain will pass, was his reasoning, cut it off and her arm is gone forever. Even *I wanted* to cut it off, I remember fighting about it. His standard reply was, 'you aren't thinking clearly, you're on too many drugs.' He was right about that, I saw ninjas and soldiers, colors for emotions, flew through space and had tiny horses jumping from the television.

> '...don't wanna see TV
> don't wanna see the news
> all I want is a big fat beat
> to dance away these blues...'

> paraphrasing Basement Jaxx

Birthday today and happy to be celebrating; I invited everyone in my phone book to a Mexican joint on Sunset. People that knew me well heard about my injury but I had work out friends, volunteer friends, acting class friends, easy to fall through the cracks friends. Most of them weren't in the stunt community. I loved doing stunts but tried to play elsewhere. I expected to be respected at work; easier to get if you're not on the grapevine.

'I don't wanna face the day
the day
today...'

—Great White

Fire in a Rhode Island nightclub—96 people dead. My old boyfriend Mr Right Now was in Great White. I remember the night we met. I was hanging with a couple of girlfriends and one loved boys with long hair. (It was the 80's) She spotted Mr and J and called them over. J was talkative and comical, an obvious player. My girlfriends were both all over him but I was interested in Mr Right Now, he was shy and cerebral. We all had dinner and drinks and because I was buzzed, I spent the night with Right Now at his hotel. I didn't want sex and he didn't hit on me. He gave me pajama pants and a T-shirt and we lay in bed giggling for hours. When they left town he sent flowers and called. I was charmed. That winter I would fly out every week or two and be with Right Now for two or three days. They were on tour with Whitesnake—who were huge—sold out stadiums. It was cool being the girlfriend of a rock star. New Orleans over Christmas was magic. Humid, smutty, alluring and anything you wanted, magically provided. Christmas lights hanging on iron balconies all over the Quarter added surrealism. One night we were in an old building that had a bar / restaurant on the ground floor. We snuck away from the crew, upstairs to have sex. (We were in heat and had sex everywhere.) Found a seemingly forgotten voodoo altar set up in front of a fireplace. There was an old pentagram chalked on the floor, left to be rubbed away by the back of his shirt.

2007

The Rhode Island fire happened because of me. Much like Latham's death, I was guilty. We woke something in the abyss and twenty years later it caused a nightclub fire half way across the country? Anything's possible I guess, though it seems unlikely now. In 2003 I was Guilty!

A freaky thing did happen to me in New Orleans, though. August of '94 I was working on a film shooting nights in the quarter, my schedule was light and my actor was a precious princess so I wasn't at the set unless I was on the call sheet, a few days a week. My actors stand in found out I was making 10 times what she was and tried to get my job. It was funny at first but she carried on for days, 'Alisa hardly ever comes to the set, Alisa this and Alisa that!' She really thought she could have my job, silly bitch. The stunt coordinator was a dick playing her, she was cute and he wanted a taste. 'You're right, Alisa is so and so,' I could hear them through the thin wall of the trailer. Annoying.

The ninety nine cent store in the quarter had voodoo dolls; I'd bought 50 to give away in LA. I cut Stand In's name out of a call sheet, pinned it to one of the voodoo dolls, lit it on fire and tossed it in the tub. The next day Stand In was ambulanced away for Heat Exhaustion! Voodoo works!

Maybe someone had a doll with my name on it. Everything was connected and everything was my fault! I would have benefited from a therapist who specialized in brain damage. My unhealthy psyche was mixing sadness and guilt into a questionable gruel.

'See the illustrious life of the disenchanted and disenfranchised
right here for your edification ladies and gents!
See Tom-Tom the dog faced boy!
See his rows and rows of razor sharp teeth!
Witness the execution of Gary the terrible tyrant today! In this tent!
WATCH—as he struggles against the bonds that bind
FEEL—the cooling flesh as his corpse is carried away before your very eyes!
Live on the inside, YES! Today! In this tent!'

~Al Christ

February 2003, Melinda's

I went to Rancho yesterday. Not sure what I was expecting. Dr Sarah and a new face, Dr Chang both asked me questions, most important, 'Where does it hurt?' I told them about the seizure-ish stroke symptoms. 'That's the most common,' Dr Chang said. It happens every morning. Right leg stiffens, toes pointing straight, I can't walk until it stops. The right arm wants to curl up and make a fist but HO has frozen my elbow.

Told them I was worried about my mug. My smile isn't straight; I can't 'wink.' When my face is relaxed the right corner of my mouth turns down, a sour puss frown. I hate my face, it's not me. Told them about acupuncture; it's helped but not enough. Acupuncture! Balderdash! Nothing but baloney, bullshit, child's play, nonsense for the New Ager's, it's not real medicine, don't waste your time! They both gave instant negative rants! It was bizarre. They gave each other a nod, a knowing chuckle, silly patient, so gullible. 'Besides you look great! It's hardly noticeable, they assured me, you look <u>so much better</u> than when you left, really amazing!' 'That's what I've been doing, acupuncture.' 'No no! Don't bother, it doesn't work. And you really look great!' 'I've had acupuncture twice a week for months.' Snort, guffaw! 'Stop, you're killing me! It doesn't work! And why bother anyway, you look fine.' Circular idiocy. Western medicine uses pharmaceuticals only. Dot. And I thought their disrespect for 5000 years of Chinese medicine was racist. What's with Dr Chang? Self hatred? Denial? Chang is Chinese isn't it? Whatever her ethnicity, she's definitely a US doctor. It's very American to be completely dismissive of other cultures.

We talked about medication: Baclofen, Ambien, and Neurontin. They were surprised I was off pain killers. Dr Chang suggested losing the Neurontin. 'Do it slowly over the course of ten days, see if you still need it.' My nerve endings were damaged, that's why Neurontin was prescribed. Perhaps the need for it was gone. The seizures I was experiencing where controlled by Baclofen so stay on that. <u>Exactly the opposite</u> of what Dr Average suggested. Dr Chang makes more sense. Dr Average was a waste of time. Not a moron, just ineffectual.

2007

Dr Average turned into Dr Asshole. He's a neurologist in Glendale, Kevin helped me find him on the Blue Cross website. I'd been thinking, there *must be something else* I could try to alleviate my continuing CVA symptoms. Dr Average charged my insurance $450 for a 15 minute office visit and me personally $190. I was expecting the Blue Cross discount, the $15 co-pay that I paid his receptionist. I sent him several letters asking him to forgive the $190, he wouldn't respond. I called his office repeatedly, he was always 'out or busy' wouldn't return calls and—unbelievably—the prick turned it over to collections. I've never paid it, eff him; I wrote a letter describing his filthy trick to the Credit Gods. Always get a recommendation to a new doctor from a doctor you know.

March 2003—Sherman Oaks, Melinda's

Ramayana 2K3—a play in Culver City Catherine and I were going to see: Ramayana is a Hindu myth / Ulysses-ish. My friends Rich and Dez are in it, they visited me in the ICU. I have striking memories of them. I was bedridden in an old southern mansion, the Bayou at the turn of the century. Louis IIIIX furniture, Indian carpets, high ceiling's, walls covered in expensive gold and pale yellow paper, French doors, white wood wainscoting. The doors were open, slight ocean breeze, creeping vines winding their way in and out of furniture and medical apparatus. They brought a circus troupe, contortionists, fire dancers, stilt walkers; not doing their acts, just quietly milling around in costume. Dez leaned over my bed, diamonds dripped off her skin like dew and she was softly glowing. Her voice meow meowing gently; I couldn't understand, she was speaking Tagalog or Elvish.

Rich and Dez came late to my birthday party last month, it was good to see them and have a real conversation. Rich (Rama) got us four tickets for the closing weekend. They were sold out but he was the star and had some pull. I called Cat the morning of (I had a feeling she was going to flake) she wanted to cancel and watch her stupid friend Stewart DJ somewhere in the Valley, insisting I come with her. No thanks—I'm going to see my friends—I like them. She put Stewart on the phone but he didn't dissuade me, he cemented my plans. He was insufferable. (This is a BIG deal for ME! I want Cat with ME! This is HUGE! You should understand how important this is for ME!) I hung up on him. He called back, I hung up on him again. I fumed around Melinda's kitchen for a minute then sat down and had to laugh. It was so Stewart. He really thought he was a Star (the nit wit) and very Catherine to avoid anything thorny, like canceling plans at the last minute. I called Friend and asked him if he wanted to go and he said yes.

That would have been the end of it except for the Cat codicil: She called at five that afternoon. 'I've been crying all day! I can't stand being between you and Stewart! You both want me with you and either way I loose!' Huh? 'Baby, I'm not between you and anything. I'm going to Ramayana, my plans never changed. Friend is picking me up. You can come with us, go watch Stewart, whatever you want.'
'You obviously don't want me around!'
'That's not what I said.'
'I heard Stewart yelling and I can't stand it! I'm always in the middle! You're tearing me apart!'

I lost it, 'Me Me Me! You are obsessed with yourself! You are not 'In the Middle' of Everything All the Time!'
'I'm a bad friend! Is that what you're saying? I'm a HORRIBLE FRIEND!' Then slammed her phone for the clichéd effect. Surreal.

I tasted metal but refused to let whack behavior ruin my evening. I needed chick support. I called Alison and Charlene, they came over with their working brains. 'She was wrong, right? Right, she was wrong.'

The Friend I invited, being male, guaranteed drama class was over for the day but I was skittish about seeing him. He was a stunt man and I hadn't seen anyone from work. I was embarrassed by my clumsy gait, my flipper arm, my crooked smile. A trapeze mantra was, 'do something that scares you everyday.' So I dressed better, no baggy men's clothing, put on makeup, combed my hair. Friend and I had a fun sexy night. He showed up wearing a maroon silk suit that matched my maroon silk sweater. We got stuck on the 405 and barely made it. They'd let our seats go ten minutes before curtain but we could look for an out of the way place to stand. Improbably, two seats were together, top row center, as we sat the curtain parted. And it was a great show! Dancing, flying, different apparatus, I know it's self absorbed but I was proud of Dez, felt big sister-ish, I brought her to trapeze years ago. Also quite entertaining to see Rich painted blue.

> '…be a fucking bastard
> lie to me scare me slap my face
> be crazee enough
> to make me hate you enough
> to let you go…'
>
> paraphrasing Shakira

2007

My friend Moe wanted me to move my stuff out of his pool house in March 2003. He was thinking of selling, the market was so bloated. I rented a storage space and hired a moving company it cost $500. Friend had given me $500 the day before from the Stunt Women's Foundation. Nice synchronicity. (Or arbitrary?) Moe wasn't home; he was moving his mother into a nursing home that weekend. Alison, Calvin and Forrest came over before the movers showed up and helped me go through boxes to see what was in there. I ended up leaving a big 1950's lounge chair in the garage and four big boxes at the end of the drive for Salvation Army. Moe got home and went ballistic! He called at seven am and woke me up swearing, super nasty. 'You Fucking Bitch! You fucking left fucking garbage in front of my fucking house! Fucking C**T! Whore! You fucking BITCH! Awakened with a filth clubbing I slowly whispered, 'it's not garbage, it's for the Salvation Army they'll be there tomorrow.' He hung up. Three seconds later he called again screaming and swearing! 'I'm sorry, I'll get someone to drive me over there this afternoon...' 'FUCK YOU! Not good enough! You hear me BITCH?' I can't even write the foul shit he was spewing. He hung up again. When my cell rang for the third time I let it go to voice mail. Maybe I was wrong but the punishment didn't fit the crime. He acted like he wanted to kill me. Surreal—was he for real? Or did I just have a nightmare? I listened to another disgusting tirade on my voice mail, narcolepsy lasted until four in the afternoon. Need for Baclofen woke me. I wrote...

> I prayed / chanted this afternoon in Melinda's hot tub. 'God, Shiva, Buddha, Allah, let me forgive my friends, God, Shiva, Buddha, Allah, let me forgive my friends,' over and over and over until I finally started crying and felt a little better. Catherine and Moe back to back; what the hell was that?

Searched Moe in my journals, found this:

February / 1992

It's been a grand week, got a couple jobs. Worked on a K-Cal promo Monday then Thursday started on Hard Copy as a P.A. for Moe.

The 'Marilyn's Death' story for sweeps. We're shooting at her house! It was for sale and the owners let Paramount rent it. Super cool to be in her house, her garden, her bedroom. I love her and imagine her everywhere…

Moe was one of many directors at Hard Copy, Paramount's magazine show about titillating death. My friend Snyder was their Casting Director and hired me a lot. I was kidnapped, murdered, was the nurse that told Elvis his mother died, a Beatles groupie and often worked as a Production Assistant.

Hard Copy called themselves 'News' I'm guessing because it was cheaper but they were always in trouble with AFTRA; they did re-enactments with actors not anchors. The producers were shifty. Nothing public, no casting calls, Snyder kept it hush hush and hired his friends, and nearly everyone that worked at Hard Copy joined AFTRA; we'd walk around with the 'killer of the week' photo seeing who looked the closest. I got to get my girlfriends work / work begets work and Hard Copy was fun. I started casually dating Moe (out in groups, no sex.) I tried to talk myself into a 'nice guy.'

February / 1992

Went to San Fran with Moe for the weekend. It was a mistake—Moe has a crush on me and I don't feel it. I really tried but he blew it twice.

1st—we get a rental car, looking for music, find Cypress Hill—I love and he HATES. He goes off on rap. 'It should be banned… bark bark bark!'

2nd—talking about trapeze, I can finally fly out of lines, I love, it's amazing I truly get the sensation of flight. He thought it was a bad idea. 'If it's dangerous, why would you ever fly without lines?' It really showed how different we are and why we wouldn't work.

'…will it matter when I'm dead
what I think or write or care?
will I leave a trace of the turmoil

and hellish all consuming beauty?
dreams tell it all every night, waking arrests
if I didn't wake what forty days would tell me then
forty years
four thousand lifetimes…'

~Al Christ

Website / March 25 2002

Greetings all, It's been a week+ since the last update, mainly because there's been no dramatic change in Alisa's condition. The medication suspect in causing the repeat-offender drowsiness seems to have now been successfully adjusted to keep her alert, although her pain level has increased. The support rod suspended off her wrist / arm was removed & is healing as expected. Some minor touch-up patchwork / grafting on her ankles was performed late last week & is also doing well. So, in general, healing is progressing fine.

The main concern is Rehab. Both neurological & physical. Physical is happening daily, albeit not ideal, but more importantly there's not a good neuro program at USC. [There was NO neuro program at USC] So after much jousting with the USC staff it looks like she'll be transferring out late this week, probably close to Friday.

The Rancho staff were in to evaluate her yesterday & the USC surgical team blessed the transfer after a group evaluation today. They've been resistant to let her go until now, as her wounds have still been critical. There's some red tape to cut this week, but if all goes well, she'll be in Downey by the weekend. So, if possible, swing by & say one last hello / goodbye to USC. Bring a good vibe as these last few weeks have been arduous to say the least! I'll drop another line over the weekend, give or take a day, with the latest, as well as the new info on Rancho.

Operation # 10: 'Patient tolerated the procedure well and was transferred to the post anesthesia recovery room in stable condition.'

NAME: Christenson, Alicia

My mind was fuzzy, cognitive reasoning disabled, I couldn't grasp normal thought processes. Trying to write with my left hand was hard, after the CVA, impossible. I couldn't remember how letters were formed, couldn't recite the alphabet. A b c …g? I tried writing numbers—got to 7—then couldn't think of what came next. It horrified me. Day after day I lay alone watching sports. I couldn't follow TV shows or films, fortunately the Lakers were golden that season.

Once I was released from Intensive Care, it was back to iffy nurses and bathing in a coffin. The Disney characters were still swirling around but luminescent; pale, salty and sad. My legs and feet were covered in thousands of staples. Every day in the tub we'd take off more metal. My legs looked like ground veal. I disconnected. The world swirling by billions of miles an hour and I was in a vacuum, barely seeing, barely hearing.

I thought I understood brain injuries before I had one. Ken's stroke, Tony cracked his skull (street luge) and was comatose four days, Georgene had a brain tumor in '00. They all explained what they were going through and I listened, empathized, thought I got it. But when I woke up from surgery and finally figured out what had happened to me, it was worse than I could ever imagine. This isn't something imaginable to an operational brain; it's a different dimensional plane, a different animal with strange animal pain.

University of Southern California
Orthopedic Surgery Associates

March, 2003

SURGERY INSTRUCTIONS

Pt: Alisa Christensen

Please make your pre-op appointment with your primary care physician 1 to 2 weeks prior to your surgery date. The

date of your surgery is Thursday **4 / 3 / 03 at 7:30 a.m.**
Please arrive at the address below at 6:00 a.m.

Please call our office should you have any questions.

Thank you,
Nesta Nestle
Patient Care Coordinator

Specialisto was going out of town at the end of March and switched my elbow surgery to the following week, he wanted to be in town for my recovery. Allritini could only be there late in the day.

Worried, I called and reminded Nesta of Allritini's schedule. I had to be last. She told me that I was the first person listed—she would change my time when someone else was added on. Seemed weird but what could I do.

We went to another peace march downtown, thousands of people. It was only covered on local news. Divide and conquer, bitches. Our national news has changed, news is now propaganda. It's too awful to think about, sheep don't think. They believe the US is still respected by other nations, our economy is healthy, the news is factual and the boogie monster lives in Baghdad.

My elbow worked while dreaming, it was the real future, I had moved forward, I woke surprised that it was still stuck. Two weeks to go.

[a week later]

I called Nesta to check her weird surgery scheduling and she told me a diabetic had the 5 pm spot. She was rude and pretended she didn't know what I was talking about. She refused to change it! Her precious diabetic took precedence. Kevin talked to her and had no luck either. I called Allritini's office and told Jane (his assistant) what Nesta was up to. Jane said she'd give him the message. I took a shower, mad and frightened. My skin broke open when I was showering, bleeding like crazy! I stood frozen, watching blood go down the drain (Psycho) until it stopped. Took forever. When I got out, a long sliver of bone easily slipped out with tweezers, no pain. IT'S SO FREAKISH! I'll never get used to it. Showers take hours. Allritini had left a message on my voice mail / he'd talked to Nesta, it was taken care of.

2007

March 2003 was the start of the illegal corporate war. My family and I were Disgusted. It was embarrassing to watch the presidents brazen bull shit; embarrassing to watch fellow citizens self indulgent blood lust. Four horsemen stomping in the new millennium; it still sends me to crazee town / WMD's? Who believed that? The whole country it seemed but only because dissenters were silenced. Colin Powell trotting around doing his best to sell the Corporate war to the UN—he should have balanced a ball on his nose too—good dog.

> '…you've taken a vibrant living country
> and destroyed it
> you think you're hiding criminal activity
> but it's clear as day to me
> and I have fucking Brain Damage!
> you stupid fucking idiot…'

> paraphrasing Siouxie & The Banshees

March 2003—Lake Oswego, Oregon

Woke at seven, flipped through TV. Caught the last five minutes of the first studio film I had a speaking part in, Another 48 Hours. (The scene I was in was the big shoot out at the end.) 'Birdcage Showgirl, Alisa Christensen' is the last cast credit.

Walter Hill was our director. I had a such a crush on him. Getting into SAG used to be hard-ish. Had to have either a speaking part or a stunt and you had to get 'Taft-Hartley'd' in. (The Company had to pay a fine to use non-union talent.) You had to have a friend in production willing to pay.

SAG and AFTRA are sisters, movies and television. (Film & video.) AFTRA was easier to join, pay their dues and you could work AFTRA shows. If you couldn't afford the initiation sum, they would let you work it off. Almost all sitcoms used to be AFTRA. Daytime Soaps still are. Extra work for AFTRA was preferable, around $100 a day, over time after eight. The first speaking part I had on television was The Golden Girls. (An AFTRA show.) They are at a Forum Seminar (or something similar) and I was part of the animatronic crowd. 'You are all individuals!' says the speaker. 'Yes! We are all individuals!' We said everything in unison, cute joke. It still pays residuals quarterly. The Golden Girls will run forever (good omen for my career) it's sweet, non-threatening and they must have shot a million of them.

I did a lot of non-union and foreign films—I had a fun part in a Korean, Born Again Christian flick called The Rapture (Elliot Hong, director)—but bible movies were an anomaly, I did mostly horror. And more than thirty music videos; MTV used to play videos all day, when they changed format they put a dozen little production companies out of business. I was considered an 'ingénue' and worked with the same models all the time; we became friends and got each other work when stuff came up. A special rate ($300–$1000) was given to sexy kittens that were 'featured.' Not a speaking part but not technically 'extra' usually requiring an audition.

I found a few pages of 'Freddy's Nightmares' dated November '89, it was a TV show. Robert Englund would introduce (Hitchcock-ish) I was usually one of the corpses hanging from hooks behind him / I'd move a little ooo! Ick! She's still alive! The pages I found are: Mrs Hancock is being hypnotized, then seduced by her corrupt psychiatrist, he begins making love to her and she suddenly turns into a corpse / he freaks. I loved jobs like that, fun makeup days, beauty to cadaver in 12 hours. Model, Photo Double, Stand In, PA (production assistant) anything to avoid non-union extra work, $40 a day, less than minimum wage.

My Extra Service sent several young blondes to audition for Walter Hill on Tales From the Crypt. Walter was one of the executive producer's. Walter also directed The Warriors. It was the first film I took notice of the director in. Released in 1979 it was pre-music video and wildly inventive. Ultra violence was sexy. I wanted to work for him. He was looking for a terrified reaction to a gun in the face. I watched him point his finger at each girl. We were standing in a line, I was last. When he pointed at me that finger was a real gun—if you don't believe—more extra work! Tears welled and he hired me. The next week on the set he told me was going to give me a few lines, it'd be more realistic. The elusive Taft-Hartley was mine! The episode was 'Cutting Cards.'

The stunt coordinator and I drive into a parking lot in a long soft top caddy. We look like Vegas idiots, his suit is brown polyester and I'm wearing a pink Kelly Bundy. The two leads were in a hot discussion. 'Hey, park the car...' stunt coordinator yells. 'Get the fuck out of here!' Gun pointed in our faces. 'Oh shit, Go! Get out! GO!' I yell at my boyfriend as he careens backward. 'Fucking lunatics!' he yells as we speed away.

Set ups take more time at night, I talked with Walter about The Warriors, I'd seen it ten times and I loved film stories. (And the end of Crossroads, Steve Vai playing the devil was inspired casting.) He told me why he liked night shoots, if you wet the streets with a water truck when picture's up it gives the flat screen a three dimensional feel. Walter turned me onto John Woo films, he was making sexy ultra violence in Japan. (When he became famous in the US he was copied like mad.) Walter is a cool cowboy. He never raised his voice, he laughed easily and often and when something went wrong (always does) he would say 'shit' under his breath and see it fixed.

He hired me on Another 48 about 6 months later. 48 got me started doing stunts. Sitting around shootin' the breeze with the stunt guys, I was asked if I had ever considered stunt driving. 'We could use a young blonde on our team.' He was playfully hitting on me, everyone did, my wardrobe was a chain bikini and thigh high patent leather boots.

> Aside: A few chains a couple of pasties and my parent's were in town. What to do what to do. I wanted to show Mom Paramount's lot but was slightly worried about her reaction to non-existent wardrobe. Maybe I could get her star struck. Eddie M wasn't around that week but Nick Nolte was I told

him my plan. The next day Mom and I were walking around, I showed her my trailer, the sound stage with our set being built, we heard someone hollering, 'hey, D! Alisa told us you were coming!' Nick was a stage away waving at us. He jogged over and was the Perfect Movie Star, charming, interested. We went to the wardrobe trailer and I showed her my chains. She said, well, you have the body for it. Cut to a few years later: The first morning of Mulholland Falls, Nick and I met at Craft Service for coffee. I asked if he remembered me, 'yes Alisa,' he said chuckling.

The little cartoon light bulb went on above my head. Stunt Driving! Finally something to get excited about! I'd stop by the airport and pick up a rental. Between 15 and 30 of us would meet in an industrial park on Sunday mornings. I learned 90's, backward and forward 180's and my favorite, 360's. Over fill the tires / silicone sand if the shot is dry, water is better / slowest is 50 faster is superb, 80, 90 heart thumping senses sharpen adrenaline makes everything slow motion / doing a 360 was having an orgasm you see coming. I also practiced precision driving, which I was actually hired for. Example: the camera truck is going 40 mph. Drive by exactly three feet away going exactly 50 mph, 25 times.

After Another 48 Hours, I did utility stunts on The Doors. Five grand for a week of watching Oliver Stone direct a concert riot and Val Kilmer channel Morrison. (He should have been Oscar nominated; he was so Morrison it was creepy.) I was hooked. Stunt people are in SAG, get residuals like actors and 'stunt adjustments.' The more dangerous or specialized a stunt (and the bigger the company) the more money you make. Actors give up to 30% of their earnings to agents and managers pre-tax. They swallow a lot of pride, they have a lot of disappointments, have to take shit from annoying assistants, wanna bee's and be on constant watch for predators.

Stunt people rarely audition and when they do, they go straight to the Director. It fit my personality better. Acting was super fun but getting work was torture. Endless, endless auditions, most of the time for angry failed actors. (Casting Directors) But I was seduced and wanted to work in the entertainment industry; I rented every movie of Walter's and asked everything I could think of about writing / producing / directing. Walter always made time for me and gave great advice; be ready to jump on opportunity when it comes because it will but not often, don't turn down any job offers (legit ones, duh) always have several irons in different fires. I loved Walter, seriously loved him. The Journeyman Artist captivated me. I wanted a mentor / lover. He had a wife and two little babies, it's the only thing that kept me off of him. Wives were fair game (if you can't keep him, tough.) But babies were a different animal, only a loser cheats on a wife caring for his baby; that wasn't Walter. We had Courtly Love—you never behave improperly—just want to. It was luscious, better than the real thing.

Mr Right Now was an actor, Walter was casting Trespass, he read for a part. Right Now knew he didn't make an impression (you can tell) scrambling he said, 'I'm friends with Alisa, she said to say hi…' they chatted about me a minute then Walter said 'don't change your hair, we'll be in touch.' He was hired. (Right Now, sure I bought Walters favor, bought me a leather trench coat to say thanx.) They shot on location; a few months later they were shooting the pick up's at Universal's lot and I visited. Walter and I sat and gossiped while the lighting was being tweaked. Right Now was in a tight set shooting CU's and couldn't come out between set ups. 'Right Now is a good actor, really good.' High praise / made me love him even more. I asked what he liked shooting more, films or television. He liked both but they were different. Films were like a book in the library and television was akin to a magazine.

He was going to hire me on Geronimo but the scene was cut. We kept in touch. (I'd call his office every month or so and he'd always return my call.) I told him about a magazine article I'd read, Ellen Barkin trashing all the annoying directors she'd worked with, I loved it, she was so fearless. The interviewer asked about Johnny Handsome—A Hill film—'I'd work with Walter again,' she said. Who wouldn't? I worked on Wild Bill (saloon girl) and Ellen B played Calamity Jane. Diane Lane was in Wild Bill and Streets of Fire in '84. Walter is loyal, he likes and understands actors, good actors have to be vulnerable, he provides protection. I still love him and his kids are almost grown fortunately, those mercenary days were over by my mid 20's.

'I'm in a circus spinning plates
I've gone down crazee lane
I'm Muddy Waters spinning plates
spinning plates…'

paraphrasing Radiohead

March, 2003—Burbank, CA

It's dawn. Staying at The Oakwood Apartments across from Universal. Makes me think of B, a lover I had for a minute. He used to live here. He was a poet, it was fun being a muse. Cloud cover and smog make the LA sunrise surreal indigo and fluorescent pink. Dawn was B's favorite time of day but we usually saw it when we were going to sleep. This place is big, gated and guarded. Pools, Jacuzzi's, tennis courts, gym's with all the amenities, maid service, room service, private movie theater and a general store on the lot. They're not cheap. I remember the two bedroom B lived in was thirty six hundred a month. I'm paying two grand for a studio, too much for long but I'm scared to be alone after surgery. B's roommate Romeo was something of a grifter. I liked him (everyone liked him) he was getting a record label to pay the rent. While B looked more than capable of taking care of himself, he was hopelessly inept. Romeo paid for just about everything and I picked up the rest. Beautiful, effed up B; he grew up hard and ran away at 16. Joined some Monks, they did relief work, hurricanes / tornados / floods. They healed him the best they could. The hypothesis behind a miserable childhood is it makes Stardom; the Rags to Riches story. Reality isn't as cool. Sometimes a person is too damaged to recover.

'…I'm outside looking in
I can see your true colors
you're a freak like me
that's why I love you…'

paraphrasing Staind & Cindy Lauper

I've been crying since I got here. It's hard to keep living out of suitcases, dragging my shit around. No home, no car. I'm living the life of a rock star without any of the perks. I've been living this uncertainty for over a year.

I've got Home Scrub with me. No more crazee meowling at four in the morning. (She was driving us nuts; I think it was the cold damp weather.) She loves the small room; almost blind, she walks around keeping a paw to the wall and learns the new space, amazing really. She adapts better than I do.

I saw Allritini yesterday and told him that I'm thinking about giving up on my hand. The elbow surgery is fine, I want my elbow to work but maybe this three fingered monstrosity is a good as it gets. I'm tired. The bubbly bloody boils, spitting out bones, maybe no fingers would be better than having stiff sore sticks. They will never move again, the cartilage is gone, the joints are fused. They're ugly and painful. He said take it one step at a time; get the elbow working and see what it does to the hand.

Speaking of pain, my left leg was killing me all night. Going fetal, I had to stand up, a huge step backward. I haven't had this much pain at night since last September. How long does it go on? I'm so fucking bored with pain. I went to the gym and that helped a little but its sad struggling to walk on the treadmill when I remember how B and I used to work out in this gym.

Saw Dr Coolchick yesterday, she did the pre-op work-up on me. She suggested doubling my Baclofen scrip and was surprised that I was off pain killers. 'So fast…' is how she put it. She thinks it's too soon. I think fifteen months is a snails pace.

2007

It was my 1st attempt at living alone / poor sweet baby / I was SO phucked up. My brain injury caused *even the most obvious* solution to a problem to elude me. I describe waking up in horrible pain and in the next sentence, I'm telling Dr Coolchick I'm fine.

'…I think fifteen months is a snails pace…'

There's no rational excuse for ignoring my night pains—I blame the CVA. I thought I could work out and *will myself better* and every month that went by without obvious improvement augmented my depression. I had no idea how long burns take to stop aching and *not one* of my burn physicians told me. My 3rd and 4th degree burns took five years to heal. (So be patient and take your medication.)

April 2, 2003 LA—Oakwood's, Burbank

I found a CD of OZ fotos. Wayne and I at an abandoned house outside of Nimben. Falling apart, overgrown with vines and grass, it used to be lovely. Now deserted, being reclaimed by land. Found some newspapers in the back entry from the '70's. What happened to the people that lived there? Unforeseen catastrophe? Illness? CVA? Burned half to death?

Melinda and Charlene are on their way over here and I am calm this minute but I don't see any end in sight. I'm in Despair. Don't want to be this crippled old hag. I'd rather be dead. To know the best has passed is unbearable.

April 3, 2003

I don't want that to be the last thing I wrote if I don't come back.

Kevin called me this morning to wish me well. It's a little after eleven and Alison is on her way over to pick me up. I feel alone, yet it's irrational. I am surrounded by friends and have family who love me. Just get through one more surgery. My elbow will work again. I won't have another stroke. And everything will be all right. This time next year, I'll be looking through new eyes and things won't be so sad.

> '…foggy morning, no sun
> but I know it's there
> there is one mystery I cant express
> to give your more and receive your less…'
>
> paraphrasing Bob Marley

Alison hung out for pre-op. Doctor Specialisto's sidekick Red Talkative came by and introduced himself. He told me about his father. He had been burned in a car fire in South America and had walked three hundred thousand miles out of the jungle to get help. Skin peeling off, covered in dirt but he made it and he's fine now. Happened years ago, before Red was born. As nutty as it sounds, I like stories like that. It calms me somehow, knowing people before me have survived.

With Alison there I was OK but she took off at three to beat rush and once alone I had frightened tears. The CVA was on my mind. I could take any outcome for my arm, I couldn't take another stroke. Specialisto came by to reassure; I wasn't having a CVA in his OR. Dot. I kept busy reading Khalil Gibran. (1883–1931) When the anesthesiologist came to start my IV, I just said hello and kept reading, even when she couldn't find a vein and stuck me over and over. Been there, that pain I can take.

> 'You are like a flower that grows in the shade; the gentle breeze comes and bears your seed into the sunlight, where you will live again in beauty. You are like the bare tree bowed with winter's snow; Spring shall come and spread her garments of green over you; and Truth shall rend the veil of tears that hides your laughter. I take you unto me, my afflicted brothers, I love you and I condemn your oppressors.'

—Khalil Gibran

DATE OF OPERATION: **4 / 03 / 03**

SURGEON: Joe Specialisto, MD

ASSISTANTS: Itsal Possible, MD
                                Red Talkative, MD

PREOPERATIVE DIAGNOSIS:
Stiff elbow, status post burn with heterotopic ossification, right upper extremity.

POST OPERATIVE DIAGNOSIS: Same as the pre-op…
OPERATIVE PROCEDURES:

1.   Release and resection of heteropic ossification, right elbow.

2.   Ulnar nerve transposition (performed by John Allritini of the Division of Plastic Surgery.)

ANESTHESIA:	General.
ANESTHESIOLOGIST:	Please Donkillme, MD
ESTIMATED BLOOD LOSS:	Minimal.
FLUIDS:	500 cc.
TOURNIQUET TIME:	64 minutes at 250 mmHg.
COMPLICATIONS:	None.
DISPOSITION:	To recovery.
SPONGE AND NEEDLE COUNTS:	Correct.
PROCEDURE:	

The patient was taken to surgery and placed on the operating table supine. Monitoring was begun. The patient was then induced under general anesthesia. The patient had an arthrodesed elbow.

Dr Allritini then exposed the ulnar nerve and transposed it. I resected the medial intramuscular septum and then started resecting heterotopic bone, removing the neocortex down to the old cortex. Eventually I got down to the trochlea.

The bridge between the ulnar and humerus was removed, and motion was obtained. The articular cartilage actually looked pretty good. There were a few intra-articular synechiae. I had to resect a significant amount of bone from the olecranon as well as between the olecranon the medial condyle. I was quite pleased with the amount of bone resected.

At this time the triceps was flipped up over the olecranon, and an Outbridge-Kashiwagi fenestration arthroplasty was performed using a 12-mm core reamer. The anterior capsule was released at this point and got to about 40 to 125 easily.

At this point, bone wax was placed over bleeding bone. Tissues were closed. Irrigation was performed. The tourniquet was let down. The nerve was secured subcutaneously by Dr Allritini. A layered closure was performed over Blake drains. A sterile dressing was applied. The patient was awakened, extubated and taken to recovery in stable condition.

USC Hospital
Alisa Christensen
Joe Specialisto, MD

First thing I noticed, my brain was the same. Second, no pain; back on morphine. I looked at pictures in the paper, couldn't read, didn't care. I was taken from recovery to my room at about eight pm. The staff were polite, the new hospital felt safe and clean.

I was there for five days. Specialisto, Allritini and Red Talkative came to check on me early, 6 am. Good news, all good news. Specialisto showed me X-rays of my elbow straight and bent. Alison took pictures / I look ecstatic and sleepy.

I was sharing a room with a distraught woman, she hated hospitals but I couldn't concur. I had a new, clean room, a big television, a phone, an IV of pain free, I was hungry and the food was edible! Pancakes and eggs for breakfast, tuna salad, apple and banana for lunch, salmon with broccoli and mashed potatoes for dinner. Bedtime snack, pb & j sandwich, popcorn and a Popsicle. I ate more in one day than the whole week leading up to surgery.

'They're hurting me, they wont help me…' she was crying, had an accent (either Israeli or Arabic, I can never tell the difference.) 'Sweetheart you're fine, I promise you're fine. Everything's going to be OK.' I gave her Khalil Gibran. I was back on TV.

I called Joni's to tell them surgery was successful and I had a message from Fred! That was a nice surprise. One Saturday night / late '90's / I was sitting outside at a bar on Sunset, laughing with a pack of Friends. Summer, hot, watching the parade of cars slide by, kids driving the strip, tons of convertibles. The guys were trying to get a car of girls to stop. They couldn't do it. (Duh.) We women would call and wave to the men driving by and they would stop, every time. Very stupid and funny; this carried on through another round. 'Of COURSE they stop, look at you! Bet they wont let you drive.' Another convertible rounded the corner. A cute Astin Martin with an even cuter boy in it. 'Hey Hey! Stop!' He did. 'Can I drive?' I said. He though about it for a minute as we all waited. 'Yes.' That's how I met Fred. He was twenty one, Parisian and studying international finance. He had been in LA three weeks. We spent the rest of the summer together and then he went home. I couldn't believe it. I called him back and told him what had happened. Fifteen operations in fifteen months. He said he'd come to the Oakwood's when I was released.

On day three the big billowy bandages came off and I moved my elbow for the first time in over a year, exactly like my dream a few weeks back.

Vision Quest delivered a CPM machine (continuous passive motion) for my elbow and I started using it while still hospitalized. I love it. The wacky contraption sits by my bedside. I strap my elbow in and it slowly ranges as I sleep. During the day I stretch and ice, being careful not to cause pain. Specialisto told me not to do anything painful. Pain would make the HO come back.

Husband picked me up from the hospital and we stopped at the pharmacy on the way back to The Oakwood's. Radiation was usually used as a follow up for HO surgery but would kill fragile skin grafts. Indomethicin replaced radiation. I took it for three months.

My cousin Lance came to visit the night I got back. He's a rocket scientist (which always cracks me up like a little kid) he works for JHL. SO Glad I have family in town. And it's been super seeing Fred again—he came by every day the 1ˢᵗ week—took me out, took the cat litter out, brought schnizzle. (Haven't smoked since Rag's visit in January.)

I had a nurse coming by for three days from Cedars-Sinai Homecare Services. The social worker at USC set it up. I liked her, a single Mom. I had a physical therapist stop by to make sure I was capable of taking care of myself. Another single mother. Friendly, funny and we knew some of the same Doctors and therapists. A week after my operation, my CPM machine broke. Vision Quest sent out a tech to trouble shoot. Once again, single mom. The Universe kept sending me woman who were fine on their own.

Tech changed out machines, the new one had an extra piece that made it taller. I was already sleeping on two mattresses, it was already too tall. We needed to take a piece out to make it fit. A simple puzzle. I knew I should be able to figure it out, it was right in front of me. I blame the CVA. (What Tech can blame, who knows.) Husband came by in the afternoon and fixed it in four seconds. 'It's just this.' He took the piece out and screwed the contraption back together. I'm sad that I've lost IQ, don't know if it will come back.

'...it is the evening of my harnessed loathing
back beyond the fair
lines drawn me quartered
empty a spine shaking rhymer
freaks pygmies Siamese babies
cruise the fairways loot the alleys
sigh maliciously shy away...'

~Al Christ

My friend Forrest helped me to get a mini van. It's a Mercury Estate, I love! Freedom! Tan leather interior with power everything. It's tall, easy to get in and out, easy to drive with the suicide ball / finally able to take myself wherever, whenever. 16 months with no tires almost made my head explode.

Brother and Nephew came out a little late. Nephew's left arm was in a cast, he broke it skateboarding. Fortunately it wasn't causing him pain. We got a lot of double takes. Nephew is seven, such a great age to be. We took advantage of the movie theater—fun to have your own private theatre. Went to Universal and Griffith Park, I have so much fun with him, we can make a game of anything. Like: Me lying on the bed—Nephew running around it—throwing wadded up paper at each other, kept us in stitches for hours.

April 2003—North Hills, Shelby's

I've moved from The Oakwood's to my friend Shelby's. A big ranch deep in the valley.

The surgery was a success, my elbow is fine but my hand isn't doing well. Amputate. I can hardly write it. The bones seem to be dying. Last summer tiny chips started showing up. It never slowed—they kept coming, month after month, bigger and bigger. Allritini used the Q-tip burn thingy to scorch away the pimples and boils when I was at Velvets. He did it again this past week and another bone came though. It's sticking out of the 1st metacarpal, almost an inch long.

At physical therapy this afternoon Therapist was concerned about a teensy tiny bit of stitching showing at the top of the suture point along my arm. I had to laugh. She hasn't seen my paw. I keep it covered with potions and bandages. I told her about it, though. It's hard to describe. A person isn't supposed to see their own bones. She called over to Specalisto's office and had me swing by. He pulled out a tiny bit of suture and asked if I wanted to keep it. Nada, I'm keeping a creepier package of keepsakes. The only person who sees my paw is Allritini.

(That weird's me out as well. It's like a horrid secret. Shelby's lover keeps insisting that I buy Green French Mud and rub it on my hand daily, he's Sure it's a miracle cure. I'd take off my bandaging and show him how unhygienic that would be for open wounds with Bones Sticking Out if I cared about him—but I don't—so I keep saying 'thanx for the tip,' and hope he eventually stops.)

Saw Allritini yesterday and brought my ghoulish little box of bones. He looked at my paw, took a pair of tweezers and tried to pull the pock marked bone out, it caused a shiver of pain from deep inside the bone. Creepy cyborg. 'Maybe we should wait a little longer...'

He looked at my collection. 'This is HO bone...' hesitant. I disagreed, I didn't have HO in my hand. Allritini thought my hand was generating new bone but the X-rays Dr Baby took still show clear drill holes. Allritini said he'd talk to Goodfella and Setjermindtoit and we'd have a pow wow in the next couple of weeks. Get another CT scan of my wrist and hand and see what's going on. I love him and trust him so I'm trying to give myself to the care of a physician worthy of trust. It's hard.

'Weed Troll drinking from a golden pie can
Weed Troll eating from a spinning ceiling fan
Weed Troll flapping all his big fat gut
Weed Troll sniffing a Chihuahuas little butt...'

—Weed Troll

I've been driving myself to rehab. Therapist is so sweet and empathetic she reminds me of Therapist in Minnesota. No strength training yet, no pain, just passive motion and a lot of massage. Therapist told me to stop trying to deal with the County and sent me to Lerman & Sons Orthodics in Beverly Hills for an AFO.

I feel stupid for throwing away the one I got from my Smallville Therapist, even if it didn't work. The AFO is a plastic brace for my right foot. It keeps the ankle flexed and the big toe up. It helps me walk normally. I had one from Rancho that worked fine but Therapist insisted it didn't. I of course didn't argue. Therapist was young. Too eager to see results and not enough experience with CVA's. She had a brace made with a hinge at the ankle and insisted it would strengthen my muscles. It was useless and would occasionally catch my skin—Ouch! It's a neurological problem. Foot Drop is caused by the CVA, not weak muscles. I tossed it in the trash out of frustration when

I was at Melinda's in February. Regretted it later of course. It cost $800, I should have donated it to a free clinic.

I threw away <u>way</u> too much. I wish someone had said, Hey Brain Damage, No! Don't Throw! I still shake my head over moving day at Moe's. I'd forgotten that a year earlier I was moving to OZ. I had already gone through my things and saved only what I couldn't part with, expensive or sentimental. I shouldn't have opened *anything* that day. I'd already given away TONS of clothing to Penny Lane, a charity that helped young women leaving the foster care system. (You're eighteen? So long bitch, try not to be victimized.) Boxes of toys, stuffed animals, books, games, pictures, candle holders, coffee cups, clocks, baskets, office stuff and unused kitchen ware to the battered women's shelter in Pasadena. Sometimes they escape with nothing but the kids.

Good kitchen stuff is pricey, pots and pans, knives, utensils, various plug in thingy's. Where ever I went I'd be cooking, I was Vegan. When looked at with chaos colored eyes I was sure I'd never be able to cook again and tossed it all. (Madness.) <u>And All My Shoes!</u> Nice shoes didn't belong on a ghoul. Didn't want new jeans, pink or white slacks, a *cool* rubber raincoat, expensive business suits that included vintage 80's Calvin Klein's and my favorite pair of twenty year old, worn, black leather, click-clacking cowboy boots. The 'garbage in front of my house!' that Moe killed our friendship over was so expensive. I was Hideous Frankenstein. Monsters don't dress up, they wear the same rags every day.

'…cold black paint chips off billboards
hissing neon sputters dim
worn heels clack and shuffle across dirty brick and boardwalk
my pets malign my hallowed halls
it is the evening of my splintered edges piercing tearing…'

~Al Christ

At Specialisto's office today I met Nelson from Lerman & Sons. If I need to get a prosthetic hand I'd be better off if I knew what they looked like, felt like, how much they weigh, how to put them on…bla bla. I talked to him before I left home this morning but he didn't bring any with him. Not even pictures. Therapist was there and said, 'Hello? Nelson? What was he thinking?' But it didn't bother me at all. The thought of cutting off my hand is harsh. I can only think about it a little at a time.

I had X-rays taken of my elbow and Specialisto said they looked good. No sign of the HO returning and he was happy with my progress in therapy. He took pictures of the X-rays with the little elf Husband gave me for Christmas and mugged for the camera. I love him.

2007

Shelby's house was perfect for Home Scrub, the sun hit the bed in the guest room all afternoon and she slept serenely. I however was in agony, could barely move in the mornings. I was taking Vicodin like aspirin with no relief. I wrote:

> 'I have to find something better. So hard to be positive when
> I'm in pain every morning....'

Still, it didn't occur to me to *get stronger pain medication!* Double duh, baby. Didn't write much about my feet, they were throbbing all day and often made me sit from pain but most of my focus was on my hand. (Maybe years of sexy heels made it easier to ignore feet pain.) Husband brought his treadmill over. We put it on Shelby's back porch and I tried to use it every day but didn't always succeed.

> '...It's nine pm. All I did today was sleep and cry. I hate
> myself for not working out, not taking a shower, not eating,
> not doing anything....'

I was falling apart and didn't know how to deal with it. Kevin came to town; his work sent him down, thank God. Kev and I went to the Getty Museum. It was his first time there. I love crazee J Paul and have been many times. I was trying to tell Kev about the granite, the blonde stone is filled with fossils. It was a hidden gift, they found them after it was paid for and hewn.

My Freakish Stroke Symptoms were in full force, searching for the word 'fossils,' I kept coming up with 'vultures'. 'No, I meant to say, Vultures. Agh! What I mean is Vultures.' We were laughing at vultures all day. Everywhere in the building were tiny vultures frozen in granite. '…prehistoric vulture formations, look closely and you can make out their nests…' Took pictures of the eclectic collection and was happy for the first time in awhile.

May, 2003—North Hills, Shelby's

Thinking of Wayne and Rag. What does that say? A shrink would have a field day. The men I miss the most are the most geographically unavailable.

Saw Setjermindtoit today. I wouldn't have recognized him. He is kind and warm, looks in your eyes when he talks, listens to your answers. 'We could do another flap in your groin area…' I've heard that scenario before. They would take my hand, excise the tissue off of the back and then sew it into my stomach for a few weeks. New tissue grows but it's weird and fluffy / puffy—it could lead to infection—and it could fail. Like the last flap. And what would it do to my elbow to be stranded in my stomach for weeks? My elbow is fragile, it needs exercise every day.

He told me how he could make me a new thumb tendon, which was interesting. (Take one from my leg.) I love that he was so into saving my hand but his options weren't very good. We started talking about amputation. 'You used to be in the film business?' 'Yes.' 'A little thing can change your life forever…' I started to cry, 'sorry I've had over a year to get used to this…' He patted my head, murmured a few platitudes. 'Do you want to see some prosthetics?' I said yes and he left. I dug through the drawers of the examining room and found fresh bandaging. I rewrapped my paw and forced myself to stop crying. One of the nurses brought me a brochure, I put it in my bag without looking at it. Put the arm brace on, sling, purse over shoulder, sunglasses, cane, walk out, 'just make it to your car, then you can break…' Waiting for the elevator was a nightmare, so many people but by the time I got to the car the storm had passed.

Looked at the brochure and was unimpressed. I suddenly wanted to keep my poor mutilated paw more than I ever had. Thought of all the X-rays I've had—I can't stand the thought of an X-ray of a stump. A glowing stump. I can finally reach my lips with my hand and kissed it over and over. 'I'm sorry little hand, what was I thinking?' I could see it gone—really see it gone—with a stump left at the end of my sad scarred arm. My poor little paw has been trying so hard to survive. I cried when I got back to Shelby's. Alone and desolate.

'...baby baby baby
you lost it today
and yesterday
you should leave but you stay...'

paraphrasing Massive Attack

Three am.

I have therapy at 8:30 am and leave at seven thirty. I took a sleeping pill at the beginning of American Idol and was asleep by the end of it but I never sleep through the night. I'm lucky to get three hours

Saw Allritini again. 'I've made up my mind. I'd rather be the woman with the gimp hand rather than a stump.' He was relieved, he wanted me to keep it too. I showed him how the bone was cooking; hideous, an inch and a half sticking up and out. The holes Dr Cookieboots had drilled showing here and there. The Thing finally 'snapped' when Allritini tweezed it. A big piece chunked off and thick healthy blood oozed out of the wound. Relief.

A year and a half and still my paw isn't healed. What's next? Monkeys fly out of my butt? Allritini put the bone in a plastic bag for my macabre collection.

'...I've got a guardian angel with a hand on my shoulder
she tells me not to fear
we shine like stars we shine like stars
one day sperm
blink of an eye dust...'

paraphrasing Moby, Santana and the unknown poet

I woke up calm, almost content. Tone from the stroke present but not as horrible as it has been lately—got out of bed and was able to walk without a painful limp. A weight has lifted off me, making up my mind to keep my paw.

Spent the morning listening to Stern and downloading fotos onto the laptop. I've been taking pictures downtown, the homeless villages, the County hospital, the graffiti, the occasional homeless dude. (When they come to the car asking for change, I give them quarters and ask if I can take their foto.) The bizarre dichotomy of wealth and poverty in LA fascinates. I'm separated from everything—a little ghost looking in—I feel kinship with my homeless brothers and sisters. There but for grace.

Thank you Yahweh for giving me a family to watch over me Thank you Krishna for giving me a union to cover my medical bills Thank you Allah for making me strong enough to survive Thank you gentle Buddha for not making me bitter, mean or crazy, for not wrecking my brain with the stroke. I pray to everyone, even Scuva, the Parking God.

Every day is spent hour by hour I have hard time thinking of the future.

'...mirage pirates and marauders entertain nightly
at the feather pillow stage
ex-annoyances become endearing
and life is worth more than spit
while I sleep
fantasies explode with the glare of old sol, stinking bastard,
and I grapple through the day
to wait
and wait
to fall again...'

~Al Christ

Alison and I saw Marilyn Manson at The Kimmel Show last night. (Her boyfriend is one of the producers.) MM was a perfect rock star. Kimmel was so out of his league it was hilarious. Their music stage is out in the parking lot and set up like a proper concert venue. Manson was polished and over the top / stage show with sexy dancers. After the first song—killing time for the commercial break—Marilyn pretended he was humping Kimmel. Poor Jimmy didn't know what to do, he tried jokes but Marilyn was relentless. Not answering him at all, just spitting water at him, humping him like a deranged animal and swearing for the crowd—who loved it.

They had Monica Lewinski (of all people) as a guest host. Jimmy was looking for anything to take Manson's attention away from him. 'Marilyn have you met Monica?' She comes trotting out on stage. 'I want to come on your dress...' She was mortified and quickly scurried off as the crowd howled approval. It's scary navigating excited crowds with a cane but Alison looked out for me, held my arm and gently / firmly pushed people out of the way.

Back inside the green room I was impressed by the party. Shows doing well don't throw shin-digs like Kimmel and they do it every day of the week. (Last night was bigger than most considering the musician.) We had made the acquaintance of a couple Brit's and found them again on an overstuffed sofa. We all had a laugh at the absurdity of Lewinsky. 'All this notoriety for giving blowjobs, Alison said with mock seriousness, I'm sure I give better head than she does.' We were rolling. Alison got up and I though she wanted to go. It takes time to get myself together, I was pleasantly surprised when Marilyn leaned in to ask me, '...are you sure it's all right?' Not wanting to be a jerk asking a crippled chick to move; it isn't apparent that I'm a gimp until I start to get up. 'It's no problem,' I assured him and sat in the chair next to the sofa. 'I want to come on your dress was brilliant,' I offered. He and his girlfriend laughed, 'she had it coming.' When we were ready to go we asked if he would take a picture. He was gracious, stood up put his arms around the both of us and Dita snapped the foto. It's on my lap top as wallpaper. Smile every time I look at it. Must admit I was star struck again all these years later. Madonna & Marilyn, something about musicians.

'...Dominique in Paris
said it was rainy and baroque, wore black silk and looked at rooftops
plenty of art

the girls come out at night and dress for the doorways
rows upon rows of them, waiting for morning
Henry Miller, it seems to Dominique
but she is Kafka…'

~Al Christ

Getting through the day / saw Allritini and Goodfella 1st this morning. They wanted an MRI so I spent the rest of the morning setting that up. Once more Shmeagle through the habit-trail to get the precious precious xray but without Alison to laugh with, no fun.

The machine is in basement of USC—I had to undress and put on a hospital gown. (I put on two of them, fore and back, freakin' hospital gowns.) I was given ear plugs. 'It's pretty loud…' An understatement, it sounded like a jackhammer. The girl at check in asked if I was claustrophobic, I could see why it was a concern. Especially for someone big, I'm small and I was cramped in there. It was a much longer process than the CT scan (an hour) and I fell half asleep. Another procedure that radiated every one of my internal organs. (Phuck.)

'There is no salvation in becoming adapted
to a world which is crazy.'

—Henry Miller

Met another idiot this week. Thought I'd try to work on my verbal communication. The way I hump and poke for words isn't getting better. I asked Dr Friendly for a reference. I was hopeful. Thoughts of my speech therapist in Portland were floating around, he was good. Friendly said he knew of someone and gave me her card, Bee Rainless, MD. I called and told Dr Rainless about my situation, the burns, the stroke, what I was hoping to accomplish, the treatment I've had. Blah diddy Blah. She sounded fine. I made an appointment and headed over a couple days later. Went upstairs to a little cubicle and waited. And waited. She showed up almost an hour late, no explanation or apology. 'Call me Bee.' Very young and Very Pregnant.

She whipped out a pack of flash cards. Doh! I had seen them at Rancho; an elephant, a razor, a coffee cup, a bathtub. 'Is this it?' I asked her. Blank stare.

'I can usually identify nouns, that's not my problem. Its disappearing words—different each day—that give me the most trouble. I also have issues with the phone, with stress, difficulty thinking ahead, multitasking...' Weirdly defensive, she cut me off. 'This is the only way I know how to do it.' 'Can I see someone else?' I said. 'I'm the only one here. I'm the head of the department.' 'Don't you have a supervisor?' 'No! I don't!'

How dare I question her authority? The angrier she became the more absurdly surreal she seemed. When frustrated, vultures wake and I get tongue tied. She finally admitted that until recently, Glendale had no speech therapy and she had *no formal training in stroke rehab!* She had taken the initiative, I was her First Patient. I stood up and looked for a hidden camera. Really. I told her I knew more about stroke rehab than she did. I needed someone with experience, and left. Driving to and from Glendale with that long wait Wasted my Whole Day. It kills me that Glendale Hospital is so casual about patient care / protocol and what the hell is wrong with Dr Friendly! Why did he recommend a new snotty bitch? (I remember reading that pregnant women get stupid, something about hormones.) When I got back to Shelby's I noticed a message on my cell, it was Bee. 'Just to let you know, I have been practicing for five years!' Angry / childlike. Practicing what? I wondered, silly bitch.

'...you cant hide your shame with bluster
don't think it's covered
you try to blame anyone but you
close down the excuse factory
shake it loose baby just let it go
it takes a few seconds to say
I'm sorry
try that...'

paraphrasing Baby Fox

Thinking suicide. My gun is somewhere in storage. Too messy. Pills are the preferred method of taking the dirt nap. Simply go to sleep one last time. So tempting.

Stopped at a strip-mall bakery in Panorama City to pick up some bread and only after I parked and got out did I see the 'We Have Moved' sign. It was stifling, air still hot and dry, the whole little sponge bob square box hovel block of shops had the feel of being deserted, though there were a couple cars in the lot. Discount clothing, Korean videos and Japanese takeout; I went and ordered a California roll and edamame and sat down to wait. A couple of teenagers came in and tried to decide what they wanted. She had a pierced lip and he was a little overweight. They were both in T-shirts, shorts and flip-flops. I gathered from their chitchat that they were brother and sister and they were also picking up something for their mother. When the woman at the counter brought my food out, the girl thought it was what they had just ordered. 'Wow that was fast!' 'No, it's hers,' her brother laughed and pointed to me. He noticed my sling, my cane. 'You want help carrying this to your car?' He walked to the van and waited patiently as I dug for my keys. 'Thanks again.' 'No problem.' That bit of interaction, that simple blip of kindness made think people aren't all bad. I can get through this day. I can get through one more day.

June, 2003—North Hills, Shelby's

The hot, dry, boring valley is making me stir crazy. Talked to Rag last night; trying to hatch a plan. Told him I wanted to spend the summer in Smallville and stay with him. Mom and I get along better when I'm not living in her house. He and his ex share their house / the kids don't move, stability / the parent's trade out. (It is The Most Mature way of dealing with joint custody I've ever seen.) Half the week he stays with Monk, so I'll stay with Monk. He has a spare room and could use a little rent. I'll make my way to Minnesota some time this month.

Was digging around the storage space yesterday and found a photo album. The green leather tome is full of negatives and proof sheets. I had an old Nikon (older then me) and would take black & white photos and print them myself. Photos of Ken and me: London, New Forrest, New York, Toronto, Sitgis. Pictures of me and Mr Right Now: Eoesaria, Maui, Lima, Nice, Machu Picchu, Montego Bay, Marrakech; vacations and work around the world. Must be careful about memories, can't let too much in at once.

'Join the 21st Century, everything's going digital.' Thank you Husband. He bought me a cute little elph for Xmas that I can use one handed.

still June 2003—still at Shelby's

Appointment with Specialisto this morning and he was pleased. I'm still using the CPM every night; elbow now ranges 85% and I know it's not done. 'Come see me in a month.' But I'll be gone. Monk figured out when he could drive back to Minnesota with me so Kev's booking him a flight on a buddy pass. I told Specialisto I needed a prescription for a hand therapist to get another wrist splint made. And another thumb splint and sleeping cast. I was stranded in slow time now rushing and hurrying in fast time. The hand therapist at USC was Robin; sweetheart of a guy. I'm dumb for not seeing him when I started therapy on my arm. I almost gave up on my hand. Silly Frankenstein, I love my stupid hand.

June June the musical fruit…

Met Rebecca at Tournasell's (the restaurant Fred works at) I was extra teary eyed. Couldn't tell her what she wanted to hear, that I'm fine, couldn't do it— didn't want to be a horror show but I'm tired of lying. She brought presents, a Waterford teapot and Christopher Reeve's new book. 'I've really missed you…' That killed me, I almost started crying again, I've really missed her; and leaving Fred behind makes me sad. He was so sweet tonight.

Spent the morning downtown with Arm Therapist, amiable as always. I called a prescription in to Dr Coolchick's office before I left her. Completely out of pain killers and it makes me nervous. No pain this minute but that means anything. [I finally told Coolchick I was hurting and needed something better than Vicoden. I was taking Darvoset.] Then back in my car for a half a minute to the Hand Clinic. I like Robin, he's warm and easy. He made me another brace for my thumb. It's an L shaped little piece of plastic / held with vultures. It keeps my thumb from pulling in. The web space has horrid thick scarring.

> Aside: Last spring in Lake Oswego, I didn't wrap my hand properly *one night* and woke up with a thick, permanent band of scar tissue, squinching my thumb in. If I had been told *how fast it could happen* I wouldn't have let my guard down. Scar tissue will form overnight <u>for a year</u>. Be vigilant.

I drove down 6th; the ghetto to Beverly Hills in half an hour; to Lerman & Sons Prosthetics to get a cast made. Finally! The old guy helping me tried to sell 'off the shelf' stuff but I wasn't going for it. 'Believe me, I've tried them all.' I showed him how my foot wiggled free of every apparatus he had. He finally acquiesced and made me a purple fiberglass sleeping cast, Thank Dog! I pick it up in a couple days, he's going to pimp it, hydraulics, rims.

Almost three—I'd been taking fotos of LA all day and had a decent collection of wealth and rubbish. Overcast, traffic is light and I'm in a good-ish mood. From Beverly Hills to Studio City via Laurel Canyon / I stop by the Shell station to say goodbye to my mechanics. (I love them, they're Lebanese.) Hit Ralph's for protein shakes and cat litter. Stopped by the Rite Aid to get my pain prescription refilled but they don't have it yet. I called Dr Coolchick's office and the prescription chick said, '…sorry, I've been trying to get them all done…' 'Can you do it within the hour?' 'Fifteen minutes.' Fifteen minutes is fine. I filled my car and fetched my mail. (The kids working there are so sweet they bring it to me so I don't have to get out of the car.)

Back to the Rite Aid. There was an SUV pulling into the one gimp space in front of the store. It's nearly five and the lot is full. I watch a pretty blonde hop out of the driver's seat. 'Hello! Are you disabled?' I yell out my window. 'You don't know if I'm disabled or not.' Tall, thin, boob job, short skirt, high heels; didn't look gimped to me. She opens the back door and takes out a baby carrier.

'Some of us really need these spots—Hey! I'm talking to you bitch—what do you think you're doing?' She smirked and waved dismissively. 'Get going honey, move along.' Bouncing along / a bobble head doll / easily into the store. I had to park a thousand miles away. I walk so slowly and painfully that by the time I got back to the Rite Aid, Bobble Head was coming back out. Carrying the kid with one arm, she opened the back door and strapped him in, then gets in the driver's seat. Perfectly healthy; lazy and had the baby, just running in for 'one quick thing'.

I snapped. 'You fucking bitch!' I banged my cane on her side window. 'Fuck you!' I hit it again trying to break it. Duh, the aluminum cane bounced off harmlessly. I went after her hood. Whack! Whack! 'Get out of the car!' The parking lot was a log jam, no one was moving and I was berserk—that bitch wasn't smirking any more—'Fuck You! Get out of the car!' Put a dozen dents in her custom paint job before the parking lot jam abated and she was able to screech away.

I slowly came back down into my body. A few people had been watching the show but now that it was over, they were moving along. I turn around and Rite Aid's security guard was staring at me, a big fat black dude. I thought he was going to throw my crazy ass out but he just looked at me, arms folded, a trace of smile on his face and ever so slightly nodded his head. Went and filled my prescription. I couldn't help but smile, too. That lazy bitch will think twice before she parks in another Handicapped Only spot. I whacked Bobble Head's SUV for everyone in a wheelchair that can't reach that high. I whacked her car for all the little old ladies who'd never behave that badly and had a laugh at the thought of BH explaining all those dents to her husband.

It worries me though, the loss of control. I went to Tournesell and nursed an iced tea, started to tell Fred what had just happened. Rebecca came in half way through my story, Fred got called away on some waiter calamity and I don't think I ever finished telling him. He'd find it hilarious, he's young, he's French. Rebecca was concerned.

'…Dominique in Vienna
lounged in hostel lobby's reading old Playboys listening to Mozart
said it was springtime and church like and quiet
children wear uniforms and laugh on the sidewalks

she thinks of Shelly
but she is Byron…'

~Al Christ

Clinical data: MRI RT HAND AND ELBOW
                      S / P BURN, SUSPECTED OSTEOMYELITIS

Exam: MR UPPER ELBOW JOINT W / O CONT—RIGHT
                      MRI RIGHT ELBOW AND WRIST

Clinical History: 39 year old female with a history of burns. The patient's
                      original injury was in January of 2002 and she has had
                      15 surgeries since then. The last was 4 / 03 / 2003 when
                      heterotopic ossification was removed. The patient also
                      had an ulnar nerve transposition. This is to evaluate for
                      osteomyelitis.

TECHNIQUE: The following MR sequences were obtained of the right
elbow through the proximal half of the forearm, and the same sequence
was repeated of the remainder of the forearm and through the levels of the
metacarpals.

FINDINGS: blippidy blap flippity flap…

Just when I think I'm getting used to the medical jargon, here come MRI
results. I needed it explained. Allritini called me back later that afternoon and
said he can't read MRI results either. They need a technician; he'll get back
to me. Spent the day saying goodbye to therapists and doctors; last massage
from Julia and said good-bye to Robin. 'Did I tell you I had a stroke? That's
why I walk with a cane,' I told him. 'Wow. You must have really bad karma!'
Huh? Whitey the White Boy? You're giving me a Hindi concept? I couldn't
answer, just as well. What a thing to say to a patient. I had a stroke because
someone fucked up in the OR.

2007

I always knew what I thought of Robin's karma statement but couldn't express myself. Metaphysically speaking, surviving a life altering injury isn't negative but (most) people that haven't been there can't see past their own fear, they can't take themselves out of the equation and only see the physical.

Back to June 2003—North Hills—Shelby's

Talked to Dr Coolchick on the phone and told her about the cane vs. SUV incident. She had to laugh but agreed that it wasn't me pre CVA. I was out of control. She prescribed Lexapro once a day and Zanax as needed for panic attacks. 'You can call me from up there whenever you want.' Coolchick is the coolest.

Allritini left a detailed message on my voice mail. He had looked at my MRI X-rays with the technician and my hand is still healing. No bone disease, no infection. 'Go on vacation, have fun, I'll see you when you get home. You can call me anytime.' Shades of Coolchick; struck again by the difference between Dr's in Babylon and Dr's in Smallville. Black and Potato.

Went to the Camera Exchange and dropped off a kinky roll of film from a hundred years ago. Photo's of my friend Winchester and I at Thanksgiving. Thought they'd cheer and I'm still thinking website (although Winnie would never agree to being on the net.) Winchester is an Ivy League friend who *acts* proper but underneath an elegant chilly exterior is a naughty schoolgirl vixen. PaulDDB was cooking Thanksgiving dinner and Winchester and I were having a glass of wine on his sofa. 'Let me take a picture of you two, you look so nice...' She looked at me with her sly half smile. 'Nice is boring, don't you think?' She tangled her fingers in the hair behind my neck and pulled me in for a smoldering kiss. Yummy. Years ago but I remember playing to the camera and how much fun in general I used to have with Winchester. PaulDDB took a couple rolls of us making out on his sofa but I never had them developed. They were put in the photo drawer and eventually forgotten. (I'd found them that day at storage.) Camera Exchange will send the disk to Minnesota.

Headed over the hill to LAX. Foggy, nice. I stopped at Ralph's in the Marina to get some snicky snacks for the road then picked up Monk at LAX. Just seeing Monk brought my spirits up. I had called a few pals who lived on the West Side earlier—Velvet and a couple of boys that work for her met us for a last supper at the Sidewalk Café. Birgit stopped by to say hello / goodbye. Velvet also happened to bring a weed fairy. 'You want a quarter? I can have it delivered in a half an hour.' Sprightly and European she hooked us up with spotchum smejum for the road. Monk ordered a Long Island Ice Tea. 'That sounds perfect!' said Velvet. I stuck with lower case tea but encourage debauchery in others. The beach was foggy and cool, rush hour came and went, we chuckled and chortled and took fotos til ten. It was a great way to say goodbye for the summer. I need to get out of here and re-group. Get my feathers nestled, paint my attic, refurbish my kitchen...Cant wait to see Rag again, I've missed him; blue eyes, shy laugh, strong arms. I need a fresh start but Smallville will have to do.

> '...friends with benefits
> working on their night moves...'
>
> channeling Alanis Morissette and Bob Seger

2007

Shelby was a nightmare. I never wrote about it / denial denial. She was separated from her husband and had asked me to move in for company. I needed company too, seemed perfect but she drank and took pain killers (often mine) and when wasted, could be vicious. The capricious quick change of alcoholics; I love you, I hate you, uh...who are you? Fred said, 'she's going to hurt you, you have to get out of there!' I agreed but how? I spent hours a day in traffic, had nonstop doctor / therapist / X-ray appointments and a cat. I could barely get through the day. I realized it wasn't me she was angry at; I was a convenient whipping boy. If I were healthy, I wouldn't have taken her bullying and we would have talked about her marriage. That's what she expected of me. But I wasn't 'Alisa likes to fix problems,' anymore, I was 'Alisa is fragile, handle with care.' My denial of the Shelby reality was hurting my mental health but I didn't understand it, I was still childlike and didn't know what to do with bad behavior from 'adults'

I stopped by my friend Hank Saroyan's one morning for coffee and broke down, he sat with me and let me cry. His uncle was William the famous writer. I'd never read any of his work, somehow he'd flown under my radar. 'What should I read of his?' I asked, scrambling for normalcy. Hank carefully looked through his library. He narrowed it down to a couple. Looked at me thoughtfully for a minute then pulled out a thin book of short stories.

'The Mexican, he said. Start with that.'

Couple hours later, I fell apart at my friend Rolly's. He's a photographer and I wanted pictures of my back. The patches harvested for skin grafts look like a cubist portrait and the railroad tracks from the lost latisimus dorsi was pure Frankenstein. Big Rail Road tracks, as if I were sewn together by sleep deprived simians. I sat on his sofa sobbing, couldn't tell him why, I didn't know. Poor Rolly; having a woman break down in front of them is hard for men to deal with. He tried. He started talking about Christianity. His church was the right one because they worshiped Christ properly. They were born again evangelicals, the crazee kind. He believed the King James Version verbatim. (Except the directions to stone adulterous women to death and kill people that work Sunday's.) Maybe that would help me. Here's a card, we meet twice weekly. It did help. It coaxed me back to my version of reality. I believe science and spirituality peacefully coexist. You don't have to choose one or the other. I believe the bible is filled with errors because humans wrote it. When sane people become wackadoo religious, it reminds me of the frailty that's in us all. Everyone has a crutch.

A couple of weeks later up at the cabin, I opened the William Saroyan book and read The Mexican. It was Perfect; calm, hopeful, peaceful. I hadn't seen Hank since before my injury but he really pays attention. He got it.

June 2003—Babbitt, Minnesota

Monk and I left town Tuesday afternoon and made it to the southern cliffs of the Grand Canyon as the sun set. We went to the edge, it was a Monet. It gave me chills. Purple, pink, lavender, rose, deep orange, burgundy and grays. Serene, the beautiful light darkening to indigo. It was incredible—the stillness—the tangible beauty. We soaked up the quiet and looked and looked until the light completely left.

The grandeur reminded me of Niagara Falls. I just looked at those pictures. I was in Toronto with Ken in spring of 97. He was in pre-production for 'Dog Boys,' and had asked me to come up and fix the script; it wasn't bad but it needed a polish. We drove down to the falls on our day off, seventy five miles away. I can't think of the first time I heard about Niagara Falls or The Grand Canyon, it was part of the national psyche. We got to the edge and felt the rush of a zillion kilos dropping a thousand miles, like The GC reality surpasses imagination.

Monk and I were fatigued. Driving through the desert had been hard on the cat. Should we have a little smoke and look for a place to stay? We filled a bowl and looked at the park map for a suitable camping spot. The weed was sweet and savory we soon were laughing our heads off. After a stop at a fast food place and directions from the kid at the window we made our way to a camp ground. Preservation Hall (an old New Orleans jazz band) was playing slow, drunken blues, headlights on, car doors open; Monk blowing up the air mattress with a loud pump we bought Blythe, Home Scrub doubling a howler monkey and me giggling giggling. A couple of white trash hillbillies with a loud camp cat laughing our selves slappy. A neighbor stopped by like a ninja, she made no sound, appearing in front of the hearth like magic. 'Did I hear an air pump?' 'Yea, I said, sorry…' 'Actually I was wondering if I could borrow it.' 'Of course!' Don't want to piss off a ninja. Too funny but also too cold to camp, we shivered up at dawn and headed back to the Canyon to watch the sunrise.

The whole drive was surreal. Tuba City, Four Corners, the way the landscape changes so dramatically from Arizona to Colorado, it's like Dorothy's Kansas to Oz. The sad wackadoo Disneyfication of Mount Rushmore.

> '…I'm so depressed I can barely hang on
> it feels like I have no future
> I'm like a crackho who's rock is gone…'
>
> paraphrasing Tupac

Before we arrived in Smallville, Monk asked me about Rag. 'He told you that he was seeing someone, didn't he?' '…uh…uh…what did you say?' Monk was pissed. 'I can't believe he didn't tell you.' Me either. Monk wouldn't say much about Glonda, just that she was his ex-wife's cousin! What What What?!

July 2003—Minneapolis, Betsy & Adams

Saw Rag before I left Smallville. Told him that I was sort of happy for him, I don't want him to be lonely, that I didn't plan on a big future for us… but honestly dude, what the fuck? He let me drive across the country, he knew *I was planning on sleeping with him* and he still wouldn't mention his new girlfriend? 'Are you afraid of me? Am I bitchy?' 'No, I'm not afraid of you; you're not bitchy at all. I don't know what's wrong with me.' He had a confused look, like a chameleon. Wouldn't (couldn't?) answer, which means; 'duh, Hideous Frankenstein, you make me want to puke.' He said his beautiful new lover was a twenty year old princess with the limbs of a gazelle and flawless skin like the dewy petals of a summer rose. Or some such shit. I wasn't going to stay in Smallville, he's the reason I was in the one whore town in the first place.

2007

Rag's careless disregard put me into an emotional coma. I sat at the family cabin for two weeks, a sad little ghost reading Saroyan, lost my appetite and couldn't sleep more than an hour or two. Purgatory. Pre injury sleep was delicious; dreams were fun, sometimes noteworthy, prescient. Sometimes a soap opera, picking up where I'd woken that morning, sometimes I'd have movie dreams, a combo of working on it and the finished product, credits would roll as I was hitting snooze.

Betsy invited Homescrub and me to Minneapolis to stay with her family in their guest room. She could see I was in free fall. Betsy has been a friend for 20 + years and is an RN with a background in brain disorders. (Alzheimer's.) She recognized and understood the bewildering scary emotional drain of CVA symptoms, knew how long burn's take to mend and she's funny; a healing trifecta.

I had lost twenty years of built up amour. I was vulnerable to all forms of assault; any bad behavior was a punch in the gut. Over and over and over, Betsy would patiently steer me back to where I was pre CVA.

'…last night I dreamed
of a different kind of sex
sex for love
it sucked…'

~Al Christ

July 2003, Minneapolis MN

Another day / week / month / the year half gone. I've accomplished nothing. Sometimes I'm fine with it, sometimes I'm the biggest loser on the planet. It's nice being around kids again. Thought I was going to spend the summer with Rag and his kids.

Speaking of Guys with Issues: B called and left a message yesterday! Fortunately I was on the other line and voice mail got it. 'Hey baby girl, sorry I missed you, I just talked to Cat…' That's how he got this number. The thought of B and Cat gossiping about me is annoying. I haven't heard from them in—2 years him and 5 months her. 'I'm back in LA…' Good for you honey, hope you don't run away this time. Finally caught myself being too harsh. It must have been awkward to call after two years, he didn't know I wasn't going to answer; he was ready to have a conversation. I checked my ego and dialed back but got this message, 'the subscriber does not accept incoming calls.' I'll admit a glimmer of relief. B loved me and my look, especially my legs and sexy j-lo butt. Can't take another Rag.

'…what the hell is wrong with you?
how could you do that to your childhood friend?
you let me drive all the way to MN
and be there for two weeks
without Even Talking 2 me?
am I going insane?
no one treats a lover that badly, Romeo…'

paraphrasing Basement Jaxx

Compared to this time last year I'm so much better; when the demons come slithering and side winding into my mind, hissing 'loser… lazy….nothing done…' I must let them hiss and be gone.

July 2003, Boston Mass

Visiting Georgene (and daughters). We've known each other most of our lives. When she heard I was in a fire she had a flashback—we were fifteen and talking about death—I had said, 'I know exactly how I'm going to die, at 40 in a fire.' I don't recall the conversation but I'm sure she remembers it right. Crazee that I knew. (Teenage women are psychic.)

Been thinking of Christopher Reeve and Lance Armstrong a lot lately (what am I saying, a lot always.) They're personal heroes but I don't have much in common with either. Reeve is East Coast, to the Manor born with a big family and Armstrong is Trailer Park Texas, him and Mom against the world. One's older than me, one younger. I'm somewhere in between them all the way around. Pop has a PhD in Biochemistry. He taught at the U of M until Nixon formed the Environmental Protection Agency (even an asshole like Nixon could do something right.) The new agency needed Bio Chemists so

Dad worked for the government. We weren't wealthy or poor. They are both married, both have children, they're both men, with the peculiar male way of taking in the world. What I would do in either situation? In Armstrong's I would have done what he did, I would look at cancer as a thing to fight, beat and win. Because if you don't you're dead anyway, right? Reeve is a different animal. Don't know if I could keep going year after year, never completely giving up hope. Precious precious Reeve. I don't know how he does it. I can't make myself go to the gym every day and I'm walking.

Armstrong's book was a success story and Reeve's were about perseverance, advocacy and hope. Me? An indistinct mess. I wonder what they'd do in my situation. Maybe it's as simple as, get pissed off because he's disabled or be elated because he can walk and feel pain…depends on where you are looking from.

> '…don't play with my heart you prick
> and treat me like some little bitch…'

> paraphrasing Mazzy Star

Got an e mail from Catherine last night and it really hurt; she's delusional. I haven't heard from her for six months and she suddenly sends me this. (I've shortened it, she went on and on about how wrong I was and how much I 'screamed' at her, the exaggerating drama queen. I *can't yell* my voice is still too weak.) Conveniently ignoring Ramayana Ding Dong and sicking her stupid fame starved Stuart on me.

> ….Alisa, I have loved you very much but I can no longer take being screamed at—and you've been abusive to me at times you may not even realize during our friendship (like our trip to the desert.)

> I've been intimidated by you because I was lacking in self-esteem, an issue I've dealt with in the last year and a half since I took over the studio. You were my friend, and I

shouldn't feel like I'm always walking on eggshells, worried I'll say the wrong thing and set you off.

I haven't heard anything about how you are doing and if things got worse or not—sure can't call any of your friends or family to ask. Where are you? Have there been more surgeries? Do you want to talk to me; can we do it without blaming or being angry?

I know that anything that has happened to me pales in comparison to your recent experiences, but my situation just keeps getting worse and I have been completely wrapped up in trying not to lose my business. Just for the record, I have been avoiding the entire old crowd and haven't done anything with anyone, just studio stuff.

I miss you. Write me back? I'll start checking this email more often than once every two weeks. Home phone is disconnected, like a lot of other things.

No sign off. It's spitting into the wind but I couldn't stop myself, I wrote back.

Dear Catherine,

The last time I talked to you was in March and you hung up on me. It hurt. If there's anything real you want to say please call, 818-307-8779. Why can't you call my friends or family to ask about me? Have you been rude to them too?

As far as getting mad about Ramayana, you deserved it, and picking a fight using stupid Stewart as a tool, rather than just saying you changed your mind is so stupid it's sick. Even if you were 100% right and I was 100% wrong, I was dealing with my own drama. I was looking at my 15th surgery in 15 months. A real friend...oh fuck it, a real friend is not you.

Re-read your letter. Would you get on the Catherine Roller coaster again? All the time I spent listening to you whine and bitch about your life, your ex-husband, your lovers, all this sad, sorry bullshit that you refuse to deal with—when I think of how much I let you lean on me—all your nonsense becomes clear; for the first time in our relationship, I was the one that needed sympathy. What I got from you was a big Fuck Off.

Have a nice life.

It's easier to turn me into 'The Bad Guy' and reminisce about some argument in the desert years ago than look at reality now. Gimps are yucky boring; they have all sorts of problems. No dancing all night party hopping, no ecstasy, no drinking.

What would Lance Armstrong do? Probably wouldn't have been involved with someone like Cat in the first place and if he got email from a bitchy sniveler, sayonara. Mr Reeve? Would he tell his self involved friend to stuff a giraffe? Probably not. He seems kind of Zen to me. These years of immobility have brought him at least to my reading a sense of tranquility.

Armstrong is a world class athlete and Reeve is completely incapacitated. What am I? Overwhelmed by circumstance, too depressed and too angry, in need of empathy, understanding and forgiveness. I suppose it was her talk with B a few weeks ago that put me back on her radar. Its good being with Georgene, she laughed as she read Cat's letter. 'What a self absorbed bitch.' She's concise.

Ditching a friend because she's been crippled is appalling but saying so long to a bitch is reasonable. In her version of reality Catherine wasn't a creepy sniveler she was the Victim her preferred role.

'…things are forever different
one and all please face truth fearlessly
change is not repentant

change is necessary
don't become lost in the past…'

paraphrasing Bob Marley

August 2003—Minneapolis, Betsy & Adam's

I met Betsy's cousin Ben. He was in Seattle's sound about six months before my injury. He and his friend caught a boat ride with some guy they hardly knew; the man was drunk and driving too fast. 'This is a no wake area, you should slow down,' said Ben. 'We'll go on stealth mode,' said the drunk and turned off his running lights. Ben was just saying, '…what the fuck are you doing!?' When the idiot crashed into a bridge. Ben's best friend was killed instantly and the drunk was thrown from the boat.

Ben looked at his legs; bones were sticking through his shins. (You're not supposed to see your bones…) He threw himself overboard and watched as the boat crashed into land and blew up. He was rescued by a couple of Argentinean fishermen and spent the next year in a wheel chair, mourning his best friend, eating pain killers and learning to walk on new titanium legs. Six million dollar man-ish. He told Betsy, 'no one understands what it's like…' There's no way to appreciate almost dieing unless you've done it. It's a secret club; the Mason's don't have anything on us.

Ben was the first survivor I sat and talked with and I was his. We exchanged war stories for hours. I have a hard time distinguishing between what's real and should be addressed and what's simply smoke and mirrors and can be ignored. Ben said he'd been thinking of joining the police force when he was a teenager. His town had a ride along program, while out they responded to a car accident. A man had his shoulder dislocated and it looked so repulsive to Ben he froze and thought he would retch. It was so disturbing he realized he could never be a cop. 'Maybe that's been happening to you.'

2007

People usually ignore each other and slog through the day but anything unusual, like a woman with a cane, catches the eye. Some people gawk at my arm with such exposed revulsion its clown-like. Now I easily ignore but in 2003 I was unable to disassociate, I was chewing rusty nails and sucking dirty change all day. Although I was aware of sheep behavior—gimps get culled from the heard—and knew I wasn't one of them, therefore technically didn't care, I did care. I was terribly lonely. When I went out I'd wear dark glasses and baggy clothes with a big sun hat and try to ignore the furtive looks, the double takes.

Life altering injury revises your personality, adds something. Wakes you up and all of the excess bullshit that used to take your interest and suck away time is blessedly gone. The horse and buggy show of it all is mercifully erased, you finally see what really matters—and it's not you—not even close. The Me, Mine and I of it all isn't important anymore. Problem: I find the Me, Mine and I of other's more nauseating than my own.

'He saw the world as a fantastic living organism, with all the different aspects of civilization busily moving around without him. He wasn't the selfish center, his life and death will be of no moment to the earth. That revelation, which many people never find, was his entrance to adulthood. He was inconsequential therefore, free.'

paraphrasing James Michener, The Fires Of Spring

The sadness I used to feel was a feather bed of self indulgence, a luxurious lack of discipline. The glorious bitter pill of it all helped me write. *This* sadness is real and I'm tired of it. I have to make peace with my body and I'm not sure how.

Sleeping at a lake house. I woke and both my hands moved. I looked at them. The left was normal, the right was still covered in burn scars and still had only four fingers but it was moving. I was elated! I ran outside to show Kevin. I had a dream lover he was happy but not surprised, as if it were just a matter of time not a miracle. (We've been hooking up in my dreams for years, a tall white boy with black dreds and lapis eyes.) Kevin came over to where we were standing on impossibly thick grass. I showed him that I was able to move my fingers. However, they were changing. I had five fingers on each hand now and no burn scars. 'I think this is a dream...' 'No it's not honey, it's real,' said Kevin. 'But I have all my fingers back; I think it's just a dream.' Euphoria fading.

I woke up sad. Paw frozen, electric seizures; I lay there holding Homescrub, sleepy purring. Petting an animal is supposed to help with recovery.

'...Dominique on the train to Prague
said it was smoky and sleepy wore old Levi's and cowboy boots
sipped scotch and talked to Americans from L.A.
they were students, they bored her
she slept and dreamed of Manns Chinese...'

~Al Christ

I've littered the dining room table with Rancho files but can't make myself open them. They create a dead spot in my mind and if I think about it too much I fall asleep. Betsy's family has been on vacation for three weeks and I'm not doing well alone. I walk around a somnambulist, go out for absolute necessities and drive myself to the gym even though it's two blocks away.

I have killed days with email, web surfing and writing letters about that moron, Sam Woodjablowme. When Monk and I drove out, we got stopped in a speed trap in the tiny town of Gilbert Minnesota. I was given a ridiculous 'Driving Under Suspension' ticket and they set a court date. Sam Wouldjablowme was the attorney in charge. He wouldn't return my calls for over a month and I was crying about it. Betsy helped me with my perspective. 'Yes this guy is an asshole but the little trolls of Gilbert shouldn't be getting to you like this. I know it's frustrating, but fuck 'em. You are stronger than that.'

I sent a letter; it helped my mental heath. (Abridged.)

Dear Mr Wouldjablowme: Do to your refusal to accept my phone calls, I am sending this letter via E-mail, FAX and certified mail. On June 21, 2003 I was stopped for speeding in the city of Gilbert. I gave the officer my driver's license, registration and insurance and waited for the ticket.

The officer came back and told me my MINNESOTA driver's license was revoked in 1991. Since I am from CALIFORNIA and gave him a current CALIFORNIA license, I was confused. I told him I was just visiting MINNESOTA. You are not allowed to have more than one state's license. I have a license from the state in which I live. The officer stated in his Incident Detail Report

'...to legally drive in Minnesota she needs to regain a valid MN driver's license.'

The absurdity of this statement scares me—I can't believe this guy carries a gun. He also stated my license was revoked in 1991. I got my CALIFORNIA license in 1988. By 1991 I was established in my career as a stunt woman. I drove in commercials, television and films, with a valid CALIFORNIA license. I have received no response from you or anyone from your office. I have called repeatedly.
(The dates and times of seven calls.)

I left detailed messages, my cell and my driver's license number and waited to hear back from you. Nothing. I tried again.
(The dates and times of eight calls.)

Jason, the young man who occasionally answers your phone, informed me the office is always empty on Fridays and 'mostly empty after lunch.' I received a letter saying 'We would request a continuance of the arraignment...' and another from Suzy B, Court Administrator that says, 'A Pre-trial Aug 6, 2003 at 2 PM before the honorable Gary J. Pagliaccetti.' I tried calling and was ignored again.
(The dates and times of seven calls.)

8 / 1 / 03—I tried <u>everyone on your letterhead</u>. [Fifteen lawyers.] No one was in, Jason said 'I told you no ones here after lunch.' You have an awfully big office for such a tiny toy town and it's been empty for over a month. Who pays everyone's salaries? The State? I find that revolting.

I've also tried to reach Suzy B repeatedly without luck. I was told by a woman who identified herself only as 'Kim' that Suzy was out, had no voice mail and I couldn't leave a message with her. Kim suggested I send *this* letter and then surprised me with a suggestion; 'if you don't live in MINNESOTA then it doesn't matter if there's a warrant out for you here.' Advice from the mysterious 'Kim' is unacceptable. I want this cleared. My friend Uncle Bill is an officer in the Smallville Sheriffs Dept. I asked him to please check my license for me. He said it was fine, no tickets or warrants; <u>a valid CALIFORNIA license</u>.

Sincerely,
Alisa Christensen

cc   Honorable Gary J Pagliaccetti
         Suzy B, Court Administrator

I received a faxed response from Sam later that day. 'We have dismissed the Driving after Revocation charge in connection with court file No. T1-03-102757.'

Took days to write. Looking back it's funny, in a small town, crooked politician kind of way but when it was happening it caused metal mouth and narcolepsy. Writing that letter was empowering; even with speech compromised, I could still communicate effectively. I wrote another letter to every newspaper on the Iron Range. Sent them packages, copies of all the stupid correspondence and the ticket. I wanted revenge. That is CVA related as well.

MORE DRUG WAR NONSENSE!

My insurance fills prescriptions a month at a time, typical. Coolchick wrote everything with three refills to get me through the summer. Baclofen for CVA symptoms, Darvoset for pain, Lexapro so a healthy bitch can park in a Gimp spot without getting WHACKED, Ambien to sleep and Zanax if I feel a panic attack coming.

The pharmacies in MN won't fill them; a boy at Walgreen's told me they can't fill prescriptions from other states unless, 'it's a state that borders Minnesota.' If I was from North or South Dakota, Iowa or Wisconsin, they could fill them but no California. I asked why he said suspiciously, 'they're controlled substances!' Good thing MN has stopped me from getting medication. The burned gimp that has trouble sleeping and debilitating bouts of anxiety needs to be controlled. Especially irritating since Ambien was filled last month in Smallville. They recognize doctors from other states up North.

> '…anything can happen
> Jah purify my vision this morning
> the sun is rising once again
> the way worldly things are going
> Jah need your strength
> to see me through the day…'
>
> paraphrasing Bob Marley

My left foot!

I woke up feeling sick and dizzy. My face was hot, found a thermometer, temperature 102! And my left foot had swelled as big as a football. I went to the Abbot & Costello ER for help. After a <u>five hour wait</u> I was told there was a hairline fracture in my big toe. Now get the hell out!

Hairline fractures are black and blue and the pain is localized, you know right where it is. Went to bed fine and woke up mysteriously feverish? Doesn't sound like a fracture to me, the whole foot was engorged and I would have remembered hurting my toe. No doctor or X-ray technician looked at the X-ray just a nurse practioner (Adull Star) who could have been reading it wrong. I don't know because she *wouldn't show it to me*!

Years of stunts gave me many bumps I seem to remember whacking a toe somewhere. Could have been the Leprechaun 4 fight or Wayne's World or the Love and War bar fight—I think it was a bar fight. Adull asked me the usual, where, when, how long in the burn unit and I told her about the CVA. She asked if I was working out, I thought she was making small talk. 'I work out a lot, 3 to 5 days a week, weights, treadmill and Stairmaster.' 'No swimming?' she queried. Such a weird question it caught me off guard. 'No. I'm not ready to be stared at.' She gave me look of *pure distain*. 'A lot of people get over their disabilities by swimming! A lot of people don't care what other people think!' She snorted like a horse and rolled her eyes. It was SO peculiarly nasty that vultures instantly woke. Must Remove Speech.

Fuck Off you weird bitch is what I was thinking. I have open wounds on my hand and fragile skin grafts on forty percent of my body. Cold chlorine water would hurt me. None of my therapists or doctors have prescribed swimming.

I stared at the nasty troll, blinking my eyes… then changed the subject. 'I need my prescriptions for Darvoset, Ambien and Zanax re-written.' I explained the strange non-bordering state rule and showed her my empty scrip bottles with 3 refills, up to date and written by Dr Coolchick. She asked if I had ever been on 'pain killers.' I didn't think I'd heard her right—such a stupid question—*I was holding an empty bottle of pain medication with my name on it.*

'Morphine in the ICU then Methadone, I went through the list. Vicoden does nothing. Lately I've been having luck with Darvoset…' 'I'll be back.' She left abruptly. Half an hour later—which made a grand total of 5 Fucking Hours—*another* nurse brought in a sheet of paper for me to sign—yadda yadda about keeping my foot elevated and a prescription for fifteen 10 mg Vicoden. 'Wait! I said as she was leaving, Vicoden does nothing for me!' She stopped, looked me up and down (filthy junkie) then stared me in the eyes pointedly, 'I don't care, that's all we're prepared to do!' 'What about my prescriptions?' 'You'll have to see a Minnesota Doctor, here's a list of clinics.' 'This hospital is full of Minnesota doctors! I've been here FIVE HOURS!' She was gone, slipped away mid sentence. They had dismissed me as 'drug seeking' and an addict, even one with a broken toe and a swollen foot is contemptible and should be debased, degraded, shattered if possible.

If I have a problem with addiction, that's for my LA doctors to address, not a shitty nurse practitioner in the midfuckingwest. Embarrassed humiliated depressed I can't come up with the right vulture / most of all, pissed that I'd let them hurt me. I sat in the living room stewing in horrid pain and impotent rage. Another day wasted at a bad hospital with a misdiagnosis from a fucking hippochristian wildebeest. Effing bitch.

Fortunately I remembered the patch. Dr Horselaugh had prescribed a narcotic patch last summer in Smallville I still had tons of them, they were too strong. Fentanyl Transdermal System. They look like see through nicotine patches and they work for three days. I put one on and went to the land of narcotic nodding; dormant, never waking up, never getting to sleep. Overkill and annoying but better than pain.

I went back and picked up the X-rays a few days ago I think I remember that hair line, I think I smacked it in the early 90's. And I Finally remembered I'm still married! Called Husband he filled all my scripts in LA and sent them priority mail. Sweet Husband. Why did I go to a Minnesota hospital? I know better, that's what kills me. Useless at best / dangerous at worst. It was my own vulture riddled fault.

2007

No it wasn't. My treatment at Abbott & Costello was unacceptable. Dot. I got a bill for $265 about six months later, the co-pay. I sent a letter reiterating the above; they responded quickly.

> '…I would like to apologize for any distress you experienced. At Abbott & Costello, we believe that patients and their families have the right to expect they will be treated with respect and concern. Most of your complaint is focused on the skill of the medical provider and our bill is not for those services. I am, as a courtesy, going to write off the

balance of the hospital bill because your experience was so unsatisfactory.'

Sincerely,
Covering Ourbutt

August 2003—Betsy & Adams

Addicted to news. California at the moment is as funny as it's ever been. They finally recalled the last idiot Governor and everyone's porn star grandmother is in the race. Arnold running for Governor (he'll win, duh) the record breaking heat wave across Europe, fires burning out of control in Portugal, Italy, Canada and The Bush Company's non-stop Wolf Crying! Yellow! Red! Orange! Watch out! Red! Red! Look under your bed! Please. Does anyone believe this? Black outs, power shortages, I had to go cold turkey! I turned off the TV and put music back on.

Nova Gel pads arrived, they were hard to find. Someone figured out if you heat scar's (any scar, doesn't have to be from fire) they get noticeably smaller. $300 for ten, thanx Producers Health Plan. Blue sticky silicone sheets, 5 x 7. I put them over my feet and ankles at night wrapped in ace bandages and my body heat creates a little greenhouse effect. Burn scars are high maintenance; it takes years to stabilize. That's what I'm hoping anyway—they finally stabilize

'How far you go in life depends on your being tender with the young,
compassionate with the aged,
sympathetic with the striving,
and tolerant of the weak and strong.
Because someday in your life you will have been all of these.'

—George Washington Carver

Slept with Damien and loved it. Broke the Rag spell. Mars out the bedroom window…

Friend Lloyd was in Minneapolis for his book tour 'Make Your Own Damn Movie.' He was taken aback when he saw me. Everyone is. Recovered quickly but hope it doesn't scare him away too. Many fun memories include Lloyd. He runs Troma, an independent film company; they specialize in low budget horror and campy satires. We met years ago (Friend starred in one of his films) and hit it off. He's intellectual and puckish. Interesting combo. Troma also distributes. Lloyd picks up films no one else will. Nothing is too poorly filmed, horribly edited or simply nonsensical for Troma to release. Movies are hard to make; seasoned producers have extra cash hidden in the budget for overages. A lot of green 1st timers go broke. Lloyd thinks everyone deserves a shot. I love that he's a maverick.

His sets are chaotic because his crews are young and inexperienced. But also, I think, because Puck likes the energy of chaos. The Playboy Mansion was a mid summer nights dream. Lloyd called and told me about the scene he was going shoot for The Toxic Avenger 4. 'Citizen Toxie! Like the beginning of Citizen Kane…' One of Troma's wanna be producers (still trying to finish her abysmal film) was a former Playmate. She was still on good terms with Hugh and had arranged for Troma to shoot a day at the mansion. Lloyd wanted to know if I would help with pre-production and be his Assistant Director on the day of. Oh Yes.

The mansion gave us a pass for fifty people, dot, but shooting at the Playboy Hut was an easy way to get press. A week before the shoot, our press passes alone had ballooned over one hundred twenty. We decided not to mention it to the Mansion's staff; it's easier to ask forgiveness than permission. Troma used to have a West Coast office in Venice. The boys there handled Troma's web site. Lloyd had long been a fan of the Internet; he had West Coast put together a second unit to do a live feed. The East Coast crew came out the day before the shoot and we walked the grounds. We entered the infamous grotto; you could feel steamy sensual abandon wash over you in a slow sumptuous feast. The DP said what we were all thinking. 'Wow. Do you think anybody's had sex in here? Today?' We laughed. It was nine am. Enormous, black gargoyles sat on the roof of the main house. 'They were put up for our Halloween party,' explained the grounds keeper, we can have them removed…' 'No No!' They were perfect. The shot list was fairly straight forward; copy the beginning of Citizen Kane. Zanadu became Tromadu.

We met in the calm, eerie quite of pre dawn and started smoothly. The early hour meant the only people on the set were working. We started our shot list. Dr Carol painting (she was also our set medic) the boy that designed the website had his eye poked out and Melinda go-go danced on top of the grotto. Between 7:00 and 8:00 the rest of our talent and crew showed up, at nine West Coast's 2nd unit. By ten the press had begun to dribble in, bringing their own crews. A woman with dozens of fabulous feather hats showed up (we used them all) and friends of Bunny's, friends of Troma, relatives, personal assistants, hangers, bangers, drug dealers, paparazzi and a few assorted pimps were all in attendance. 2nd unit was doing a live feed and looking for things to catch their interest. They weren't disappointed. They went into the dressing rooms and talked to partially clothed models, they did Q and A's in the monkey cages. (Melinda did an interview and little fellas tried repeatedly to take off her string bikini.) At one point, they were in the grotto shooting hot, tattooed girls having sex. It got over eight hundred thousand hits before it crashed late in the afternoon. (I believe it was an internet first; free, live, lesbian porn from the Playboy Hut grotto.)

In the eye of the storm, I heard about these shenanigans peripherally. Our unit was First, our shot list the most important. By the side of our fearless king, I kept the pace and plowed ahead. It was getting late in the day. Magic Hour it's called but in reality it's only magic twenty to forty minutes, when the setting sun makes everything golden / perfect. I wanted to put myself in a shot, so we perched Noxie on top of the grotto and on 'Action' he threw me into the pool.

We worked into the night. The grotto was filled with Troma loyalists and exhibitionist's as we staged a silly, voyeuristic wet dream. Thirty people having an orgy, massacred by the evil Noxie. Lloyd was asking the girls to get topless (no takers) when suddenly on take two—a boy ripped off his shorts and did a crazy naked dance all over the entire set—a good minute, we were laughing our heads off. At scene's end everyone is dead as Noxie screams and beats his chest, a mutant Tarzan.

Slowly the press faded, Bunny's had enough, the extras were done. Our last shot was Noxie snorting a pail of cocaine saying '…nose blood…' With that, a snow globe falls from his mutated paw and rolls towards camera. Just like Citizen Cane. Brilliant.

September 2003—Smallville

Back to feeling like chucking it. Driven up to Smallville to see the parents and give Adam and Betsy a break from me and Scrubber. Though she's been a perfect guest, no howling, just endless kitty sleep in the sunny spot on my bed, I know Pop would like to see her. They nap together, support system for the seeing impaired. Am sore, achy. Hard to stand it. Mom was showing me pictures from last summer. I was a wreck. Sideways face in a wheelchair, I didn't look human. Shrunken apple doll.

The 'You're a Bitch!' Lady Story: It was a breakthrough. Betsy the kids and I were at the Renaissance Festival. We sat down early to watch Friends sing. (Their show fills up; we wanted to make sure we had seats.) I settled down on a hay bail with Betsy and the kids to the left of me. A woman sat on my right. 'Could you put your purse on the ground?' she asked. A goofy Puca Bag Betsy had just bought me in Scotland. The ground was fine dry dust. 'No, it's new,' I answered. 'Well put it in your lap!' she ordered.

Flap flap.…

My right arm is in a sling and I was holding a water bottle with my left. There was no room on my lap. 'No,' I finally said after an endless struggle. 'You're a BITCH!' She barked. I was stunned, hurt. Betsy had been talking to her daughter. She turned around incredulous, 'did I hear you right? Did you just call my disabled friend a bitch?' 'She is a bitch!' I looked at Betsy helplessly, unable to speak. Betsy stood up. The theater was filling, she had a decent audience. 'I cannot believe you sat down next to a disabled woman and started *swearing* at her, what's wrong with you?' 'You're making a fool of yourself!' You're A Bitch Lady hissed. 'I'm making a fool of myself? Let's ask them. Which one is a bitch? Her? (hand over my head) Or her? (hand over You're a Bitch Lady) the audience clapped and laughed. Funny.

Betsy noticed I was still quiet an hour later. 'Did she really get to you?'
I shrugged. 'You have GOT to toughen back up sweetie, assholes are
everywhere. You cannot let them do this to you.' We sat in the shade and
drank lemonade. 'Do you remember when I broke my leg?' I didn't. 'We
were at 1st Ave seeing some band and I was on crutches. This drunk chick
kept bumping into me. You asked her politely to watch what she was doing,
didn't work. You yelled at her. Nothing. You went to the bar, got a double
shot of cream de menthe and poured it in her purse.' That broke the evil spell
/ I laughed, I didn't remember doing it but it was definitely me pre CVA.

A few hours later we ran into You're a Bitch Lady in a shop. I gave her a
little poke in the butt with my cane. It sent her SCREAMING into the street.
'She hit me with her cane! She hit me with her cane!' Her mortified grown
children dragged her away. Had to lean against a wall I was laughing so hard,
Betsy beaming.

September 11, 2003—Cleveland, Ohio

SEPTEMBER 1, 1939 (abridged)
by W.H. Auden

'I sit in one of the dives
On Fifty-second Street
Uncertain and afraid
As the clever hopes expire
Of a low dishonest decade:
Waves of anger and fear
Circulate over the bright
And darkened lands of the earth,
Obsessing our private lives;
The unmentionable odor of death
Offends the September night.

Accurate scholarship can
Unearth the whole offence
From Luther until now

That has driven a culture mad,
Find what occurred at Linz,
What huge imago made
A psychopathic god:
I and the public know
What all schoolchildren learn,
Those to whom evil is done
Do evil in return.

Into this neutral air
Where blind skyscrapers use
Their full height to proclaim
The strength of Collective Man,
Each language pours its vain
Competitive excuse:
But who can live for long
In an euphoric dream;
Out of the mirror they stare,
Imperialism's face
And the international wrong.

Faces along the bar
Cling to their average day:
The lights must never go out,
The music must always play,
All the conventions conspire
To make this fort assume
The furniture of home;
Lest we should see where we are,
Lost in a haunted wood,
Children afraid of the night
Who have never been happy or good.

All I have is a voice
To undo the folded lie,
The romantic lie in the brain

Of the sensual man-in-the-street
And the lie of Authority
Whose buildings grope the sky:
There is no such thing as the State
and no one exists alone;
Hunger allows no choice
to the citizen or the police;
we must love one another or die.'

Rest in Peace.

Two years since the towers went down and our government is making the world worse. Marches and protests ignored, diplomacy not even tried. The hawk's crapping with glee.

I'm in Cleveland at the World Burn Conference. I was contacted by Friendly Social Worker from USC about a grant from a charity called 'Firefighters Quest.' They sent a bunch of us out. Firemen are a big part of it and Firemen have always had my heart, they are what cops are supposed to be; they really do protect and serve and mysteriously, more often than not, they're eye candy.

Dr Approachable gave the opening speech and what sticks in my mind is he misquoted Shakespeare. Attributed '...a rose by any other name would smell as sweet...' to Gertrude Stein. (Gertrude Stein!?) He was a sweet grandfatherly cat but some of his philosophy I disagreed with, ('burns are an incurable disease'? No honey, HIV is an incurable disease.) I had to stop myself from telling him about his Shakespeare gaff—have to laugh—my period started two days later. The next speaker was a chick, 'Helping families to Recover after a Burn,' going into the psychological effects of burn injuries. Dealing with loss, trauma and the steps to rebuilding your life. She was fun, humor, anecdotes. WBC provided lunch and had an open mic. People that felt like talking got up and told war stories. Nice, camaraderie.

The Rock and Roll Hall of Fame was unexpectedly cool. Tour start's in the basement. Exhibits were great, we were all pleasantly surprised. The Gravity Games (an X Games type of thing) were going off next to the Rock and Roll

Hall and their crew was also staying at the Renaissance. It added surrealism, outside the whirlpool, watching the world swirling by; a year and a half ago I could have been at the Gravity Games. Not in them, I'm past the 18 to 24 I'm never going to die thing, but working on them. When I would see them in the elevator or the bar, I felt like I had on the wrong badge.

I'm at the airport, processing the last few days while it's fresh. Good overall with occasional human foibles. Men saying 'Smile!'(always a winner) and a woman saying, 'at least your face wasn't burned…' as she stalked away on perfect legs. Men can be idiots no matter what they look like and the callous woman was obviously having difficulty with her own disfigurement. What a Horror Show to suddenly have no face. Easy to ignore the occasional remark and make friends. We who have nothing in common but the survival instinct; I find myself thinking of Armstrong and Reeve yet again. I'm not burned beyond belief like so many here but I'm not wearing the Gravity Games badge either.

It was a good experience and I'm glad I went but the existential angst intensified. I continue to feel nothing. I'm not cheerful and smiling, not lonely and crying, I'm far away caught in a swirling vortex, life goes on at its normal speed and I'm in a CVA dimension. Sometimes it's a comfort admittedly but most of the time it just is what it is.

I went to the support groups. I didn't participate but enjoyed hearing stories. I did ask if anyone there had suffered a stroke, a young man said yes so I made sure I talked to him later. A young woman asked when she should bring up the subject of burns to a prospective lover. Her injury wasn't apparent and it was hard for her to decide when. She didn't want to get to the point of no return and have him be freaked by scars. But didn't want to talk about sex as if it were an invitation. I tried to answer, I thought I had a good one but stumbled through clumsy, halting speech and eventually apologized and gave up. Vultures were circling the whole trip. What I was trying to say: Take him to an action movie and when talking about it afterwards say, 'that scene where they blew up the compound reminded me of when I was burned…' Or go out for a drink and say, 'did I ever tell you about the fire I survived? I don't talk about it much but…' Have the conversation away from the bedroom and sexy thoughts. He won't get that you're sizing him up as a lover. Men are simple that way. It's a real anxiety, the fear of being rejected for damage; you're vulnerable. Part of foreplay now but better than the alternative. It was scary letting Damien near me after I was dumped by Rag; super glad I did though.

I used to have a lot of good friends. They came when I was hospitalized, when I needed them most, they were there. I'll always love unconditionally for that. That helped save my life. Eighteen months later though, most have turned to ghosts. I thought it was my fault. A survivor asked me if any of my friends stuck around, it surprised me and helped. He explained the weird sad phenomenon that happens to all of us. When you become disabled—especially disfigured—friends leave. Usually between years one and two, when it becomes obvious things have changed permanently.

Most aren't outrageously cruel (like Moe and Cat) they are simply too busy to talk and won't return calls. I don't understand the subtle brush off anymore. Emotionally, I'm twelve. I kept calling many many embarrassing times before the light bulb finally sputtered on. *You are being avoided on purpose; they don't want to know you anymore.* I wish I'd been aware of Friend Drop Phenomena sooner. It would have helped to keep me from feeling so crazee. (Although it still would have ached.) It's not something you think about preparing yourself for.

The closing ceremonies and banquet were fun. Dinner, slide show, dancing. I didn't try to dance but sat at a table with Friend (the boy who'd had the stroke) and we laughed our heads off at the shenanigans of the drunks.

Vultures circle lazily overhead, waiting for some part of my brain to malfunction. There goes my sense of time. I've found myself at the airport *three hours* ahead of departure …swoop! Food for vultures. I'm sitting at the café next to the gate still in a bizarre, time travel mode; I would swear I left the hotel with two hours to get to the airport, check my bag and get a wheelchair. I remember looking at the clock…a mystery. And how did I mix up Sunday and Monday? Vulture snack. That kibble cost $139 and change. I had to re-do my E ticket or sit in Cleveland by myself for another day. They don't make a lot of noise considering they're huge birds; you'd think they'd be hard to miss but they catch me off guard all the time.

HO is starting up again; my elbow is painful and hot. Disconcerting but Specialisto told me that it always comes back a little, as long as it doesn't impeded movement in the joint, don't worry about it. I've stopped pain medication again; Minnesota makes it too hard. Winchester thinks I should call my book 'Vultures,' not just for the words, numbers and IQ points that disappear but the medical profession, the pharmaceutical companies, Medicaid, Medicare, insurance, hospitals, doctors, social security disability, the list is endless. Example: Yolanda is a young woman I met at the conference. We were talking about plastic surgery; she said 'people are always asking why I don't have more. I can't afford it.'

There ya go. Vultures. You can only have surgery that's OK'd by Insurance Companies and what you look like is not a consideration. Too bad if how you look is married to how you feel, if your sense of self is locked in with your face. And who's isn't, really? One in a hundred? A thousand? But plastic surgery is only for the rich. That was presented for our viewing pleasure by a Congress speaker. He was a plastic surgeon who was burned as a teenager. It was a house fire, he lost some family but managed to save two brothers. (Hero) Both hands and arms were burned, he had gruesome photos of his recovery. Right after the fire his skin was cut open. (I remembered them doing that to me at USC! In a flash back I remembered being in the plane, saying 'cut it open, please cut my arm open…' it was going to burst like an over cooked bratwurst; they wouldn't and told me to wait for the hospital.) He showed slides of his paws one-year post fire and they looked awful, two years after and they don't resemble the previous photos. He had tons and tons of reconstructive surgery. Now he's a plastic surgeon that specializes in burns. It was amazing, really brought home how far the medical profession has progressed in such a short time. As long as you have Insurance that's willing to pay for it. Our country needs to keep feeding the war machine; there's nothing left for universal health care. Fucking vultures.

Still September 2003—Smallville

Damien is going to take some time off and drive back to the west coast with me. We leave Oct 1st

Kevin called with good news about SAG's Insurance. The fiscal year is up at the end of the month, I need to make twenty G's a year to keep it; easy enough when you're working but I only made seventeen in residuals this year. Kev and I were hunting around on the Internet for options. 'Cobra' is a plan where you can keep the insurance you have for another year to eighteen months. SAG's insurance is five hundred a month. There are charitable organizations that will help to offset the cost and I was gonna go down those habitrails next, but no need! SAG informed Kev that since I'm still on Case Management status they would continue Plan 1 for another year.

Kiss Kiss Kiss
everyone in that office.

In the early 80's I was living in Dinky Town (U of M's campus town) with a sliding scale of other friends. We rented a trashed frat house that had lost its vulture and had kegger's once a month to pay rent. Damien was a cute under age teen that came to our parties. He had a crush on me but I liked adults and thought of him as a friendly pet. Cut to 20 years later: Damien was coming to Betsy's once a week to give me massages, he still saw me as perfectly nineteen and four years age difference disappears in your 30's. Both lonely, we hung out a lot. He was easy. Witty and amusingly self depreciating.

His blues were looming, he'd made dumb decisions. Around the time I was burning in the desert, Damien was getting arrested in Kansas for transporting five thousand pounds weed of across state lines. He was in limbo waiting for justice to creak along. He'd sold his house and hired a criminal lawyer off the television. Finney the Shark could keep him out of Folsom but he was gonna do prison time. Damien was an emotional wreck, trying to 'Make the Best Of It.' I convinced myself our situations were the same. (In reality, only abstractly.)

Damien and I took Hwy 94 across North Dakota and Wyoming. Wyoming is my favorite state to drive through, beautiful colors and no billboards. Then bitch slapped by ugly Montana sprawl; hurried Mc Mansions, no foresight or planning, ugly pink houses for you and me. We left Hwy 94 in Missoula and took the 12 through the top of Idaho. Soaring trees, Seuss like mountains, crisp fall, so dramatic. Fun driving across country again. We took the back door into Portland. Hilly, dry farm land. Great to see Kev and Y and say goodbye lost summer.

Damien and I were on a honeymoon. Life is easier with a partner. I was lonely he was lonely—we were smitten and had sex a lot. I never wrote too much about intimacy but my orgasms were affected by the CVA. It's easier to have one, they're stronger, last longer and once I have one, I can have three or five more. Definite mood elevator.

October 2003, Los Angeles—Montecito Heights

Thinking Henry Miller. Woke up in Watsonville. Driving the coast was magic. We took four days to drive down Hwy 1 through ancient trees, Marin county, San Francisco, sunset along the dunes, rocky cliffs, the sky turning magic west coast lavender, the moon full. Big Sur is my favorite part of the CA coast and bits of Millers description's floated back. (We stopped at his museum but it was only open a couple days a week.)

In love again for the third time in three years; Wayne, Rag, Damien, what a trio. Wayne torn away by the Fates, Rag dumped Frankenstein for precious Glonda and Damien…? Going to prison. I have to laugh, I've always been unlucky in love, but love being in love anyway.

I had several friends with guest houses and spare bedrooms, I picked Alexander & Tweak's for the view. Montecito Heights overlooks downtown LA from the north east. They are in a 1970's over size ranch, the house is a comfy tear down, but the location is outrageous. You can see the Long Beach Harbor on a clear day. Curvy drive to the top, click open the gate, then drive ½ mile down a dirt road, surrounded by grassy fields. A church owns most of this property with a few privately owned chunks scattered about. It's a dream. Tweak had mentioned finances were tight so I'd called to see if they wanted to rent their downstairs for a few months. Yes. Damien and I spent a week making love then he flew home (thanks Ross) with plans to come back.

2007

Homescrub was staying with Friend in Minneapolis, Damien would bring her back in his truck, get a part time job and spend the winter. Sounded perfect. I joined a gym in Pasadena, got back in touch with Coolchick and Allritini and resumed acupuncture. Called Calvin to see if he was still interested in doing a website, he was. CafeDeb.com seemed like it could make money. Loosely magazine-ish. I had nude fotos of myself and friend Cee Cee ready to put up. It was good therapy to learn new things, how hard could it be? Pretty hard, it turned out but it was good to take on tasks *that I didn't want to do* to kick start my brain. Café Deb was the perfect foil, lots of thinking in different directions, with enough of an artistic bent to keep me interested. Alexander worked all day, came home sad and started drinking. Freaky Tweak was crippled by meth addiction and hardly left the house. Hard to hide when I'm living there. I ignored them both (denial) and felt great. I'd go downstairs and write. Calvin and I went to a street party downtown with the usual suspects. Decompression from Burning Man. Fun to see the party pack again. I wrote eight pages but I think the following sums it up:

> I saw a boy from the sheriffs department sucking a super-model's nipples. She was an impossibly perfect brunette and he was bent over her chest with both hands cupping her tits. They both laughed as she pulled her tiny T back down. 'Thank You' he said and walked off smiling as his two cop buddies laughed appreciatively and slapped his back.

I can't see that happening in Minnesota. Stupid Babylon, I've missed you.

November, 2003—Montecito Heights

'…hazardous
baby I'm falling
men like you should wear a warning…'

paraphrasing Britney Spears

Saw Allritini this week. He told me he loved me, so easily too. We were talking about recovery and setting up my next surgery. He said the ICU nurses at USC still ask about me. 'I love you, Alisa, I really do. Not everyone would be able to go on, but not you. You never gave up.' Started to give him the usual, 'I fall apart all the time, I'm a mess...' But I caught myself and simply said, 'I love you too, baby.' I do.

And I love Damien and forgive my friend Rag and I sleep the sleep of children and dream the dreams of angels. The pieces of angst and chain coiled and tucked aside for now.

'...these are the times to remember
for they will not last forever...'

—Billy Joel

I cried at Calvin's the other night. He was giving me a lesson on HTML, we downloaded 'alisachristensen.com' to use as a tool. I used to use a vanity site for my headshot's and résumé's. Calvin went to pick up take out and left me alone, remembering. I think it was Face Off—maybe Deep Cover. Waterworks. Face Off was a John Woo film. I doubled Dominique Swain, only for one night though, it's just such a cute picture of us, a Polaroid in the makeup trailer. Had a part in Deep Cover, I read for the director, Bill Duke. They wanted a good looking stunt woman who could act. The part was small and they didn't want to hire two people. I had to laugh at my tears. Deep Cover was a hundred thousand years ago and Face Off at least seventy five. Calvin's so sweet, he pet my hair and told me everything would be all right.

And the children? Those little bastards sleep like the coyote's howling in the canyon below me. I woke at 4:20 and couldn't drop off again. Laid there and watched the rising sun turn the canyon purple. Listened to Howard Stern. Tarantino was on, talking about 'Kill Bill.' He's clever and gave good interview. We met in Spain, at a film festival with Ken.

Journal / Nov 1996

Ken was foreman at the Sitgis film festival and Quentin Tarantino had entered a film he produced. Technically producers weren't supposed to fraternize with the jury but who was going to tell him no?

Ken was annoyed at first, didn't care for Pulp Fiction but I talked him into giving QT a chance. Tarantino loved Ken's films and was excited to meet him. QT was charming chatty and quickly won him (all of us) over (Ken said Tarantino remembered his films better than he did) but he hadn't changed his clothes. Day after day the same t-shirt. We didn't think he'd been showering. He started to stink.

I finally asked him why, lost suitcase perhaps? He said something like, if you wear the same shirt all week at a festival, you'll always know where the paparazzi shots were from. Made sense but TWO t-shirts would do the same thing, no? The members of the jury and friends took up a little wager for champagne. Mira [Sorvino] was coming for the closing ceremony. Will he change his clothes? Have a shower & a shave? The men said no, he's a guy, he's Quentin Tarantino for Christ sake, he'll keep doing his thing. The women thought not.

Of course we were right (and chose Dom) when Mira showed up Tarantino was showered, clean shaven, wearing a nice jacket and hopefully had burned that shirt.

November 2003—Montecito Heights, Los Angeles

Went down to Vignes and 2nd and slowly wound our way west, giving stuff to Homelet. It was pouring, thunder, lightning, brilliant. I had bought $25 of

Charles Krueg cabernet (2 buck Chuck) at Trader Joes earlier; went by the .99 store for bottle openers, water and some brightly colored tins of shortbread cookies.

It started raining thick sheets as the sun set. The kind of thunderstorm I'd been missing all summer. Thunder so loud it shook the house. Tweak was blessedly passed out and Alexander and I were sitting in the kitchen talking about our days. He was a sad clown, worked eight hours and then had a flat tire in the rain. He has one of those toy tires on his car. I told him about my plans for the evening, hoping I could talk him into it. Alexander was starting to say, 'not tonight, the weather is too bad…' when the phone rang. It was his Friend needing a ride, she works for a costumer downtown on the corner of Urine and Heroin. Yippee!

'I'll drive.' We picked up Friend smoked a little spotch, put on old Cypress Hill for mood and slowly began to meander. There was something going on at Staples and the main throughways were bumper to bumper. Homelet avoids high traffic and I get nervous when too many people surround my van and avoid big box villages.

We finally found a guy standing outside of two small tents smoking a cigarette. He watched me getting out of my new warm van, 'Hi, how you doing tonight?' He gave me a look that said, lady I'm in no mood to be saved. 'I'm doin' OK…' resignation. 'Do you want a bottle of wine?' 'What?' …sure he hadn't heard me right. 'I have some wine, if you'd like…' 'Yea, thanks.' 'You you know your neighbor? Do you think he wants a bottle?' He started to chuckle, 'I think he would.' His name was Tom and the guy in the tent next to him was Chicago. They were so sweet. I gave them bottles of water and tins of short bread cookies as well. 'These are my favorite kind,' said Chicago smiling at the container.

Zombies noticed my van, they began to amble over. 'What do you have? 'Can I have some cookies? 'Got a blanket?' Yikes! Time to bail. On to the next lonely tent / tarp / box. Alex and Friend were getting into it too. It's addictive, making people happy just by doing something fun and easy. We gave this one cat a ride a few blocks to get him out of the rain and under a better awning. He was a little out of it, not too bad, talking about having had an epiphany about something or other. He wanted to go to a shelter in South Central. 'No sweetheart, I'm not going that far…' Dropped him off at a dark doorway with a big overhang, I helped him get his things from the back. I took his hand, it was so cold. 'Your hand is warm,' he said. We looked into each other's eyes; connection with a fellow human being. 'Good night baby…' 'Good night.'

Saw only one woman, a black chick. She was wasted; drunk, cracked out or a little of both. I had just given the last bottle of Cab to a Mexican gentleman. I turned around to hand him the last tin of cookies and she appeared (like a ninja) and snatched it from my hand. 'I'm homeless too,' she said defensively. 'It's OK honey, you can have them.' I nodded and smiled, she relaxed a little. The Mexican and I made eye contact. She could have the cookies, he was happy with the wine.

Fun for an hour visiting Homelet in the rain and cold; what can I do for them? Their problems are myriad, how to address them is beyond me. All I can do is one on one, not much. No money, no housing, no medication, no safely net, yet I come home feeling good. It's addictive and selfish, the sin of pride but that's fine 'cause I'm a sinner.

'There is an imaginary line
between those that conform to society's rules and those that don't.
The great majority of people are distinguished and defined by their
incomes. Dot. Everyone who has spent even a short amount of time with
Homelet knows this.
There is no 'us and them' we're the same.
The problem lies within the cliché 'out of sight out of mind.'
When do we ever get to share an hour with the poor?
We keep the humblest wedge of society segregated.
The majority of educated working people know nothing of poverty.'

Paraphrasing George Orwell, Down and Out in Paris and London

Alexander was out of town for the weekend and Tweak was looking for someone to bitch at. Alexander doesn't listen to Tweak, he tunes him out, kind of funny. When they're fighting, or more specifically, Tweak is going off and Alexander is ignoring him, I'm Switzerland. I come down to my basement hideaway and send dirty email to Damien (the new preferred past time.) Not my yard, not my problem. Come after me because you don't have a depressed lover to bash? Wrong baby.

I sent e to Damien:

> Tweak barked at me, been doing it for days then acting as if nothing happened. I finally said, 'I am recovering from a serious brain injury, I can't stand stress. 'Is that so? Well you should have gone on a cruise then. This isn't a house for you to sit around in.' I just gave them a grand for two months rent. 'I can't stand being talked to like that. Alexander lets you do it to him but don't do it to me.' He started yelling—went on and on about their altruism—if I'm so hurt then go on a cruise. Cruises must be precious to Gollum because he kept bringing them up. Then, 'you think you can just lie around and recover in this house?'

> I went OFF! I was walking around the kitchen like a mad woman! I called him every name I could think off...of course I couldn't think of much.

> WHO THE FUCK DO YOU THINK YOU ARE? YELLING AT ME LIKE I'M YOUR BITCH? YOU'RE LUCKY I'M GIMP YOU FUCKING PRICK YOU FUCKING JUNKIE FUCK! I PAY FUCKING RENT AND I DEMAND FUCKING RESPECT!

> I had a coffee cup in my hand and was waving it like a wackadoo! It was all I could do not to smash him in the face with it. I scared him, he shut the fuck up and ran back to his room.

> Geeezzzzzz......

Damien wrote back in the morning.

> Aww babee, that really sucks. Sounds like you both said some awful things, very unfortunate. For whatever stupid reason you triggered hurt, anger, angst. You're in a vulnerable place in your life, he has to see that. I feel really bad for you baby. I understand why you got mad, your swift response drove him into a hole, so what's going to happen next? I hope you muster up a peace offering. The stronger heart has to move first, in my experience.

> I wish I was there to help make it better for you baby. If only I could be there to give you a hug and a shoulder… and other parts. Whatever you wanted, as often as you needed, maybe more than you think you want… It's OK to have make-up sex when your lover has a fight with someone else, isn't it? Maybe we could start a whole new movement of having restitution and recovery intercourse for all the major hurts and annoyances received outside the relationship.

> We could practice and practice and write a book, maybe a script, call it 'The Stupid Planet's Guide for Intimacy' or maybe just practice.

> I think about you all day, lovingly, longingly, lonelyingly, lustfully, yeah baby. Take care. XOXOXOOOXOXOOXXO-OXOXOOXOOOXOXO

I knocked on Tweak's door late that morning, 'truce?' I stepped in. 'I'm fine.' Still wearing clothes from the night before, twitching, chain smoking, no eye contact, so disturbing; I left him alone. The following evening, after he had slept, I tried to explain what happens when I get that mad. I can feel it like a wave building in my stomach, although it's my screwed up brain that's doing it, it's definitely building, building, before it comes crashing in. When I snap, I want to kill. Like some Nordic berserker I no longer care what happens to me, just seek vengeance. It's pretty crazee. 'I warned you a few times. I suppose you thought my saying 'I can't take the stress,' meant I was going downstairs to cry. 'Actually I did,' he admitted. I had to laugh at that, which made Tweak laugh. Armistice this minute but it won't last. As soon as he gets high again he's a golem. No has given me a road map. The Middle East has nothing on my brain, its napalm, anthrax, shoulder launched missiles.

2007

Living with a methamphetamine addict is Dangerous. I had done it in 2000 (not on purpose) and had seen the horrid transformation up close—Live on the Inside! Human to Ghoul before your eyes!

Mike was a good roommate didn't smoke or drink and he was funny. We had the same sense of humor. (We decoupage'd our coffee table with porn, gay and straight, almost died laughing, it took days. The living room was flesh colored so it took people awhile to notice. Then what will they do? Laugh or freak? That game never got old.)

I liked living with a man, gave me a sense of safety. Short lived. Mike was trying to leave his problematic lover. They were done when Mike moved into my guest room but within a month Rob had joined him. I naively thought their problems wouldn't become mine. They'd been together since they were teenagers, more than ten years. Not my yard...Rob was fine sober. Street wise and easy on the eyes but he loved the club scene. Wanted to drive the right car and wear designers. I'll make Easy Money; he thought, started dealing meth and was quickly addicted. Mike told him that he wasn't welcome high and none of his friends could visit. Ever. We'd see him every five or six days, coming down and needing to crash. He'd show up with black and blue pinch marks all over his face and try to have conversations. He'd fall down the stairs, actually roll down some stairs, make the turn, and roll down more to the floor. He'd drop food everywhere, sleep 24 hours, stay another day feeling miserable and repentant, then back to hell. I could see his IQ dissipating from week to week. It was fast BOOM six months! The personality of a human was replaced with that of a rabid rat. Malicious and volatile.

One night when they were alone, Rob squirted lighter fluid on Mike while he was sleeping and tried to light him up. I came home late to a couple of police cars quietly parked on the drive around the building. Mike had called 911 but they were both being arrested. After the OJ fiasco, cops in LA take spousal abuse seriously and arrest the accused. If it's two men accusing each other, they both go. Being sent to jail was Mike's last snail. He left Rob and the state. Mike is living happily with an artist in Dallas and Rob is doing porn in West Hollywood. Methamphetamine is repulsive. I knew scratchy, scabby, skeletal Tweak was lost even if Alex didn't. Although I didn't write about it, I was very aware of the problem and wasn't living with it again. I signed up for 'Westside Rentals' online and began to search for a new hut. Damien would help me move when he came back.

'…Ladies and gents step right up…
See Bissa the snake woman!
She was found sunning on a large rock in Kenya!
See Louis the human pincushion!
We'll let you pierce the skin yourselves, unbelievers!
Live on the inside! If he's not real, you can keep the truck!'

~Al Christ

My left foot! For crying out loud / again with the left foot.

A spot on my heel constantly ached. I remember mentioning it to Allritini when I was at Shelby's it but he didn't take me seriously. My guess is he didn't understand what I stammered about my foot and I let it go. I was ridiculously passive and couldn't explain the *simplest* problem. Poor combo. All summer a lump of scar tissue would stab and force me to sit. I went to Allritini prepared to be firm but he just said 'yea, we can take care of that. It's an outpatient thing, take about an hour…' There was a Little Drama with the foot, it healed slow and hurt like mad. I drove to Santa Monica weekly to have it monitored.

Big Drama at home! Alexander kicked Tweak out in a raging, break whatever's in sight, run for your life fight. Ding-dong the witch was gone!

We went to the desert for Thanksgiving. Alex filled the van with tent's and pillows, an awning for the sun during the day and we had the blow up mattress Monk and I got in Blythe. Alex's friends ran young; a couple of DJ's had speakers set up in Box Canyon. Friday night was fun, low key. There was a dirt bike shindig going off a mile down the canyon. A bunch of people—presumably young men—were playing loud rock, zooming around and shooting guns. We were far enough away not to eat a stray. They had set up a lighthouse with flashing red and green lasers; you could see it from the freeway, convenient for people looking for us, farther up the canyon.

'Bureau of Land Management' land is supposed to be free for public use. Saturday evening six pm, our modest encampment of twenty people was swarmed by Rangers. We were told to get out NOW! 'They have stuffed animals, I heard one tell another, that's one of their things…' He was referring to big fluffy Get Well gifts from my hospital stay. 'I SAID Get UP NOW!' a fat cop yelled at me. Alexander was letting the air out of our mattress while I idly sat on a lawn chair next to an offensive Bunny. Cop walked up to me until our knees were almost touching. (A big man bullying a woman is a Pathetic Worm.) 'MOVE YOUR ASS! You are going to spend the night in jail!' Unable to speak, I pointed to my sling, picked up my cane, gave him a shrug. He deflated and went to yell elsewhere.

We were thrown off public land for *stuffed animals?* Did that really happen? The dirt bike jamboree was still blasting away as we drove to the canyon next door / they were fine. Surreal police.

December 2003—Montecito Heights, Alex's house.

Allritini had asked me to sign and FAX a release last summer. He'd kept a photo record of my surgeries. He wanted to use them for a paper he was going to publish. I'd been bugging him for copies all year. He finally gave me a CD today. Bizarre white and gray tendons showing, flesh debrided. And wires around my fingers! That wasn't a dream, it was a memory. My feet bloody red, toenails burned black! I realized it was dark blue polish. Poor sweet little feet, I used to get pedicures.

'In searching for help he had naturally turned to his friends, especially those he had succored when in need. And they had failed him, every one of them.'

—Henry Miller, Big Sur

Alexander had a horror show. He was fifty thousand in debt and the credit cards were in his name. Tweak fetched the mail and had hid the trail for a long time. The enormity of the nightmare had Alex shell-shocked.

I helped him with the numbers mumbo jumble and started to come out of my figures fog. I called each creditor, told them about the identity theft, the hidden addiction, I was a third party mediator, soft spoken and patient, politely calling back repeatedly, I got results. Late fee's stopped and reversed, interest frozen, a few even knocked off some of the principal. It helped build my confidence. I wasn't stupid, I could help my friend. I could do mail, make sense of it, organize it, post-it note it, and help Alex send the checks on time. I voted bankruptcy but he vetoed. He wanted to refinance his mortgage and consolidate the bills. First, he wanted to fix up the house, it would take a couple months.

'…I'm surrounded by people in quiet desperation
worn out sleepwalkers, beaten warriors
slugging their way through their day
going nowhere, going nowhere…'

paraphrasing Tears for Fears

Saw the film 'The Station Agent.' A dwarf lives in a city, hates it. He inherits land in Nowhere, New Jersey, a tiny train station in a tiny town. In Smallville, everyone's in everyone else's business and *everybody* was curious about the dwarf. He was generally pissed off and prone to drinking. Made some quirky friends, one was a woman more hurt than him. (Her child died.) His friendship saves her; saving her, he lightens up and saves himself. Loved it. I'm a little preoccupied with Little People.

Back in the ICU of USC: Four am, every morning, a technician would wheel in a glow in the dark portable apparatus, clattering and noisy. His assistant was a dwarf; a tiny fellow, like Mini Me. The technician would raise the bed, help lean me foreword and then stuff the midget behind me. 'OK, go ahead and lean back.' 'Are you sure I won't hurt him?' 'No, no, it's fine,' he would assure me. I would lean back, slowly, carefully and I would feel the little guy struggling to breathe under my weight. Occasionally he would grunt or softly moan. It always felt inappropriate, squishing the midget, but when they were done, he would hop down, no problem. We didn't speak, rarely made eye contact but there was no malevolence in him. I recognized it was a delusion but the midget didn't know I was hallucinating. He was there to get squished. Even after an entire day mirage free, at four am there he was, squirming around behind me. I wonder what the technician thought when I would ask if I was hurting the little guy. Was he surprised that I could see him too?

> '...I might like you better if we fooled around a little
> still you say no
> maybe that's a veto
> but never say never...'

> paraphrasing Romeo Void

Went to General Hospital today to have Allritini look at my foot; I didn't want to wait another week, it looks bad and hurts. We can see USC / County Hospital from the picture window in the kitchen. Allritini works at the burn unit one week a month, I called him yesterday and he said to come by at eleven.

The nurse at the Burn Unit's desk looked from his book annoyed and said, 'he's not here, he'll be in the outpatient clinic at noon.' Rude / dismissive. I didn't argue. Maybe I made a mistake; my short term memory is so effed. I meander my way back out of the cavernous contraption and go to the building next door. It's now eleven thirty, I check in at the start of the habitrail. I don't have an 'up to date card' go to window number two, I need to fill out a do dah form, go to window three—horrid, fucking boredom sets in—I think of leaving but can't believe it's taking this long, surely it will end soon. At 2:30 I am escorted into the wackee little out patient clinic. Allritini says, 'why didn't you come upstairs at eleven? I was waiting for you.' Agh! I told him about the Lying Troll at the gate! He looked annoyed but in true Buddhist fashion didn't say anything mean. Just, 'I guess I should have had you come to the office. Sorry about that.' Then looked at my foot and said, 'it's coming along fine.'

I can't stop thinking of that Lying Villain on the twelfth floor. He wasted my entire day. For what? Fun? I curse that lizard with cancer. Grisly, painful, inoperable cancer.

'Weed Troll waitin' on a DSL line
Weed Troll say net porn lookin' mighty fine
Weed Troll addicted to his little window screen
sniffin' gak & eatin' corn & smokin' Mr Green...'

—Weed Troll

2007

Alex's basement got sun all day. Once the malignant tumor of Tweak was removed, everything was better. Scrub would sit in the sunny chair next to my desk and I finally opened up my medical files from Rancho Los Amigo's. I'd been putting it off for over a year. Rancho was hard to get used to, I was defeated. Until the stroke I'd been preparing myself for dealing with life post burn. It was going to be hard, not impossible.

Hope dissipated with the CVA. Rancho handles 10,000 patients a year. Stroke, car accidents, spine injuries, gun shots; the worst case scenarios the hardest to recover from. They're located on acres of space in the city of Downey, south east of LA. Most of it closed. Building after building, blocks of them, still and heated by So-Cal sun, slowly falling apart from disuse and kipple. Forgotten classrooms, commissaries, vacant operating rooms, a ghost town. Closed now, birds nest in broken windows.

Blocks still remain in use and I was told it was a great facility, I was lucky to get in, they had a waiting list. I took an ambulance down there. I didn't know what to expect. Three months at General Hospital had been hell; I was ready for clean and edible. I was completely helpless. I couldn't sit up in bed without assistance. Three months on my back had emaciated my muscles and I was ten pounds thinner. (123 to 113.) A chunk of hair on the back of my head broke off from laying on it so long. I was wheeled in on a trolley bed by the paramedics. It's a different view, seeing the world from a supine position. Around and around long poorly lit hallways that seemed to last for miles. The ceilings were dusty. Great, another gothic County facility. I have good insurance, why why why?

Then we turned a corner and voila! The Polanski Building! It looked shiny and smelled new. It was like being taken from the Roman Coliseum, complete with tourist's garbage, to a new condo filled with contemporary art. The color scheme is Southwestern, beige and salmon, non-threatening, boring, lots of light, big windows.

County of Los Angeles   Department of Health Services
RANCHO LOS AMIGOS NATIONAL REHAB CENTER

DATE OF ADMISSION: 3 / 29 / 02

CHIEF COMPLAINT: '...unable to perform basic activities of daily living.'

Couldn't dress myself, brush my hair or teeth, I hadn't thought about it except abstractly. I got there on a weekend and a half a dozen friends came out to see the new pad. I was still under quarantine and had a private room.

Tatiana was my morning nurse. She looked like an angel. She came in at seven, her thick black hair was either blown straight or set with curlers, her makeup was subdued and perfectly applied. Her skin was flawless, her smile mischievous; having her in my room was comforting but she added to the surreal tint of everything. She and another girl took me across the campus to have my hearing evaluated. They were both young, chatting amiably, switching easily between Spanish and English. They pushed the chair slowly;

it was amazing to be outside in the spring air. Except for the quick jailbreak with Jerry, I hadn't been outdoors in more than three months.

The Rancho campus is enormous, when we got to the screening room; they left me alone saying that they would be back in an hour. I remember how odd it felt, finally being alone. I savored it then another nurse came and got me. I was put into a small, glass walled room and given a headset. It was an interesting. Old and antique looking, the earphones were as big as baseball gloves. I was instructed to listen closely and indicate to the left or right when I heard a tone. It reminded me of the hearing tests we were given in elementary school a thousand years ago. Even the tones sounded familiar, as if I were waking up with a memory intact. The room was dark, cool and soothing. The screener was just a disembodied soft voice out past the glass, somewhere in the shadows. Made me think of work. Sometimes, especially in an action sequence, the sound isn't acceptable. Then Post Sound will have you come in, usually months after principal photography is over. You stand in a dark room in front of a microphone with headphones on and watch yourself on the screen, then recapture the frantic screaming, crying swearing, whatever it was. Always fun. My eyes were also tested, at another time, a day or so later. It seemed to me that my right eye was lazy, unfocused, it *still* feels weak but I passed with 20 / 20 vision in each eye. Again / elementary school. The same eye test that's been used for decades. Hold a card over one eye, read the lines, hold card over other eye, repeat.

'…you're standing there yakking away
like nothing's changed
while I'm torn to pieces by lions
spinning plates in a 3rd rate circus
I'm rolling down crazee lane
I'm Muddy Waters singing the blues
spinning plates
just spinning plates…'

paraphrasing Radiohead

Website / March 30ᵗʰ, 2002

Hi Everybody, Tony here with the latest news and update from the hospital. First, the biggest news, Alisa moved yesterday from USC to the 'National Rehab Center Rancho Los Amigos' in Downey. A big Thank You to the doctors and nurses and staff at the USC—Burn Ward for making it possible and for putting up with my incessant questioning.

Directions from LA: 5 South to the 710 South and exit east on Imperial Hwy—More info is available on their web site: www. rancho.org / So, it seems after everything so far Alisa is at the beginning of the second big cycle in her recovery and if timing is any indication, it should be a good one. She was admitted to USC on the day of the full moon and was released there on the day of the full moon 3 months later.

I'd like to sincerely express my thanks not only for everything you have done for Alisa but for all your help to me as well. Thanks for helping me help Alisa. Everything looks as good as can be expected at this point and I hope everything is set for an amazingly fast and complete rehabilitation.

Kevin and Y flew in again yesterday and will be here through Wed. It looks like we can find a place for the family right on campus at Rancho, so everything is falling into place for the immediate future.

More soon... p&l, Tony

It cracks me up that Tony pays attention to the moon, he doesn't look the type. He's 6' 4 and weighs 190, sinewy muscular, short light brown hair, perfect teeth. He looks like a jock and acts aloof and disinterested. Add a few tattoos and he's the portrait of my perfect man. That's what made him so hard to leave, he was beautiful. But he was a prick. It's funny that he thanked the Burn Unit staff, I know they were doing the happy dance to see his back. He was a bastard and didn't care who he offended. Once in awhile it was appreciated. I remember this one nurse, a grossly overweight troglodyte, always bitching about her 'disability.' I couldn't stand her. Talk about being oblivious to another's pain, I was laying there like a cooked vegetable and she would go on and on about how she couldn't lift this and couldn't do that, her back hurt, her hooves were sore and her pointed horns needed sharpening. I suggested working out to her one day just to shut her up. 'It will improve your back if you build up your muscles,' I said. 'I can't work out, I uh…it's too hard, I don't have time, it hurt's…' All the fat excuses. 'Well then think about at least changing your diet, because carrying around all that extra weight isn't good.' 'I have gland problems, I hardly eat anything!' she sniffed, wiping cookie crumbs from her mouth. Whatever, honey. Self Deluded, party of one? Trough's ready.

She was my nurse one afternoon—I was fading in and out—Tony was sitting there reading the paper. She had to test the pain response of my right hand and stuck my finger with a needle. I moved it…ow. *Then she did it again*, the sick bitch. Tony went ballistic. He went off on her so furiously she flew from my room; he followed her and screamed at the whole staff. 'What the fuck is wrong with this woman? She gets some kind of psycho kick out of causing pain?' I didn't wake up from the pin pricks but Tony screaming in the hall brought me around for a minute. I never had to look at Poor Fat Disability Nurse again. She wasn't allowed near me.

She wasn't fired though. She could have poked fifty holes in my hand and nothing would have happened to her. No matter how useless or sadistic, that bitch can't be fired. Just move her to another floor. Poor Fat Disability Nurse could hurt the working poor who don't have recourse. She could stick needles in homeless schizophrenics and illegal aliens. What are they gonna do about it? They don't have insurance and a pit bull sitting by their bed. They should be happy that they're taken care of at all. Shouldn't they?

County of Los Angeles   Department of Health Services
RANCHO LOS AMIGOS NATIONAL REHAB CENTER

PAST MEDICAL HISTORY:

'The patient was born in the Midwest. She has worked as a stunt woman in Hollywood as a double. The patient states she was married at one time and is now separated or divorced. She has no children. She has a history of tobacco use, occasional alcohol.

Denies intravenous drug abuse.

> Denies intravenous drug abuse? I deny stabbing puppies, too. Annoyed until I read the next one.

REVIEW OF SYMPTOMS:

'Denies any headache, but states that she has profound itching x 2–3 days and does not know why. She states that her dressing changes are painful. Denies any premorbid history of any problems in her vision or neck.

> The itching! Of course I knew why, it was the graft sites and donor sights. I would scratch until I bled.

'No history of shortness of breath, chest pain or abdominal pain. She is tearful when she discusses the camping trip and the burns that occurred as the sleeping bag melted around her. The patient is unable to continue due to labile emotions.'

Once I was in bed, I couldn't move. My feet and knees were propped up with pillows, my fragile right arm encased with more pillows and I had a few under my head and shoulders. I was Itchy the Michelin Man unable to scratch. Before my injury I would fetal up on my side or sleep on my stomach. I was starting month four of sleeping on my back. Hell. I would turn on the television and wait for my pill to work.

Website / April 4th 2002

Hi All, Quick update on Alisa... The transition out of USC went pretty smooth & she's been at Rancho for a week now. It was quite difficult the first few days, leaving the familiar faces & surroundings of USC (as cold & sterile as a trauma center is) for a new facility. Combined with the reality that the "real" work is now beginning, it ended up being quite emotional at first. However, things are changing.

It took the staff a few days to assess & get the programs in motion, but speech / physical / occupational therapy is now in full swing, if she keeps pushing, the best estimate on her stay is 4–6 weeks. Her legs are coming around. Her left ankle, first predicted to be useless due to extensive tendon damage is moving & gaining strength. Her right ankle stiffened up after the last round of skin grafts at USC, but is now showing signs of improvement. Her right leg has come back somewhat after the stroke & the long-term prognosis is that she'll eventually be walking, perhaps running, on her own.

The right arm is still the problem. She hasn't gained any use of it since the stroke & it's becoming increasingly unlikely that it will ever be functional. The wounds are still quite severe across the back of the hand. Also [HO has] formed in the elbow in response to the trauma, stiffening it up & posing a new problem to deal with. Another surgical cleaning session is also looming. They're trying to decide the best way to deal with all these issues.

Back on the brighter side, her speech is improving. She still has a hard time choosing the right word now & then, but it's remarkable how much she's improved in the last month. Her pain medication also seems to be back on the mark. There's still a fair amount of discomfort of course, given the condition of her wounds. But the balancing act of remaining alert enough to participate in therapy, while also having some relief, seems to have been achieved.

Couple misc things.... she can wear her own clothes now & we brought what was left in her old apartment over. She fancies the hospital pants because they're comfy & baggy & easily pull over her leg bandages, but mentioned she could use a few more T-shirts. So if anyone has a couple she could use for, please bring when you visit.

I moved most of the vides / DVDs to her new room, so they're available for pick-up. There are still two boxes of movies at our temp family apartment on Rancho's campus, if you need them, please coordinate a pick-up with Tony. The need for movies has dropped-off somewhat. She's busy during most of the day and starting to sleep better. However, there are several weeks to go... so if you have something special, I'm sure she would love to see it. We hooked up the vid / dvd player just in case she's in the mood.

Finally, she has a phone in her room, so please give a buzz & say hi. The best time to reach her is early evening. Direct dial is: 562-401-8325. In general, Rancho is a country club compared to USC & the staff seems great. I'm extremely pleased she's there & now working hard toward recovery. Thank you everyone for the good vibes, prayers, meditation, tantra, feng shui, sweat lodge dances, or whatever positive energy you've put into the universe on behalf of Alisa. She needed it & it's been helping!! Talk to you in a week or if anything changes dramatically. As always, don't hesitate to call. ~Kevin

'...I know you hear what I'm saying
a revolution is coming
the sturdy un-killable children of the poor
aren't going to eat shit forever

don't you be the one apprehended
don't you be the one who is offended...'

paraphrasing Third World

I had spent three months in a news cocoon. General Hospital barely had TV reception and no cable. I watched the Lakers and loved the Zyrtek advertisement.

(Shot in Black and White: A tall thin model says she's allergic to dust, something-something and pet dander. Her old allergy medication wasn't good for pet dander. Close up of her Papillion: 'It was either get rid of it, or get rid of Rufus...' Rufus looks anxious! Oh no! Cute little Rufus! Don't worry, she switched to Zyrtek. The wacky, stringy Zyrtek music plays while Pretty Model and Papillion frolic in the park. Don't know why—another morphine mystery—but I *loved* that ad.)

Rancho had basic cable. I couldn't believe what I was seeing on CNN. Bush had signed orders declaring the Geneva Convention didn't apply to Afghan detainees? We had a prison camp at Guantanamo Bay? People were being held indefinitely with out being charged? What the hell had happened? My country had gone mad.

A thousand years ago I fell in love in Morocco, in Essaouira by the sea. Khalid had gone to school in Paris and lived in Barcelona. Everything about him was flawless. (His birthday was the same as my fathers, January 17.) Enchanted, I loved him. I wanted to know what being an Arab man was like, they seemed so serious but he was playful sweet, amusing sublime. He told me all sorts of things, good, bad and neutral.

Morning coffee was served hot and ink black in demitasse cups. We never went out without a guide (body guard) but Friend and I were technically inside of our hotel in Marrakech, the coffee shop was open to the street. A big fat hairy bearded gross in every way man walked up to us and tried to take my hand. I snatched it away, repulsed. 'You are staying in this hotel? You will come to my room at nine tonight.' Smiling, he took my hand again and put his room key in it. I threw it into the street! 'What is wrong with you? Fuck off! You can't talk to me like that!' 'All right, he said nonplussed, you can come at ten?' Friend was laughing so hard she was holding her stomach. The bearded goat thought the prostitute was angry about the time. 'Yes?' He was still smiling. 'Yea, you wait for me.' He walked away happy. It was hilarious—we were bleached blonde Americans—of course we were whores.

Khalid was exasperated when I told him about it later that am. We talked about westernization. The US is generally considered unlawful, cow-boyish, wild wild west. Uneducated men don't understand 'equality' of the sexes; does it mean American women want sex like men? They think American movies are a true view of the culture and I looked like Sharon Stone. You can just ask her for sex, no? Morocco considers herself above vulture when compared to the US because they don't have capital punishment. He also told me when Arabic men argue, yelling and waving the arms, it's often tradition and meaningless. He said it drove him nuts, that's why he preferred Europe but he would always come home to visit his family. He taught me an old Arabic saying:

'…me against my brother
me and my brother against our cousin
me and my brother and cousin against the world…'

County of Los Angeles   **Department of Health Services**
RANCHO LOS AMIGOS NATIONAL REHAB CENTER

CLINICAL PATHOLOGY LABROTORIES

Urinalysis   4 / 18 / 02

This chart tracked my urine. From 3 / 30 / 02 to 4 / 18 / 02 they faithfully recorded Color, Appearance, Glucose, Bilirubin, Ketones, Occult Blood, (Occult? Huh?) Protein, Urobilinogen, Nitrates and Luek esterase.

I had a urinary track infection caused by the catheter. The results slowly came back down to Normal. Apparently it was hard to cure. 'All I need is cranberry juice,' I remember telling Dr Sarah. She laughed like I was joking. Rancho only used pharmaceuticals, duh.

Going to the bathroom alone was a big priority. One of my nurses would help me to move from the bed to the wheelchair, take me into the big gimp equipped bathroom, help me pull my pants down, help me transfer to the toilet and help me up again. There was a gorgeous male nurse from South African working in my unit. Chiseled features, sexy accent, perfect skin, straight white teeth, he looked like a soldier who had just been through Navy Seal training. One afternoon I buzzed the nurse's station for bathroom help and he came in. Friend was visiting. I looked at her, she looked at me. We were thinking the same thing. 'Sweetie, you can't take me, you're too good looking.' We started laughing and embarrassed him, which made him even cuter. Shy smile, 'I'll send in a woman.'

'...Dominique in London riding the subways
said it was crowded and charming wore red and bought flowers
stayed in a friends borrowed flat up by Baker Street
went to the National, saw wax abnormalities
there is a small gallery by Regents Park, seems no one goes there but her
Conan Doyle, thinks Dominique
but she is Cocteau...'

~Al Christ

Damien is back—it's great to see him but...I don't know what's going on in my head. I get angry at every thing he does. Damn, I don't want to be like this. I don't want to be this high maintenance bitch. I'm trying to be neutral.

2007

Once again, I was in denial. I refused to look at the complex picture of the Real Damien. I preferred the one I had Photoshop'd in my mind, that Damien was perfect. Then I wondered why I was getting upset by his behavior. Damien's reality was that of a mid west pot dealer's. He was smart enough to do other work, he was good looking and had a natural ability to make people like him but he was lazy as a stick. Friend had been taking care of Homescrub while I got settled in LA. The morning he was supposed to fetch her he was a no show. He had no excuse except to admit he didn't like cats. Why not mention this a month ago? I had Homescrub shipped airfreight for $150. That was the warning shot across my bow. I didn't recognize it consciously but sleeping bear did and was turning over, hence the bitch. Damien and I had been emailing every day. He was going to get a part time job and help with my bills, which were $1300 to $1500 monthly. I was receiving $430 a month from Social Security Disability Income. My quarterly residuals were shrinking fast; I was worried about an uncertain future. If I didn't find income before my money was gone, I was screwed. I wanted a grown man's help. Damien was a big kid. And I knew that! All of his ex girlfriends hated him—red flag-o-rama—but somehow, I thought he'd change a lifetime of laziness for me. I needed mental help.

> '...I never knew I could be such a bitch
> it surprises me, I honestly don't get it
> I can't see where we went wrong
> but I don't feel the same
> and I don't think it's coming back...'
>
> paraphrasing Gordon Lightfoot

My Temper and Chicken Slaughter: 'Post Traumatic Stress Disorder' Goodfella pronounced it but it's nothing that simple. My brain is malfunctioning. I try to take neutral ground and most of the time that works but I almost bitch-slapped a stupid girl recently.

They were silly, chickens aren't the smartest but they were part of our pack, the white rooster and his two orange girls. They had chicken food but every morning they would poke their noses in the window of the kitchen door looking for goodies; old bread, stale crackers, last nights popcorn, vegetable peelings, they'd Hoover. It was farm-ish and they were easy to love.

Chandelier is a friend of Alexander's. He told her she and her boyfriend could stay the weekend. She has a hundred fifty pound wolf / malamute high bred. She let it loose in the yard and that fucking dog killed our pets. I was doing a load of laundry and Alexander came over looking ashen. 'The chickens are dead…the rooster put up a fight, his feathers are all over…' We stood holding each other for a minute. 'I can't deal with it right now, I have to go to work.' He left broken hearted. The wolf had busted through the latch of their cage / they were toast. When Damien woke he buried them in the yard.

The morning of the chicken slaughter (as yet, unaware of the carnage) Chandelier told me her sob story. She'd been kicked out of Mommy's in Vegas. Mommy is co-dependant and step Dad is a jerk. Mommy told her to move out because Chandelier couldn't get along with her husband. If she was eighteen I might have sympathized but Chandelier is twenty-eight—get your shit together honey pie—stop leaning on your poor mom. Let her be with The Jerk if that's what she wants.

She came back that night, it was Saturday and we were having the usual party. After avoiding me all evening she finally said, 'what's wrong, you look sad.' 'Not sad, mad. Your wolf killed our chickens.' Unbelievably she gave me attitude. 'He's a wolf that's what they do…and most absurd, Alexander said it was OK to let him go in the yard.' So it was *Alexander's* fault her big, feral dog went ballistic. I couldn't stop myself—I didn't smack her or call her a stupid fucking idiot like I wanted to but I told her a thing or thirty-eight. If she can't handle a wild animal and shouldn't have one. If she can't care for her own basic needs—like shelter, for fucks sake—she shouldn't be hoisting her high maintenance pet on unsuspecting friends. Alexander gave her permission to let the wolf loose in the yard because he thought it would behave like a *domesticated dog not bust through a locked gate!* That she wouldn't take any responsibility was idiotic and put her on waivers. (Someone you wave bye bye to.) Her boyfriend thought he was helping and kept saying things like, 'he *always* kills birds, that's what he *does*.' 'Shut up Timmy!' she would snap but he wouldn't listen, '…that's what happens when you have a wolf!' When you find yourself arguing with imbeciles you must stop for your own sanity, nothing you say will get through. That I get so steamed is…tiresome. Waivers, baby. You're on waivers, that's all.

However, the appendix to the Chandelier story is funny as hell. She and Timmy slept on the sofas in the living room with her wolf chained outside the yard. The morning found her still with attitude, puffing around but avoiding eye contact. She was sitting in the living room writing something as I was heading for the shower. 'Damien and I are leaving in an hour.' Alex had already left for work and we park half a mile behind an electronic gate, it takes some organization. 'I just have to finish this letter then Damien said he'd let us out.' I had a laugh over that. With a little ambition Damien could have been a diplomat. He'd said to me the night before, 'you know she's sorry but for whatever reason she can't bring herself to be accountable. Don't let her stupidity get to you.' Talking to Chandelier of me he said, 'people get very emotional over their pets and yours needs to be kept under control.'

We went through the day. Alexander gets home at five thirty. He goes into his bedroom to change out of his suit and comes back with a bemused look. 'What do you think Chandelier wants?' He had the letter she'd been writing. 'To stay here?' I guessed. 'We could turn the old chicken coop into a kennel.' Damien was cooking dinner and we all started laughing. That's the correct response to a dip-shit like Chandelier.

> 'War is another thing. I am by nature warlike. To attack is among my instincts.'

> —Nietzsche

Georgene had sent me a hand held tape recorder when I was at Rancho. She knew I kept a journal and assumed (rightly) I was going bonkers without an outlet. On / Off / Record / Rewind; the mysteries of Zoroaster. So I put it aside. I couldn't figure out the words. I couldn't recognize numbers. Not like dyslexia, where numbers get rearranged, it was more like trying to read Chinese or Russian. Kev and Tony hooked up my VCR and DVD player but I never used them. I could use the VCR and DVD at USC because it was the same set up pre CVA. The same VCR and DVD in a new location was a hazy and uncertain; I avoided anything that I didn't understand.

County of Los Angeles   Department of Health Services
RANCHO LOS AMIGOS NATIONAL REHAB CENTER

ADMISSION ASSESMENT AND PLAN

1.   Status post left middle cerebral artery cerebrovascular accident infarct with right hemispheris; this appears to be an embolic infarct; the etiology is unclear.

2.   There is report of a thrombus in the left jugular but this most likely was not the cause of this patient's cerebrovascular accident. Will admit patient to neuro stroke service and begin rehabilitation evaluation. Continue Lovenox subcutaneously.

The 'cerebrovascular accident' *was* caused by the 'thrombus in the left jugular' but Lovenox was shot twice daily into my stomach to prevent blood clots anyway. Dime sized black and blue marks covered my lower belly.

3.   PBSA, 30–40% of the right upper extremity and bilateral lower extremities. We will consult plastics to follow her wound management. Laboratory studies in the a.m. Continue dressing changes as indicated. The patient is also status post split thickness skin grafts from the torso, the abdomen and the quadriceps area.

The dressing changes were a nightmare. Because it took two hours, the morning staff didn't have time. The night nurses bathed me and rewrapped my legs. We'd start at five am and finish by seven. My arm was placed in a plastic bag. My new Occupational Therapist would tend to it later in the morning.

4.   Depression, follow up with psychology for support and to review medication management.

This was a good idea in theory but the Psychologist, Mr Roger Insipid, was a creepy little worm of a man. Skinny with a whispery voice, he would come lurking into my room and talk incessantly of drugs. 'Did I do drugs? How much, how often? How about alcohol? Did I drink too much?' As if I didn't have a reason to be depressed, no real problems, it was all drug related. Didn't he see my bandages? Didn't he know anything about strokes? This was a famous STROKE rehabilitation facility. Help me with THAT! He made my depression worse.

5.   Allergic reaction, etiology unclear, it may be secondary to new medications, possibly Baclofen. We will review all the medications before continuing. Maintain Benadryl around the clock q.6h.

I had an allergic reaction but was on so many medications they couldn't tell what caused it. I was covered in red splotchy patches that itched like crazy. Added to itching from the graft sites, it sent me to the third moon of Jupiter.

6.   Oxacillin resistant Staphylococcus aureus. Will place patient in isolation room.

Visitors still had to wear surgical gowns and gloves but at least the facemask was gone.

7.   Pain control. The patient transferred on methadone 10 mg p.o. q. 12h. Will continue along with Neurontin and monitor patient.

That wasn't enough! Off Morphine my pain was Acute and Unmanageable. They eventually upped the Methadone.

8.   Prior history of substance abuse.

This was thanks to Mr Roger Insipid. I told him I used 'No street drugs!' Which wasn't true but he was so unbelievably crawly, there was no way I was going to discuss teenage LSD or dancing on X. I envisioned him slinking into the janitor's closet and jacking off.

He was a skipping disc, talking about cocaine and heroin endlessly. I finally told him out of sheer exasperation that I had done cocaine socially _twenty_ *years ago in the 1980's.* Didn't everyone? I didn't care for it, it made you talk incessantly about the same boring things. I'd seen people lose everything to coke; family, friends, dignity, self worth. I was ambitious (Devils Dandruff we used to laughingly call it) and I know nothing of heroin.

I had a fantastic life, the kind of life people dream about and I missed it, so much I couldn't breathe sometimes, how could I ever get used to being a gimp? He could have given me hope, the burn community is connected, there are retreats, chat rooms, people to talk with, people that have been through it, that would have been good to know. I didn't find out about any of it until Firefighters Quest sought me out and sent me to The World Burn Congress 18 months later. Insipid gave me nothing but stress. Heroin / Cocaine / Heroin / Cocaine.

County of Los Angeles   Department of Health Services
RANCHO LOS AMIGO'S NATIONAL REHAB CENTER

BEDSIDE SWALLOW EVALUATION

Diet / Liquid consistencies	Solid with thin liquids
Medications	Whole
Level of supervision	Supervised
Aspiration Precautions	Maintain patient sitting at 90 degrees during meal
Use safe swallowing strategies	liquids via straw, check for pocketing
Dysphagia Therapy	oral motor exercises
Patient / Family / staff Education	Re: Risk of Aspiration
Discharge Goals	Solid with thin liquids

At USC everything I drank was out of a straw, before and after the stroke. I didn't realize the CVA had paralyzed my mouth. I couldn't drink out of a cup; it would pour down the right side of my face. Frustrating.

The 'risk of aspiration' I still deal with. My motor responses (things you do automatically) are screwed. I have to be aware of my windpipe and would actually visualize it shutting before swallowing for months. Still, I choke and cough. Annoying.

'Pocketing' is food getting stuck your cheek. Like a chipmunk. Humiliating.

January, 2004—Montecito Heights

Saw Dr Coolchick for the yearly pap smear. I feel so ugly, exposed, the scars all over my legs gleaming in the bright sterile light. Coolchick was cool, fast and professional. My period is out of whack. I didn't have one for almost a year and now it's coming every two weeks. I wanted birth control to manage it. She wanted to ask someone's opinion before she prescribed it, worried about the stroke.

Ironic that I always said I didn't take birth control pills because I smoked and stroke is in the endless list of side effects. Truth: it was easier to say, 'I'm not on birth control…' than have an HIV chat. Good way to weed idiots. If I heard whining about 'decreased sensation' or the worst, 'I have complete control…' Yuk. Lust gone. Waivers.

There's no arrogance in Coolchick, if she's not sure of something she says so. I thought (knew) my CVA was human error but had her call Allritini. He called back the next day, carefully agreeing with me. 'There's nothing to suggest it will reoccur.'

2007

Coolochick asked me again if I wanted pain medication and again I declined, even though I woke up in aching pain every am. My denial of reality was causing my pain to become chronic. When the brain gets used to sending pain (about a year) it makes it harder to reverse.

County of Los Angeles   **Department of Health Services**
RANCHO LOS AMIGOS NATIONAL REHAB CENTER

CLINICAL PATHOLOGY LABROTORIES

Chemistry—Renal
UNITS
LOW NORMAL
HIGH NORMAL   bla bla bla…

Can't handle the Rancho paperwork. I blew through USC's foot of paperwork with a lazy South Pacific breeze. I can barely make myself read the Rancho slop, let alone transcribe it. Meditated on why. Maybe it's Insipid's assessment. Having that panty sniffing nose picker trying to entice me into drug talk was repugnant. But I did like a party, 'exhibiting alcoholic tendencies' according to the AA test. It's hard to recognize, accept and change negative behavior.

Maybe it's my hand; my right hand seems to have been destined for a horror show. Looking back with cloudy eyes everything has more meaning than it deserves. Smoke and mirrors. At sixteen I was cooling my heels in Woodland Hills. Not the suburb in LA, a group home in Minnesota. It was an experimental program. 'Positive Peer Culture' or PPC—it took delinquents and turned them on each other. Being attacked by people your own age was going to socialize you properly. Load of crap of course, if you were smarter than the average bear, you ran the place. I had been in juvenile court for almost three years and my judge made me an offer I couldn't refuse. If I got through the program at Woodland Hills without running away or getting tossed, he would emancipate me. The Golden Carrot.

The third finger of my right hand got infected under the nail. Rather than taking me to a doctor, getting antibiotics and being done with it, the WH staff tried to heal me themselves. (Though no one had any medical experience.) Someone had the idea that if I soaked my paw in Epsom salt, that would be the miracle cure. For the next month, I carried a plastic jug of hot water, as my finger grew steadily worse. It was twice its size and turning black before they would admit defeat. The Smallville ER Doc said, 'I'm afraid that finger's going to have to come off.' No thank you idiot, just give me antibiotics. I refused to let him or anyone in that hospital touch me. (Even young, I knew small town doctors were suspect.) The WH staff freaked and didn't tell my parents. Fortunately drugs did the trick. A few days later a pearl size hole under the nail opened and blackish puss popped like a zit. It never healed right, the nerve was damaged. When I would hit it just so, playing the piano for example, it caused pain and the hole where the icky go came out didn't close normally. My hand is so disfigured it's hard to see but that bit on the tip of my FU finger was caused by WH morons.

I broke my right hand at twenty-five. I was living with Dena in Los Felix and dating a director, we met on a music video. No love connection but friendly, easy and forty was my magic age, Mr Right Now was 39. We went to Palm Springs for a relaxing weekend and it was for a minute. Massage, facial, manicure, pedicure, Right Now played golf while I did aerobics with a private instructor and we met at the pool for a beautiful desert sunset. The second night we got bored. Palm Springs rolls up her sidewalks; we could find nothing to do. We ended up drinking martini's with a couple of lawyers until we were ridiculous. Back in our room, he had what some folk playfully call whiskey dick, it embarrassed him and he said something rude to me. I punched him in the face and gave myself a boxer fracture, called that because it happens if boxers land a glancing blow. (Or a drunk roundhouse.) My fifth metacarpal snapped like a little stick.

Over the years I must have broken or fractured the 3rd (F you finger) forty thousand times at trapeze turning around to return to the bar and jamming my longest finger into it. You'd think after doing it once, I'd have learned to keep my hands flexed and open but my flight was faulty at best. If I was coming in low, I would stab out for the bar every time.

County of Los Angeles   **Department of Health Services**
RANCHO LOS AMIGOS NATIONAL REHAB CENTER

CLINICAL PATHOLOGY LABROTORIES

Hematology—Coagulation

Proteome INR Therapeutic Range for Oral Anticoagulant Therapy…ho hum, dee dumb.

It occurs to me that since I broke my *left* hand *twice*, my theory that my right hand was destined for anything is silly. When Mr Right Now and I got home from Palm Springs, my roommate Dena took one look at us and started laughing. 'Nice relaxing weekend, huh?' It was so obvious what had happened, Right Now with a shiner and me with my hand in a cast. The cast was temporary according to the ER Doc in Palm Springs; I needed to go to a hand specialist to have it set properly. Boxer fractures are tricky, if they're not set right the pinky will curl under the other fingers. Right Now had someone in the production office find a Beverly Hills hand specialist and we went in that morning. As he was escorting me to X ray, Doctor Beverly Hills turned to Right Now, '…how about you? Are you all right?' 'I'll be fine.' We knew we were in for it. A man with a broken hand and a girlfriend with a black eye would be appalling but the other way around…amusing.

My hand was set in plaster with my little finger pointed straight. I was told it would come off in four to six weeks. Beverly Hills gave me a prescription for Percocet, told me to keep my arm raised and to come back in two weeks. Couple days later: It was the start of the holiday season. Dena and I thought it would be fun to take Christmas pictures on the beach to send home to Minnesota. Friend was a photographer, living with her actor boyfriend in Santa Monica. I had a clutch but could shift with my cast so I drove.

Dena and I dressed like sexy elves, green and red swimsuits and furry Santa hats. The first thing Friend said to me was, 'I had a premonition that something horrible was going to happen to you!' 'Maybe it's a reaction to my broken hand?' I suggested. 'I don't think so. It was so strong that I had to tell you. Be careful!' Bay Watch was slowly cruising by in a yellow pick-up. The boy driving was so intently staring he headed right for us and almost hit me. He stopped on our pile of clothing and purses. 'Oh shit, sorry!' 'No problem, honey.' All three of us were laughing. 'Well that must have been it said Dena, you had a premonition that she was killed by a life guard.' Friend was unconvinced. 'Maybe…' skeptical. (Maybe she felt *this* drama.)

We shot a roll of film frolicking in the sand and then our attention wandered to the kiddy swings. There was a circular ride that you held with <u>both hands</u> as it spun around. I got on and it started to turn much faster than I had anticipated. I lost balance almost immediately and my left paw got caught in the spokes. Snap! Ouch! Oh no! I couldn't believe it! We went back to Friend's apartment and tried to decide what to do. Neither Dena nor Friend could drive a manual transmission. Her boyfriend could but they were waiting for his mean EX to drop off the kids. It would be dangerous to leave Friend alone with her. 'I think I can drive your car,' Dena ventured. The three of us piled in my little Sunbird and headed for Santa Monica's ER, grinding, humping and thumping through the gears, we were dying with laughter. 'You're doing great, baby.' It was still a few years before affordable cell phones, I spied a payphone. 'Let's call Doc Beverly Hills, maybe we can just go over there!' We and ran over. A short, squat Mexican gentleman was having a conversation. 'Emergencio! Emergencio! Dena yelled at him, we need the phone!' He surveyed us, two sexy elves and their blonde bombshell bodyguard. He wasn't impressed by whatever the 'Emergencio' was, he snorted, turned his back and kept talking. I was in no mood to negotiate my hand was swelling up like…well, like the last one did a week earlier. I kicked him in the butt so hard he *lifted up off the ground*. He dropped the phone and took off running without looking back. We were laughing again. Dena picked up the phone, 'sorry,' and hung up. I gave her Beverly Hill's phone number. His X-ray technician had already left for the day, he said to go to Santa Monica's emergency room and come in tomorrow. They confirmed the snapping sound I heard spinning off the kiddy swing was a hairline fracture. They gave me a temporary cast, complimented us on our holiday attire and we drove Friend home.

It was dark, five-ish, rush houry. Dena had kind of gotten the clutch and slowly wound our way back into Los Feliz. A few blocks to go, she stopped suddenly at the end of the exit ramp, the car stalled and she was freaked! 'Something's wrong at the apartment!' 'What do you mean?' 'It's such strong a feeling, look at me!' Her arms were covered in goose bumps. 'When we get there it's going to be on fire, or robbed, something!' Good God! Another premonition! I believed her! Filled with trepidation but when we arrived, it looked fine. Dena unlocked the door and we peeked in. It looked fine. Dena walked around the first floor turning on the lights and it seemed fine. Fine,

fine, fine. We both breathed in relief. 'Maybe it was just a reaction to our day,' she said shrugging it off. She went upstairs and started turning on the lights. I plopped on the sofa.

We lived in a 1930's apartment. High ceilings, arched doorways, French windows, deco tile in the bathroom and a wrought iron railing going up the stairway. From my vantage point I could see her walking back and forth on the floor above me. Suddenly she looked at me and screamed! Then she laughed, stumbled down a few steps and collapsed into tears! I rushed up to her. She couldn't talk, she was shaking! As she left my bedroom and turned to come down the stairs, she felt someone behind her and heard My Voice say right behind her head, 'Hello Denise...' The same moment she heard The Voice her eyes lit upon me, sitting downstairs on the sofa. The hair on my arms stood up like her goose bumps in the car. Doppelganger?

The production company Right Now worked with was having a Christmas party that evening. Right Now wasn't going to be there, he was shooting a commercial in Mohave all week but we'd been dating awhile and Dena and I were friendly with everyone at their office. We went wearing our Santa hats. 'What happened to you?' An obvious question for the girl with two casts. I started thinking—what exactly *did* happen to me? Bay Watch almost running us over, the evil kiddy swing, Friend's premonition, Dena's ghostly encounter, too much to explain in a few short sentences of party chatter. 'I was cheating on Right Now,' I said laughing.

Maybe the reason I don't want to go through the Rancho paperwork is simply that reliving it is hard. Dealing with reality now is arduous. My impression of Mr Roger Insipid is correct; he is a smarmy rat working for the County. He is A Fucking Loser. Probably a recovering cocaine / heroin addict himself, which would explain his obsession. A couple days ago, I was gloomy and everything looked doomed. Today I feel better and can trust my instincts again. I've got to remember my emotions have brain damage too.

> '...you've forgotten what's important
> it doesn't matter where or what or who you are
> if you're alone

> watch an ugly old couple walking by
> he's got her and she's got him…'

paraphrasing Romeo Void

Six months later Dena had bungeed home and I got my first wackadoo roommate, Psycho Cherry.

> Aside: The Bungee Theory; people are born, live and die in within 50 tiny miles. There's a word for it (it's a vulture I think it starts with P.) They may go off to college or spend a year abroad but soon ZOOM back to their safety net. Advice from Mr Right Now as I was leaving MN was, 'don't be sad about leaving the nest, your friends will be right where you left them when you come back to visit.'

Psycho Cherry was striking. Turquoise eyes, white skin, jet black hair. Snow White, tall and thin. The month she moved in I was working my ass off—literally—I was preparing to play another stripper. I did two hours of aerobics in the am and jogged the hills at sunset. I never saw her, she bartended at a local club, seemed perfect.

The first sign of trouble: I came home as the sun was setting and Psycho Cherry startled me. She was sitting on the stairs in the gathering dusk—turquoise eyes staring with a preternatural luminescence—a living statue. 'I haven't been to bed in two days and I have to be at work in an hour.' A month later, she slit her wrists. Psycho Cherry, high on coke and cheap red, had the paramedics kick in the door for drama as she reclined in a sexy teddy. I came home from acting class at midnight as the cops were leaving. She had told them *I hit her* but believed my forty-person alibi. I was left with a splintered doorframe and a blood spattered living room. I called Mr Right Now and had him come over to protect. I picked her up from the hospital in the am. 'Why the slander?' The Drunkard's Excuse, 'I'm sorry, I don't remember.' 'No jumping from a moving car,' I joked, but I had had enough.

Psycho Cherry was out and my friend Snyder moved in. He was one of the first friends I made in LA, he was a casting director who did tons of music videos. (And Hard Copy.) I liked living with Snyder but I finally made enough money to move and I was tired of street parking. (The building was old and didn't have a garage. I got so many parking tickets I was booted thrice in one year.) Snyder's friend Sky Boy moved into the second bedroom and I rented an apartment in Hollywood. Cut to a couple months later: A film Snyder cast was having a Cast & Crew screening on the Disney lot. Sky Boy came with him. We don't know each other and we're chitchatting. Sky Boy asks, 'did anything weird ever happen when you lived there? Anything at the top of the stairs?'

Uh-o…

He said something had *violently pushed him* but he caught himself on the railing. Another time he woke up being smothered by something big and green on his chest. Whatever it was, it was in my old room. There *was* something at the top of the stairs and in the master bedroom. One night I came home late with Right Now. We were talking on the sofa in the living room when our attention was grabbed by movement above us. My two cats came strolling down the hall on their back feet, *as if someone were holding their front paws.* They walked slowly, deliberately, out of my bedroom and into Dena's. 'Did you see what I just saw?' Right Now asked. 'Yep.' 'Just checking.' I thought of the nightmares I had living there. Once I woke punching the pillow next to Right Now's sleeping face, *barely* missing him. I also got smothered, a lot. I would wake up to a heavy black shapeless thing slinking off my chest. I told myself it was dreams. Nightmares.

'I have a friend who's a psychic, Sky Boy continued, I asked her to come over. I didn't tell her anything just asked her give me a reading, she said a young woman recently tried to kill herself downstairs and different woman *did* kill herself upstairs about fifty years ago. Hung herself in the stairwell, she's still pissed. She committed suicide over a guy.'

Sky Boy's psychic friend knew about Psycho Cherry, the other one was a possibility. Maybe Psycho Cherry was victimized by Ghostie, drug use making her susceptible. Poltergeists, spirits, demons, other dimensions, different planes of existence, swirl around my brain. Coincidence, synchronicity, serendipity, fate, luck, karma, destiny, nothing feels random; maybe some malicious entity had been sitting in the desert waiting for someone to show up; someone high and easy to kill.

> '...later that afternoon
> my boy came by with a bottle of tanguery
> and a bumble fat blunt of bubonic chronic
> shit this smoke aint no joke
> I had to back up
> and sit my ass down
> tangery and chronic? yea I'm phucked up now...'

> paraphrasing Snoop Dogg

January 2004—Montecito Heights

Damien and I took off for Phoenix to spend New Years Eve with Georgene and Co. Six hours on Hwy 10. Pomona, Ontario, Rancho Cucamonga, Fontana, San Bernardino, all the eyesore sprawl littered on the 10; Fast Food chains, Wal-Mart's and new housing going up in the middle of hot dusty desert. Flytrap condos stretching as far as the eye can take it. Nothing neighbor-hoody, no center of town, no libraries, no museums, parks or public pools, nothing that won't make the developers money. Just endless chipboard housing, the cheapest possible, each one the same as the last, crammed together, waiting for a merciful earthquake.

Past Redlands, Banning, the big gothic windmill farms outside Palm Springs, past Indio and the turn off to Box Canyon and Joshua Tree, we finally saw nothing. Except the Prison, barely visible off in the Chuckwalla Valley. 'Don't pick up hitchhikers' said an ominous sign. We didn't see any. After New Years we headed north. Up Arizona and into Nevada through Vegas (Vegas yuk) and drove around the Hoover Dam. Water was low and sad.

'Don't let the sun go down on your black ass in Kingman.'

—graffiti in the girl's room

Kingman is the little crackho town on the border of California and Nevada, meth shacks are tossed on the rocky desert floor like children's blocks. Racist monsters live in the desert.

Damien had become an expensive pet. That gets old fast. The plan of Damien getting a job and helping with bills had been abandoned. It started off well, we'd made resumes and he left them all over Pasadena. He tried to get a job at The Ritz as a masseuse and his feelings were hurt when the girl hiring looked down her nose at him and said no. He was offered a job at a massage / facial place in Pasadena but turned it down! (I found out weeks after the fact.)

I love Death Valley, magic and enchanted it's my favorite National Park. Furnace Creek Inn in DV starts at $200 a night. I wanted to drive another hour down the road and get a $45 motel room. Damien talked and cajoled and joked and got the desk kid to give us a teensy closet on the 1st floor for $120. He was *so proud of himself*; in his mind, my money had become 'our money.'

County of Los Angeles   Department of Health Services
RANCHO LOS AMIGOS NATIONAL REHAB CENTER

'Patient complains that Berbert, who has taken over her bathing and dressing (since the usual girl is on vacation) today did an unsatisfactory job. Was rough, took a long time, did not wrap dressings well. Patient requests a female to do this job for her.

Patient denies any hot flashes. (I asked to follow up on the secondary amenorrhea in three months) Patient was very sensitive to thought of early menopause, began to cry. I tried to reassure her that it was unlikely due to her young age.

Denies insomnia.

Vitals: Temp 98.6, pulse 58, respiration 20, blood pressure 100 / 53

Am Young / Dr Zee'

Am Young would come and check on me every am and faithfully record my vital signs. She was Dr Zee's intern. A tall waifish Asian girl, Japanese I think. She was shy and sweet and was always wrong.

Berbert was a night nurse, I liked him. (He was nice; most of the nurses I dealt with at Rancho were nicer than GH.) He probably had never bathed someone with a serious burn injury it's not easy. I needed to be demumified from miles of bandaging, helped to sit up in bed, slowly put my feet on the floor and transfer into my 'shower chair.' A hybrid of the wheelchair, it was metal and plastic, had an open toilet seat, was taller with four small wheels.

We put my right arm in a plastic bag, taped it to my upper arm and went into the spacious, gimp friendly bathroom and under the shower. Five am came early and I was always freezing when naked. Rancho had Central Air Conditioning set for polar bears. I hurried through my wash, shivering, teeth chattering and then dried off. I didn't get out of the chair. I would get wrapped up in towels and flannel blankets and then wheel back to bed. Putting humpty dumpty back together again proved too much. Skin grafts need to be patted not rubbed dry and I was bleeding from various points. Silvadene lotion, Xeroform pads, gauze and ace wrap all took time and he got flustered. 'No offense Berbert but I don't think you should bathe me anymore.' 'None taken.'

'Patient denies any hot flashes…' cracks me up now but then, Am Young upset me to tears. I hadn't gotten my period since the fire and I mentioned it to her. 'Maybe it's early menopause,' she offered. 'WHAT?' I burst in tears. 'The ICU nurses said my body was shutting down unnecessary function, I just wanted to know how long it would last.' 'Maybe that's it…I'll ask Dr Zee,' she was obviously distressed that she'd upset me. I never heard another word about it. What's interesting about this is her take on it. It's true but she leaves out one fact; *she was the one that suggested early menopause.* There are countless inconsistencies in these records. (I've never 'denied' insomnia.) Chart Lore. Making things up, stretching the truth, leaving out important or damning info. Doctors are prone to the same mistakes and are as capable of intentional omissions to cover their butts as any one, it makes me crazee when people take what they say as gospel.

'...free your mind, no one can do it for you
no one stops time from rolling
how long will they kill our prophets
while we stand still and do nothing?
some say it's all pages in a book
written long ago
playing out as planned...'

paraphrasing Bob Marley

My attorneys told me I'd have to submit to a physical. Sleeping Bag Co wanted proof that my injuries were real; it would be performed by The Glorious Doctor Groseman. They sent a Sheila to help me hold my temper; she gave me a pep talk before the horror show began and stayed in the examining room with me. When he asked questions, I'd look at her and she would say 'No Comment.' I'd seen The Glorious Doctor Groseman in action a few months earlier. The burn unit he works at had a Survivors Meeting. For most of the hour, The GDG regaled us with his achievements. He'd saved an Afghanistan girl; he had a trophy wife he'd been on Oprah! Sickeningly narcissistic. I remember being annoyed at driving all the way to the valley just to help feed his ego.

Finding out The Glorious Doctor Groseman was taking Blood Money from Sleeping Bag Company's law firm sent me into orbit. The thought of him PROFITING from my BURN injury made me want to scream FUCK YOU HIPPOCRITE! I took 10 mgs of valium an hour before, that and The Sheila got me through it. She was slick and pretty, told me to stay cool and say little.

He told me to undress. I wore 'shorts' underwear but I did take off my bra. It was unnecessary, my rack wasn't burned but I like to watch men stare as if it's uncontrollable, the call of the boobs, they're always chagrined once they come out of the tit-coma. And he was, that was somewhat satisfying, but his posture was patronizing. He made clucking noises to indicate he was superior at plastic surgery and he was very annoyed that I wouldn't show him my puss. He even had the gall to tell me he was going to take fotos. I looked at Sheila and she said 'no.'

I hate that mutherfucker with the heat of a thousand suns. Tap dancing, smiling, phony fucking bastard. 'I love burn patients! Tippity tippity Tap! As long as they're *my* patients, Tippity Tap! Otherwise, I want to be hired as an Expert Witness for the Defense! THAT pays a LOT!'

Tippity fuck you tap.

February 2004—Montecito Heights

Damien sleeps but I'm up as usual. It's 7:30 in the morning and I just did a one-e. (Self-indulgent.) We've transformed the basement into a nice apartment. Paint Paint Paint! Faded blue walls, lighter at the top, cobalt blue floor with wine colored accents. Door, cupboards and post. We cleaned a thousand pounds of spiders and dust, stuffed the old filing cabinets into the closet and washed the windows.

I love it here but Alexander invited the devil back. Tweak the addict. Still snorting and smoking meth, crazy mean and unmanageable. Alexander let me spend money fixing up his guest room and then gave us a one-day warning before the Tweak Show began again. A Real Asshole Thing to do. When I objected he said, 'Tweak loves you!' I stared at him did I just hear right? 'Tweak hates us all.' 'No No! Alex insisted, He Loves You!' He had a trapped animal look; he'd invited an ugly little troll that stole money for drugs back into his life and I don't think he knew why. I certainly didn't.

Damien and I moved all our stuff down to the basement and got my microwave and coffee maker from the storage space. We only go up to use the shower and once in awhile the oven. The last thing Damien did was change the faucet for the sink. One little leak turned into a two day ordeal, pipes, washers, vultures but it only cost twenty bucks! The whole transformation was under $350. If Alex had given us a warning, I wouldn't have spent time and cash fixing up his guest room, I would have been looking for another place to live. Tweak drove non-stop from New York and showed up high. The first thing he shrieked about was Homescrub. Damien cornered him and said if he fucked with me or my cat, he'd beat him. It wouldn't be hard to do. Stalemate; Tweak had good self preservation instincts and believed the big straight guy who looked at him with disgust.

County of Los Angeles   Department of Health Services
RANCHO LOS AMIGOS NATIONAL REHAB CENTER

PROGRESS NOTES

They range from moderately good to unreadable, as they're hand written. The first page has a drawing of my hand with all the open spots where the bone was showing through and a couple pins coming out the side of my wrist. That was my occupational therapist. She's no artist but you get the picture.

My hand was so swollen it truly looked like a Frankenstein paw to me. Huge white twisted and gnarled—so sore I could hardly stand it—bones showing. I actually wanted it off it didn't look like part of me. Therapist told me that I might have to remove it anyway, so let's see what we can do in the meantime. She would patiently wash and then re-wrap my swollen fingers with Cobain, a spongy tape that comes in a myriad of colors. It worked the swelling went down considerably.

PSYCHOLOGICAL EVALUATION

Mental Status Evaluation: Conducted over four days, it was a paint by numbers evaluation. Check off appropriate boxes and then fill in extra information.

Level of consciousness: Alert

Orientation: Person, Place, Year, Month, Day of Month, Day of Week, Purpose

Attention: Impaired, Sustain problems appear when [unable to mulit task]

Audition: Intact for conversation.

Speech / Language: Impaired, frequently use expletives and mispronounces words

Memory: Impaired, Recent memory, recall improves with cueing

Problem Solving: Although pt has the ability to perform, may lack motivation to work through recovery process i.e. easily frustrated, gives up

Appearance: Thin, sometimes Good Energy, often Low Energy

Attitude: Cooperative

Self Report of Adjustment: Overwhelmed

Interpersonal Relations: Can interact without difficulty / conflict

Affect: Sad, Worried, Labile

Mood: Anxious, Depressed

Neurovegetative Symptoms: Vegetative, Affective, Cognitive, Crying, Guilt Feelings, Sadness, Pessimism, Concentration, Insomnia, Indecision

Present Suicidally: None

Behavioral Dyscontrol / Violence / Aggression: None / Minimal

Impressions: Ms Christenson has moderate to severe depression. She is presently coming to terms with the reality, physical disfigurement and inability to be as physically active as in the past. Her history suggests that motivation and wherewithal, i.e. ability to persevere and complete tasks may have been limiting factor premorbidly. Currently her depression [may be seen] as presenting a threat to her succeeding in rehab as it may exacerbate her tendency to give up and feel frustrated by what she has to do.

The patient [is] currently on a low dosage methadone and has been on other opiates at her acute care hospital. Although she may require narcotics for Analgesia, pt has history of psychoactive substance abuse would suggest that use non narcotic exclusively for pain control as a prudent measure.

Treatment Plan & Recommendation: Continue anti-anxiety medication bla bla...

    Patient: Christenson, Alissa

Steam is coming out of my ears I've become a cartoon. Mr Roger Insipid said that I had the tendency to slack off, never finished what I started and had a drug problem. I don't know who he was talking to but it wasn't me. Alissa Christenson, perhaps.

People tend to see themselves in a favorable light. (Try putting out a casting notice.) Smarter, stronger, faster than we really are, more physically capable, more mentally sound and I'm sure I've been guilty of that, BUT: Not only would I aggressively 'persevere and complete tasks,' I was a dog with a bone. I wouldn't be satisfied until I was finished. Nothing half assed either, I liked things done right.

'Substance abuse' pisses me off to the point of insanity. Mr Roger Insipid puts this shit in my files and everybody who reads it believes it. People think Chart Lore is True. They didn't know me before I was hurt. My Doctors, nurses and therapist's saw a fucked up woman in a wheel chair. Someone who couldn't put three sentences together. Then they read an Insipid fairy-tale. 'Oh...that explains it, she was a drug addict.'

'...and still you call me co-dependant
somehow you lay the blame on me...'

—Garbage

February 2004, Montecito Heights

Goodfella and Silver Aquacell: A new potion. I went down to his office because the skin grafts on the top of my left foot were getting hard and scabby. He had something new to try. Aquacell is a piece of light gray felt. Take scissors and cut a larger piece than the size you need. Dribble some water and it Morphs into thick slippery goop, put on the worrisome skin, change daily. Two weeks later, foot skin fixed.

The skin on my the back of my hand is still bubbling and boiling, it's different. It's the bones cooking underneath that are making it erupt. Goodfella wants to remove the top layer of skin, clean up the bone and then do a flap over the back of my hand. Still with the FLAP TALK! No means no! When the middle metacarpal finally releases the dead, it will close for good. I have macabre fotos to go with the bone chip collection. You must see, words don't do, it's fantastic, like great horror makeup.

Robin and the Cyborg Paw Thingy: I can pinch and carry with my right hand! That's huge, George! I could always pinch my thumb down but couldn't lift it up again. (Nerve damage) Robin made me a contraption that I Velcro on. It's a simple brace with a couple strings of metal that act like a spring. I put my thumb in and the spring holds it up, ready for action. I pinch down and the wires pick my thumb up. Pinch down, lift up, pinch down, lift up!!! I can start using my right hand again. I can open my purse, read the paper, I can hold things! My elbow ranges 95% and my hand now has limited but useful function. Thrilling and a little hard to believe. The potatoes in Smallville won't believe it either.

County of Los Angeles   **Department of Health Services**
RANCHO LOS AMIGO'S NATIONAL REHAB CENTER

CARDIOLOGY PROGRAM

REFERRING PHYSICIAN: Dr Zee   Date 4 / 25 / 02
CLINICAL INFORMATION: CVA   STUDY TYPE: TTE

Every morning the nurses would check blood pressure and my heart beat. My BPM (beats per minute) was always low, between 40 and 60. I remember Right Now getting a blood pressure device and it amused us for a minute. Someone gave it to him as a joke for Christmas if memory serves. I would get up; have some orange juice, maybe a carrot and a run in the canyon. Right Now would have a bagel with cream cheese, coffee and the morning paper. My BPM were 45 his 75. Rancho gave me a battery of tests. Stroke can mess up internal organs. Fortunately, my heart was fine. Lungs were fine. Liver was fine. Chemistry Lipid's were fine. (Whatever a chemistry lipid is.)

My hand was the problem and *of course it was getting worse*. The reason Kevin let Rancho rehabilitate me was the Grand Build-Up. Rancho was 'excellent and attached to USC.' I would get further surgery—that I needed—from the team that had already been working on me. It was a load of shit. Goodfella was in Miami the month of April and Allritini was endlessly waiting for bureaucratic paperwork, he wasn't even allowed to touch Rancho patients. I was warehoused, my hand decaying.

> 'Vexation, morbid susceptibility, incapacity for revenge, the desire, the thirst for revenge, poison-brewing in any sense—for one who is exhausted this is certainly the most disadvantageous kind of reaction.'

—Nietzsche

Social Worker from USC–LAC called to see if I wanted to do extra work on Cold Case. They had a story line that involved a fire and wanted burn survivors for a rehab scene. I said yes if they would hire Damien too. It was a one day job. Being on a set again scared me, I didn't know how (or if) I would react emotionally. They were shooting at the Biltmore, (again with the Biltmore?) Damien was an orderly, they gave him a seven am call, five other survivors and I at two. It's always nice to be with other survivors (the secret club) and I enjoyed myself. I walked by the deco pool wearing tennis shoes, sweats and a backless swimsuit; harvest scars on my back (presumably) making an interesting shot. I didn't miss it; I'm glad I had a career in the entertainment industry and am just as glad it's over.

'…if I could peek into your brain
what stories I could find there
paperback novels by the hundreds
like the drugstore sells…'

paraphrasing Gordon Lightfoot

The We Ho DVD's with the director's commentary arrived. Three of my male stars and Charlene (we used her house for a location) helped record it. We sat in a studio watching the show with headphones on and recorded our chatter, silly gossip about the show. When my weird stutter—that suddenly cut's off sentences—would stop me, I would motion and they would JUMP in, pretend they were talking over me. It worked and turned out pretty funny. I sent the DVD's to my cast and crew, I have to laugh, the crew is six people. Cast is big though and kept me busy for a minute.

We Ho is West Hollywood Stories. I wrote, directed and produced. My old distributor Harry called me up one day and said he had an idea to do a Gay Soap Opera. He asked if I wanted to write and direct. He would executive produce. Harry was cheap and problematic but also funny and creative / a trade off. It was December 1997, I wasn't working on anything else and I knew boys would be fun. I wrote a three hundred page script in a month, four one hour episodes. I like writing with a deadline but I worked so long and hard that I gave myself carpal tunnel. (Fortunately cured in a few weeks by acupuncture.) Friend came over and helped me finish typing. We sat cackling away as the script took shape.

We Ho Stories had good Doctors and evil twins, love triangles and lost weekends, kid napping, kleptomania, drug use, blackmail, insanity, a nude maid and a cross dressing nun. It was provocative, sure to offend right wing wackadoo's and everyone agrees controversy is a great marketing tool.

I had gotten rid of my last bad roommate and my spare bedroom was free. Friend was a struggling actress looking to get out of NYC for the winter so I invited her to LA to help me. The two of us were a three ring circus for the next four months. I put out a casting notice and got pre-production in started January '98. It was my most ambitious project to date. Ignorance is bliss. Casting was hilarious. Always is. We received more than a thousand submissions over the next few weeks and slowly waded through them. I'm always amazed at the things people submit themselves for.

We scouted locations. Most production companies use a Location Manager but we were on the 'no budget' budget. We needed locations that were free or just a handful of beans. Like Melrose Place, most of the main characters lived in the same building. My apartment complex became We Ho Manor. My neighbor's apartments became various abodes and friends houses filled out the rest. My chiropractor's office became the Holloway Free Clinic run by good Doctor Rosenblume and his mercenary partner Doctor Whitley. Vivian's Café in Studio City became the diner across the street from the clinic and the No Tell Motel with Jacuzzi's in every room became the Catholic convalescent home that housed crazy Sebastian.

LA has a huge talent pool of good actors, many of whom are homosexual. While I didn't discriminate against straight guys, and had a few brilliant straight actors playing queer, most of my cast was openly gay. Reading actors for different roles, I had the luxury of incorporating what we saw into the story lines. John P. was good and looked younger than his twenty some years so I wrote in the story of a teenage runaway. Bob, a nice looking gentleman, could transform himself into 'Bobby' a tired, frazzled and frayed six foot seven crazee lady. Friend and I couldn't believe the pictures he was showing us. Perfection! I wrote the character of Gigi.

Five major story lines with various intertwining sub plots; twenty five actors. Friend and I climbed aboard the We Ho roller coaster and began principal photography in February. We had organized over a hundred wardrobe changes picked picture cars, wrote and re-wrote scenes with specific actors in mind; we were prop department, art department, transportation and catering; with Murphy's Law in full effect, (it usually is.) I was most proud of the shooting schedule. I had over three hundred scenes to organize. Actors with paying jobs that weren't available on such and such, locations that were only available on so and so, equipment that was cheaper to rent over the weekends and always plan for problems. (Keeps me from getting bitchy.)

I hired the 'crew.' I 'quoted' the word because I couldn't afford a real crew. I hired a makeup artist and camera man with his own equipment and he promised production assistants. He was my first mistake. Mr Magoo I like to call him, Thievery Magoo. Harry thought we should have a gay camera man. He envisioned long, steamy, soft core scenes. It was the first of many fights. 'I'm not wasting my time on soft core, gay porn, give me a break!' I envisioned something for television, maybe not network but not Skin-a-Max either, HBO or Showtime. He was thinking straight to video, I thought why not both.

I had known Harry for years. He was locked into 'sex sells' thinking. He had long relationships with other distribution companies and had a formula, and while it never made him filthy rich, he did all right. His production company did the Witchcraft series. I was an actor in Witchcraft 7—Detective Lutz—a tough cop tracking down vampires. (Lutz was a 50 year old balding man in W6, 'continuity is for sissies,' laughed Harry.) It was schlocky fun, nobody was under the illusion we were making Ibsen, it was a paycheck and we were all friends by the end of it.

A few months after W 7 wrapped, Harry and I were having lunch and got to talking about the perfect vehicle for low budget R rated drama. The first thing was to shoot it on Beta. (Digital, now.) Hard to sell in the US but the foreign market isn't so addicted to film. 'It would have to be about one character, preferably with voice over said Harry, day in the life kind of thing.' 'Tiny cast takes place within a week,' I offered. 'Get a big house that you can shoot different locations in.' 'No stunts or FX.' 'No extras.' 'Maybe a coming of age story, it has to have a lot of sex.' 'Hey! I have a short story like this!'

I had written 'Jane' a year or so earlier. I had recently read Catcher in the Rye; thinking of Holden Caulfield running amok in New York, looking for love. He was short on change and dying to get laid. What if the character was a female having teenage angst in Bel Aire or Malibu? A pretty girl with an expense account could have sex whenever she wanted, which would cause its own slew of problems. I faxed him Jane that afternoon. Harry called, 'Do you want to shoot it?'

Yes I did. I wrote a 90 page script and asked Friend to help me produce. We shot Jane in Director Friend's big, roomy house. It was a freshman effort but turned out fine. The only thing I didn't like were the love scenes—too long—but that's the only stipulation I had from Harry. ('You have to have a love scene every 15 minutes' he drooled.) Other than that, he didn't care what I shot. Watching a character from my mind come to life was too cool. My lead, (Tupelo Jeremy) was great and I loved the whole process. I loved directing, loved producing, loved editing, I was hooked.

Harry sold Jane internationally but I never saw a penny. At the time I thought, okay fair enough. Instead of spending a fortune at UCLA or USC, I was given a fist full of dollars and pushed out the door. Go forth and create! It was worth it to get a project under my belt but I wasn't going to work free again. When Harry tried to hit me up with the same kind of Dickensian paper work (no broken fingers and a bathroom break every Tuesday) I said no. Back end gross / and its firm. During an argument, he admitted the idea for a Gay Soap came from two gentlemen that ran a distribution company called Ariztical Entertainment out of Tucson. He was trying to freeze me out because he was just a go between, he wasn't going to distribute it himself. We couldn't work out an equitable compromise so I gave him back his money. Producing a project with your own cash is a big no-no, too many things can go wrong but I got hold of the boys in Tucson and they still wanted to distribute it domestically if it was ever finished. 'It's not going to be soft core,' I warned them. 'That was Harry's idea,' they assured me. I already had this train rolling, so full steam ahead baby, watch for livestock on the tracks.

Thievery Magoo had to go, unfortunately not fast enough. He had shot the first three day weekend and most of his scenes were soft focus and / or couldn't be heard. We tried but didn't have enough time to re-shoot everything Magoo screwed. A half blind camera man who steals? He seemed like a badly written character out of a French farce. His last horror show was stealing a credit card and maxing it on the internet. (Photoshop and porn, if memory serves.) The production assistants he brought with him were young cuties that he was hoping to seduce; they'd never been on a set.

I persevered. I fired Magoo and hired my DP from Jane. A great camera man but turned out he was homophobic. Would it never end? I sat him down for a talk. 'Listen baby, women view homophobia as a clue to hidden identities, where there's smoke, you know? A real man doesn't care what anyone else does.' He got me and stopped being a pussy. He also hired a decent sound guy. The boys Magoo hired wanted to stay, they just needed instruction and ended up being good PA's. We shot long weekends through the month of February and into March. That was the year of El Nino. Rain hardly let up. The sky was overcast and gave the shoot a surreal overtone. Always the rain, dripping, pouring, water-falling in, around and on the set, every once in awhile letting up for a minute, when we would hurry outside to grab exterior footage. The cast was great, agreeable, humorous. Friend and I handled production like a team of ten. When we finished shooting 12 hours, there was work to do on the next day's schedule. Organize the props, craft service, put ducks in row. I slept two or three hours a night.

The office manager at my chiropractor's office was a friend. They were closed Sunday's and I could use it anyway I wanted just be done and clean by Monday am. That Saturday at midnight, my phone rang. Rebecca calling to cancel, something seriously wrong with her kidneys, she was in St Josephs waiting for emergency surgery. She was to play Dr Whitley, the bitch on wheels. She was in half the scenes at the 'Holloway Clinic' and we were shooting more than thirty. I said 'Oh my God, of course you have to cancel! Call me when it's over!' Then fell to pieces helpless with laughter. Friend and I laughed until we couldn't move. Midnight with a six am call and one of my leads had to bail. The only thing to do was play her myself <u>and that</u> was funny. We were rolling on the floor of my bedroom clutching our bellies. I was already wearing too many hats Actor was the icing.

We were almost finished shooting and taking a breather, walking through the American Film Market. AFM happens like Brigadoon every spring in Santa Monica. Hundreds of independent production companies meet at the Lowe's Hotel to sell their wares. I loved the Kasbah feel of the place, the circus side show of it all, always amusing. Friend and I stopped in to say hello to Lloyd (Troma) and after listening to crazee We Ho stories he said, 'Alisa, put me in it! I want to be in your soap opera!' I scraped around my brain and thought of what we had left to shoot. 'Well…you could be the nun who throws Sebastian out of the convalescent home.' 'I'll do it!'

When principal photography was done, I still had to edit forty odd hours of footage down to four one hour shows and lay a sound track. I looked for help with post production from Friend (Ex Mr Right Now) he was the senior editor at a huge, busy post house. Friend introduced me to Hank Saroyan, who had an edit bay in his pool house and a late mortgage payment. I did the rough edit at Hank's and Friend did the final polish and opening and closing credits.

We Ho Stories was fun and I learned a lot but it took 100% of my time, I couldn't do stunts. Financially, it was a drain. Car needed repairs, cell bill was overdue and Friend wouldn't even pay for the wine she drank every night. Exasperated one day, I snapped at her about money, buy groceries buy anything! She reminded me that she had been working on my project for free, how could I be so cheap? I backed off but the water was getting hot. We had been together too long without a break. She had the luxury of a boyfriend (now husband) who paid her bills and she'd been with him for years, her reality differed from mine. The day she came home with her arms full of shopping bags was the snail. 'There's a big sale at SAKS!' Incredulously, I watched her pull out suit after suit after suit. 'This one was only $400, can you believe it?' I couldn't. I sent her back to NYC with a sigh of relief and got a roommate with a job.

I finished editing the fourth installment in May then went to the UK to see Ken. I was super tired and needed the escape of Old Tinsley's. While there, I got the idea that Channel 4 might be interested in We Ho. Channel 4 had recently done a week of 'Gay programming.' (Channel 4 is like ABC or CBS / Network, corporate giant.) The UK was more open to new concepts than the big four in the US.

Back in LA, I got a heads up from a producer friend of Ken's that a producer from Channel 4 was in LA. After a bit of phone tag we connected and I got my chance to pitch We Ho Stories to Maria Mac Monster in June '98. She was attractive, intelligent and about my age. She couldn't say yes on her own but could bring it back and show the decision makers. I gave her a copy of the finished episodes along with all the marketing and promotional stuff I had been working on. I was so naive. I honestly thought that since it was a finished project, complete with a soundtrack and dated copyrights, I was safe from larceny. Two weeks later, I got a call from Mac Monster, back in London. 'We looked at it quite seriously, it's very funny but we're going to pass. Good luck with it.' I didn't have any reason to suspect foul play. I was a stupid retarded baby playing with snarling beasts and filthy vermin covered rats.

When I first heard about Queer As Folk, it was more than a year later.

It started airing in the UK in fall '99. Ken called when he noticed it. (Being straight, it took awhile to blip his radar.) 'There's a show on here that looks suspiciously like yours, sweetie…' Surprise, bitch. Channel 4 had hired a production company called Red to do a gay soap opera a month after looking at We Ho. There was so much buzz about their new show that Channel 4 released a 'Making Of' video, available at my local Video Store. They interviewed the head writer, a cute gay Brit. He enthusiastically told how exciting it was to write the pilot. 'They told me exactly what they wanted and then it was put on the fast track! I first got the call in July of '98 and we were into principal photography by February of '99! 'That's unheard of! Usually Channel 4 takes years to get an idea going…' Indeed.

I rented the first episodes of the UK version of Queer As Folk and watched as actors with British accents re-did the show I had produced almost two years earlier. The attorney with no morals, the runaway kid with a girl friend who was black, even the opening scene with two sexy men making out in a steamy shower. It was an unconcealed robbery. I was sick. Having a 'Created By' nod from a network, (yes she wrote this and look how much money it's making) would have put me in the game. They could have bought my rights for fifty grand—peanuts. I had ten more shows in my head and with a track record; I would have been taken seriously.

I shopped around for a lawyer who specialized in plagiarism cases and found one in a Century City tower with help from Friend. He had recently represented Mike Myers in a plagiarism suit against Paramount and did some pro bono for Friend's film festival. He listened to my tale and then asked to see the two shows. A few weeks went by with his minions carefully watching each show and the smoking gun of 'The Making Of Queer as Folk.' He asked me back. You have a case he said, I will waive my [four hundred an hour] fee but you'll have to pay for litigation expenses and we'll have to file suit in London. You'll probably win but they will appeal. The time line we are looking at is at least two years, maybe longer. Are you ready for a big, drawn out battle? That's how the networks work. They know it's wrong to steal it's just so easy. They have many lawyers on retainer to handle their many *many* plagiarism cases and know most writers don't have the resources to combat them. He said I'd be appalled to hear how established this practice was but I believed him. Plagiarism had happened to many friends. It was easier to sue for breach of confidentiality. Did I notify Mac Monster that West Hollywood Stories was not to be disclosed in any of my correspondence? No, didn't think of it.

It would cost thirty / forty grand to cover air fare, court costs, hotels, hookers, did I want to spend all disposable income fighting Channel 4? Think on it. The statute of limitations for plagiarism is two years, we'd have file soon. I thought about it for a week and decided to let it go. I think I was still in shock, Goliath take a bow. In hindsight, giving up was a BIG mistake for my psyche. I had always thought positively, one of my projects would make a fortune, I knew it. If I worked hard, nose to the grindstone all that clap-trap, tenacity and perseverance would win. The reality of the corporate network system had been slammed into me with a couple body shots and a punch in the kisser. Yes sweetie, you are very good—we're having you for a light snack—Cheerio.

Why do anything if it will get ripped off? Downward spiral. I started drinking too much, sleeping too late, pissed off employers, gained weight. I couldn't recover. Every where I looked, Queer As Folk leered at me. HUGE Billboard's on Sunset Strip, tons of advertising. The show about LA's Boys Town made here, stolen in the UK and brought back to Boys Town. Everyone loved it. Friends and Cast called to congratulate me, it was so obviously the same show. I disconnected.

An underground party scene thrives in LA, secretive, illegal and sexy, no annoying stars, paparazzi in tow and No Tourists. It used to snake through downtown, into tha' hood, the desert on BLM land and then back to start the loop again, a step ahead of the cops. It was hilarious / internet directions to a café or pub / let them get a look at you, then pay cash and get a map / sometimes it would be to another map site / I had a year long 'lost weekend.' I would do X and dance till dawn on a Tuesday. I hung out with beautiful (vapid) party people. Told myself I didn't care.

Journal July 91

Phone tag with Walter all week but finally connected tonight—he sounds depressed and sick of dealing with Fugitive. Says the project is dead—I've been hearing that for 9 months—but I'm pretty sure he means it this time.

The Fugitive came out in '93. I know how he felt when he watched it. Stomach gets queasy mouth dries up. Changed just enough to raise a reasonable doubt, not hard, it's from a television show, everyone has to follow the one armed man. Every memorable stunt in The Fugitive was written by Walter: The train crash, the frantic race from the court house, the gunshot to the face stopped by bullet proof glass, even the death defying leap 'Harrison Ford' (stunt double) takes out of the drainage tube into the churning river, that location was scouted by Walter.

When Moe was directing for Hard Copy, they went to Canada and did a show on a guy that teaches orphan geese to fly with his hydroplane. Moe immediately saw movie potential. He paid for the rights from Mr Nomorals to shoot it. Called an 'option' it's legal and binding, you have X amount time to make a film and if principal photography hasn't begun in the allotted time, its back on the market. Options are made for years and I think Moe bought it for three. Hard Copy aired the story a month later and FOX saw movie potential as well. They convinced Mr Nomorals to break his written contract with Moe. Give back his money they advised, they would pay so much more and they'd handle any icky legal mumbo jumbo if Moe tried to sue him. He didn't have to worry his sweet Canadian head about it.

Everyone in town has a horror story; mine got added to the endless list. Dormant since my college experiment, existentialism finally reared its goofy head and saved me:

'Life is meaning less and devoid of reason.'

—Sartre

Winter of '00–'01 was cold. I went through my three walk in closets and shook off some self pity, I was so lucky; I had an email blanket drive and brought clothing, umbrellas, blankets and water downtown to Homelet. The poor, the hurt, the disenfranchised, the old, schizophrenics, alcoholics, drug addicts—they're more than homeless, they're voiceless, invisible. I avoided drunks, junkies and big box villages but not every homeless person has made a choice to be on skid row. Sometimes you just get fucked.

I'd give away a sweat shirt, a blanket and listen. The Native American couple, their old pickup had had died on the way to her sisters in San Diego, they were otherworldly. White hair, soft spoken, I had to lean in to hear them. Teenage boys pushing a sleeping girl in a shopping cart, they'd been evicted from their squat. They bummed cigarettes, were animated, funny and loud as they told about the places they'd been that night. The girl slept through it all like a baby. As I traded hatred for compassion I finally let go of some disgust (not all) and said goodbye Underground hello Vegan.

Ariztical Entertainment distributed We Ho domestically and it made back it's production cost and some change, it was nice to see it on the shelves of the local video stores but it was bitter sweet. I'd been shaken like a rag doll I needed to re-group.

'...Los Angeles makes you feel isolated
it's a big sprawling city
20 million people in the basin

but it's got no soul
eat or be eaten…'

paraphrasing Gerald Rafferty

Website / April 17th 2002

Hi Everyone, Mostly great news!!! She's walking in small intervals—maybe 100 steps max & almost able to get in / out of her wheelchair on her own. Speech is getting better. She still has a hard time finding the right word, and this is the most frustrating part for her, but there is noticeable improvement from week to week. When you talk to her, just be patient when she fumbles. She'll usually think of another way to express the thought & eventually get it out.

The BIG news is she moved her right arm!!! Granted, it was only a shoulder shrug & a tiny thumb wiggle, but this is monumental. Ever since the stroke there has been no movement at all with that arm. But at least we now know there's some hope for a partial recovery. Now it's a matter of what controls the brain will restore....and when... time will tell, but this is thrilling news. This new development affects some future activity planned for the arm however. Current status with the arm is there are still open areas across the back of the hand & elbow.

More importantly, there is also significant bone build-up in the elbow in response to the [HO], which currently prevents any movement. Originally they were delaying any surgery to address this but now that it's probable she'll regain some control, they want to free that arm to allow rehab work to begin. It's a difficult decision to put her back in surgery when she's currently in such an excellent recovery mode, but given the latest development, it seems necessary & somewhat urgent.

They will probably do a couple more activities during the same session—remove the remaining two pins sticking out of her wrist & add artificial skin over the remaining open areas of her hand / elbow to further accelerate healing. In general, the elbow is the main concern right now. It's also the major source of pain... No date yet for the surgery. Still unknown as to when exactly she'll get out. It seems a ways off. She'll surely require additional medical attention, but she'll be able to get that, along with continued rehab on an outpatient basis at Rancho or another facility.

Best guess is the middle of May. Still not sure exactly what the outpatient requirements will be, so it's hard to plan the next move...So, all in all, really amazing progress in the last two weeks!! There's long way to go of course, but it's so exciting to observe significant improvement!

Couple of misc items: * Still getting a few e-mails kicked back.... Anybody know these people or identify a mistake with the address? Please also get back with me if you know of anyone else who needs to be added.

* I apologize if any unsolicited recipients still remain on this list... just reply back & you'll be removed. (I've been receiving phone messages from someone who was obviously added by mistake. Freak, I need your e-mail or give me a call-back number—anything to clue me in as to who you are!)

* Need a temp home for Alisa's cat "Home Scrub". She's a sweetie. Give me a call if you have any ideas.

* Alisa now has a laptop, with e-mail hookup, in her room. But she's so tired by the end of the day she hasn't been using it much, plus she just doesn't seem ready for it yet. I'm sure she enjoys reading them periodically, or will at some point however. Snail mail is probably still the best right now. ~Kevin

Kev and Tony's letters kept getting more removed from reality. I don't fault Kevin, he was calling from Portland for real news and was hearing Rancho Stories.

So many exclamation points!!! I wasn't having that great of a time!!! The HO was incredibly painful and my word retrieval was getting *worse* not better. (It probably had a connection to pain.) I don't have an excuse for Tony, he was there every day and he wasn't easily snowed by medical professionals. He seemed to be playing to the mailing list.

I was unable to comprehend the laptop mystery, I turned on the machine once or twice but it scared me—sneak attack horror—why was I afraid of a *computer*? I didn't understand my CVA symptoms and no one at Rancho EVER talked about them. I was fully engulfed in stroke fog. Rancho didn't test my brain for proficiency or loss of ability. It makes me furious. I was given therapy for *physical symptoms only* and even that was poorly done, like we traveled back in time 20 years. My brain having such major and obvious malfunctions should have been addressed.

The Big News about my arm!!! Still pisses me off!!!

All of the Rancho Experts agreed my arm wasn't worth working on. It was too injured, why bother. It had been an experiment and would be amputated. No one had me doing simple shoulder shrugs, or asked me to try and make a fist, do isometric exercises or any of the <u>many</u> things my *next therapists did*. If you are recovering from a stroke, <u>get the affected side moving as quickly as possible and don't stop.</u> The 'shoulder shrug and tiny thumb wiggle' was my own stubborn refusal to give up. Every day as I sat in the wheelchair I would look at my tragic hand and try to move it. One day I was sitting outside with Friend talking about amputation when my thumb moved. We both noticed it. 'Try it again,' he urged…wiggle wiggle…it was my thumb trying to communicate! 'Don't give up on me don't give up on me…'

Therapist suggested I stop working out altogether because it made my tone worse. Thank God I didn't take that idiotic advice. Rehabilitation in two more private hospitals made it shockingly obvious that Rancho was a County

Facility years behind in every ugly malpracticing sense. I couldn't write about it until 2004, couldn't let myself remember / process my anger.

Website / May 8th, 2002

Hi All, Here's the latest: Rehab is progressing well at Rancho. Alisa's pushing hard & noticing small, incremental improvements week by week. She has movement in nearly all muscle groups now, although some muscles (toes, fingers, shoulder) only flicker. But knowing the nerve messages are getting through is extremely exciting. She can now touch her right thumb to her index finger!! All movements are delicate, weak, slow & difficult but it's all good & simply amazing given her condition 4 months ago.

She's walking, still extremely slow, with the aid of a 4-prong cane. Still a hundred or so steps at a time, but says she's starting to feel stronger as time passes. The wounds on her legs / feet are nearly closed, except for a couple tiny patches & small areas that open / close during the healing process.

She's wearing a cast on her right ankle at night to stretch & both feet are nearly back to 90 degrees again. She was fitted for compression garments & will start wearing them shortly. Speech is improving quite well, although she's still often fumbling for words. This is the most frustrating part for her it seems.

When she wiggled her thumb a couple weeks back the urgency to free that elbow to allow PT stepped up a notch. They've been going back & forth on what to do ever since. It's (literally) a million-dollar arm now & every decision is made with great care. After much discussion it was decided that invasive surgery to free the elbow is not the best choice right now, mainly due to continued infection (which is not threatening, but a concern), but more importantly they didn't want to disrupt the blood flow / vascular bed of that wounded region. They finally reached an agreement, and last Thursday put her under to free the elbow by brute force. It went well & she gained about 40 degrees of movement. They took advantage of this time under anesthesia to perform range of motion in the shoulder, as well as remove the remaining two pins in her wrist / arm. Follow-up surgeries remain, but will be done at a later time.

So, the new target date (we learned today) for her release from Rancho is 5 / 17. The target date has moved several times, but is now starting to sound more definite. So, if you have videos or anything you'd like to reclaim down there, please try to collect soon. Alisa's planning to donate any media left behind to the hospital. Well, that's about it, I think, for now.... She's getting better...long road to go....The milestone of leaving a 24 / 7 care facility after 5 months will be a welcome one for her I'm sure. Thanks everyone for your continued good wishes & support. p&l Tony

PS: To the stunt coordinators on this list: I hope this will not be perceived as an inappropriate solicitation but I will be looking for work again now and if you have a day or two on something, it would be greatly appreciated. Please call me directly since I'm not w / any answering service at the moment. I still love stunts and am ready and willing and crazy enough to give it 110%. Thank you.

'I hope this will not be perceived as an inappropriate solicitation' in **bold italic type** couldn't be perceived as anything but. Idiot.

My speech wasn't improving. Speech Therapist wanted to try electrical stimulation on my facial muscles. Speech Therapy was *the quietest hour of the day*. I would sit in blissful silence and let her run a battery powered thingy over the right side of my face. Muscles flex, release, flex, release. It was interesting and it worked a little but it was NOT speech therapy. Kevin was out of town. He wasn't ever told the truth. (I still can't 'touch my thumb to my index finger' more Rancho Stories.)

I remember being skeptical about the proposed procedure. Forcing my elbow to range by brute force? That sounded cave man-ish but I wasn't clear headed enough to say no. I remember trying to talk about it and being rudely dismissed. I had Rancho Experts telling me it was the right thing to do. I was shown an X-ray of my elbow, it looked normal except for a teensy chip sitting at the tip. That was the HO. 'It's so little, we can just push past it.' They had to put me out to remove the pins anyway; they would do it at the same time.

County of Los Angeles   Department of Heath Services
RANCHO LOS AMIGOS NATIONAL REHAB CENTER

DEPARTMENT OF: Orthopedic Surgery   OPERATION DATE: 5 / 02 / 02

ATTENDING SURGEON: Ima Idiot, MD

OPERATING SURGEON: Dono Whatimdoing, MD

PREOPERATIVE DIAGNOSIS:
Right shoulder, right elbow flexion contracture status post pinning of wrist.

POSTOPERATIVE DIAGNOSIS:
Same as the pre-op…

INDICATIONS / FINDINGS:
The patient is a 38 year old female who has sustained a stroke and also a 30–40% total body surface area burn secondary to a bed catching fire when she was camping. The patient has developed flexion contractures in a pronator position, both in her elbows and in her shoulders.

She was noted to have right elbow flexion and contracture of approximately 70 degrees and was only able to forward flex and abduct 80 degrees. The patient was given the option of surgical or non-surgical management. The patient gave informed consent and opted for surgical intervention.

OPERATION:
1.   Manipulation under anesthesia.
2.   Pin removal.

ANESTHESIA:
General Mask.

PROCEDURE:
The Patient came into the operating room and was induced under general mask anesthesia without any complications.

We then slowly manipulated her shoulder, just by slow manipulation under anesthesia, and we were able to abduct it to approximately 110 degrees, externally rotate 70 degrees and internally rotate to around forty degrees. We were able to cross-shoulder abduct to halfway across her shoulder. We then slowly ranged her elbow.

We noted at this time that we were not able to get her out of fixed pronated position; we were able to get her flexion to 80 degrees, so a range of motion from 40 to 80 degrees. We then felt it was satisfactory, that was as much as we could get without causing some iatrogenic injury.

We then proceeded with removing the 2 pins, getting a needle drive and removing the two pins distally. We then placed Silvadene cream by removing first the cellular debris and placing Silvadene cream over the wound site distally near her wrist region. We then covered it up with 4 x 4's and Ace wrap over it.

The patient was then stable after she woke up from general anesthesia and was transferred to PAC Unit.

COMPLICATIONS: None.

POST OPERATIVE CONDITION / DISPOSITION:
The patient was stable and transferred to Post Anesthesia Care Unit.

ESTIMATED BLOOD LOSS:	None.
IV FLUIDS:	350 cc.
TOURNEQUET TIME:	None.
SPECIMENS:	None.

POSTOPERATIVE PLAN:
Our plan is to continue aggressive Occupational Therapy, given that she does have heterotopic ossification of the right elbow. Then, in approximately 1 year's time, we will consider excision of her heterotopic ossification. At this time, we will continue Occupational Therapy with range of motion exercises.

NAME:	CHRISTENSON, ALISA
WARD #:	1 NORTH

I woke up in the recovery room and felt pain coming. I asked for medication. The first thing I learned about pain management is to stop it early. If you wait until it's acute, it's too late. 'I can't give you any in the recovery room,' the nurse told me. Huh? As the anesthesia wore off, pain grew steadily worse. I started moaning and begging for relief as the staff looked at each other helplessly. The nurses couldn't give medication without a Doctors prescription and the fucking idiots left the building without leaving one.

It's hard to describe pain…never does it justice.

Migraine is a sharp beaked maggot digging out your eyes from inside your brain.

A broken arm (or foot) is a snap…wait for it… wait… Ka BOOM! Bulldozer agony. You feel a wave of nausea, black spots float in front of your eyes but it passes quickly and you can keep your senses and seek help.

Broken ribs are insidious. You don't realize it's happened at first. Just took a hard hit to the floor and everything is perfectly still for a few seconds, then the director yells cut. Bell rings, work starts up again. I hold out my hand and the stunt coordinator pulls me up. Take a deep breath and WAMMO! A stitch in your side gone ballistic, a stab wound. You double over for a second and take shallow breaths until it sort of, kind of, goes away. 'Honey, that doesn't look good.' 'I just had my breath knocked out, lemme sit a minute.' That's one you can keep working through if hard stuff is over. If the set medic finds out you've cracked ribs, work is over for the day and you get a free ride to the ER. Making over a hundred an hour? Keep breathing shallow and see your regular physician tomorrow.

Throughout the years I've dealt with pain and the burns were the worst until this. Nothing could prepare me, my elbow was a white hot sun radiating gamma rays and broken glass through my body every heartbeat a horrid throb / stab / throb / burn / throb…

Until this procedure, my elbow looked normal except for skin grafts. I remember the X ray and the joint itself looked normal. After the attempt to *force* my elbow to move, it kicked the hetrotopic ossification into overdrive. Screaming screaming until I lost my voice—still trying to scream—trying to hit to escape—I was tied down screaming shrieking crying begging for relief! I wanted to kill them! Kill them!

The procedure was in the morning and Doctor Idioto checked his messages late that afternoon. That he hadn't thought of *pain medication* is unbelievable. The whole procedure was unbelievable. Occupational Therapist was watching in the OR. She told me a year later (when I visited Rancho February '03) they were wrenching on my arm so hard she thought it was going to break. Why didn't *she* say anything? If she was right there and it was <u>obvious</u> they were causing damage, then STOP it! Rat bitch, rather sacrifice a patient than speak up, that's something to be proud of honey. Pat the rat on the back. (And, she thought it was a good thing to *tell me* a year later?)

Every part of the elbow joint started to grow bone IMMEDIATELY, the moment they tried forcing it. It froze solid and created the 'Elephant Man' elbow that resembled a squashed baseball. What I had to lug around like a flipper for another year, what Dr Stupidio in Smallville looked at and pronounced 'un operable.' What Dr Beast told me to cut off. It took days to be able to get out of bed and start therapy again / I was given a shot of Dilauded every twelve hours in addition to Methadone and Neurontin and still it was horrid, tense pain. The doctors still had my therapists trying to move my elbow! 'If you don't move it, it won't work,' said Dr Idioto, trying to make me feel bad for his fucking mistake. And I did, that kills me too. Every kind of shameless nasty behavior *killed* me. (And Remember Specialisto's caution last spring: 'Be careful about causing any pain, pain will bring the HO back. Keep it iced.') My elbow was being destroyed by fire over and over. It was hot to the touch and bright red— bone burning under skin—yet no one thought of cooling it with ice.

The handwritten 'Ortho R3 Consult F / U—P / N' on May three says: 'Patient complains of pain not being properly managed. Otherwise no acute events on.'

No acute events on? That my elbow was growing new bone like crystal in a subterranean hot spring didn't warrant comment is telling. He knew how badly he'd fucked up and wanted No Written Evidence. USC had left me to ROT, literally. USC was done using me as teaching tool; I was forgotten and left to be tortured by county hospital idiots! Everything single fucking thing they did was wrong! Monsters!

WOW

There's the reason I couldn't write about Rancho / I'm furious about being a test monkey!

> '...I want revenge screaming for revenge
> I've been angry too long
> its killing me inside
> when I channel rage into a positive direction
> I get a lot done...'
>
> paraphrasing Pantera

2007

Two years to process is crazee! Having No One to talk to (no one allowed to see me, nobody told) I blocked it out like a *childhood trauma*. I didn't remember being tortured except in weird dreams, so horrid they can't be real dreams. No wonder everyone was looking at me strangely when I went back to visit; they probably thought I was armed.

Website / May 17th 2002

Greetings All, Alisa will be discharged from Rancho today & tonight she's catching a plane up here to Portland. She's going to come stay with Y & I for awhile, continuing rehab on an outpatient basis at Legacy Emanuel Hospital & Health Center. Legacy is the best place in this area for her condition—they have burn, neuro / stroke & rehab centers all integrated within the group & she should continue to receive first-rate treatment. Her therapy will resume here starting Monday.

As of today, she continues to improve.... the latest milestone this week—successful navigation of (a few) stairs! Her doctors have OK'ed this transfer, indicating her wounds are still healing at a great pace & they don't anticipate any required surgery for some time. [Playing the part of concerned doctor for my brother] It will still take many months for the arm to completely heal over, and for now, they'll monitor & let her continue to mend on her own. We'll be obtaining a sanity check on that advice from the team up here.

Now that Alisa's out of the hospital & entering the next phase of recovery, she should be able to resume contact on her own, so I'll be signing off. I want to thank all of you who reached out in any way to support her. The cards, e-mails, messages, money, hopeful thoughts & positive vibes all contributed toward her miraculous recovery. When this began four & a half months ago she was suppose to loose both feet & her arm, if she survived, today she has a hopeful future.

You can reach Alisa here at our house & she'll probably resume e-mailing shortly. Thanks everyone, Signing off ~Kevin & Y

2007

The family wanted me in Smallville. Seemed best, the Rents weren't working and I needed skyscraper maintenance but I begged Kevin to let me go to their house in Portland. I knew I needed more surgery soon, my fifth metacarpal was turning BLACK and I didn't trust Smallville Doctors. Tony picked me up from Rancho. (He wouldn't let anyone else do it, controlling to the last minute.) I had a teary goodbye with my nurses. I had started packing days earlier; I had a ridiculous amount of kitsch. Tons of T-shirts (thanks to the email list) plastic dinosaurs, wall hangings, boxes of DVD's, silk flowers, a huge bag of get well cards and a million stuffed animals.

Treasures, everything was from someone sending me love. I kept it out and surrounding me like a fetish I could draw strength from. Unfortunately I couldn't fit it all in two suitcases and a carry-on; I donated half to Rancho. The drive to LA from Downey is ugly, cement, industrial, dull. But I saw the opening scene from Blade Runner, emerging from the womb, everything was new.

We stopped at We Ho Manor for hugs and kisses, BBQ, cake, presents, love, stories and jokes. Friend started crying and it made me cry. Emotional, nice. They gave get well prayers, luck, control, strength whatever was lying around. They were so sorry this had happened; take a little more love before you go honey, so much love. Good bye beautiful neighbors, goodbye Avalon.

Tony drove to Burbank Airport; he got me a wheelchair then left me on the sidewalk and parked. I was abandoned again to 'the first time.' Almost dying is driving along in a mono-tone sepia colored life when BAM! Your lens gets changed to Technicolor and the sound becomes stereo. You wake up a superhero, spiritual, improved and inexplicably (stupidly?) happy. I was certain I had lived for a reason. Memories hit me, translucent and crazee beautiful, everything was swirling around my cracked brain looking for a new place to chip in with a ludicrous high-speed sense of recall that gave it crazee metaphysical meaning.

I love Burbank Airport. It's an Oasis in Ugly Airport Land. LAX is a water buffalo, Burbank, a slender gazelle. Every episode from Burbank Airport came flooding back into my mind at once: Phoenix hundreds of times to see Grandma and Georgene. Married in Vegas, skiing in Breckenridge, Aspen, Keystone, Monarch, Reno for Burning Man, work in San Fran, a pack of us picking up Friend in a limo to see Pink Floyd at the Rose Bowl… Tony came and brought me back to reality. We fetched my ticket and the guard thought I might be a terrorist. Tony lifted my suitcases onto the table and Guard unpacked my kitsch stuffed bag. Ka Pop! Zillions of stuffed animals all dying for air jumped out, CD's, trinkets, coffee mugs, beanie babies.' All right. You can pack this back up.' 'I can't,' I said. I couldn't. 'I'm not touching it said Tony, I'm just taking her to the plane.' That was funny. Too much authority in an idiot pisses off Tony as much as it used to piss me off. I'm neutral now. Stupid people with boring jobs try to perk themselves up by making other's jump through hoops. They're to be pitied.

My first experience out in the world as a gimp, everyone stared, I felt like I was watching a movie. I took an elevator up to the plane. (Burbank Airport is so cute you still go outside and walk up the stairs to embark.) Tony watched from the terminal, I was crying—<u>tears of relief</u>—to be escaping Tony! A guy in Business offered to trade seats with me. I told him no, it was a short flight but thank you. My first clue as to how traveling as a disabled person was going to be. Took an extra 20 mg of Methadone but the flight still hurt. Portland's airport was a crystal cathedral, driving over the freeway was through Vincent's painting, Starry Night / glowing surreal circus boats in the rivers below / baby skyscrapers blinking multi colored lights / so beautiful it gave me soft exquisite pain.

Kev was organized he had a wheel chair, he had appointments set up, occupational, physical and speech therapists and Dr Cookieboots, the head of the Burn Unit to see about my paw. He had directions from OT on my bath routine, I needed a shower bench and I needed a handle to help me get in and out. I even needed the bed in the guest room raised; I couldn't bend my knees to sit down that far. We loaded up on gimp friendly wares at The Barnacle (Pops name for Home Depot).

We went into Legacy Emanuel the following Monday. Dr Cookieboots was kind, nice bedside manor, eye contact, waited patiently when I was speaking. He put me at ease. 'How committed are you to keeping the hand?' He was skeptical about my paw it looked Horrid. The fifth metacarpal had turned black and the rest of them were gray. '100%, I guess. I don't know anything about prosthetic's. I can always cut it off later.' I started crying. He scheduled me for his first available surgery ten days later. 'I think I'll drill some little holes along the open bone, might stimulate granulation, bones are porous, full of blood; then I'd like to take what's left of your fifth finger and turn it into a flap.' He didn't know how long it would take to heal. Ditto HO. He was dubious. 'Would you mind calling Dr Allritini and talking with him about it?' Dr Cookieboots responded like a barking poodle! He didn't like the idea AT ALL! BARK BARK GRRRR!

Such an Extreme negative response, a total reversal of the 'bedside manor' persona he'd been using, it freaked me. Arrogant surgeons don't like to be second guessed and are very irritated by 2nd opinions. I'd seen it before, not unusual behavior. At the time, I remember thinking it was type A, pissing on fire hydrant nonsense and blowing it off. Now I think maybe it was: Hey! Brain damaged dummy! CVA under anesthesia during a DRESSING CHANGE? Out of control HO? Left your surgeries unfinished? Left you warehoused in a county run facility while the bones protruding from your skin turn black and start to ROT? You *want* me to call those idiots after what they did to you?

Just a guess.

Cut to 6 mo later: It was the winter of 2003 and I was staying with Kevin & Y. Bones spitting out and freaking me out. I wrote:

> Dr Cookieboots told me to expect it, so it's not a complete
> surprise. But I wonder what is happening underneath there?

Is new bone growing and taking its place? Or is it simply riddled with holes, weak and brittle? I think I need to go back to Cookieboots for a check me. I need some reassurance.

We went for X-rays / nothing different / Cookieboots said again that it might not work, the bones may be infected. I innocently asked when my fifth finger was going to fit into it's new spot. I had expected it to meld into my hand; instead, it just sat there, a backwards finger sticking strangely out of my paw. BARK BARK! GRR! 'Why don't you ask A PLASTIC SURGEON!' Grrrroowwl! (Wasn't he a plastic surgeon?) What a weird fluffy pudgy mudge Cookieboots was. I didn't think he'd done anything wrong until HE Red Flagged it. He was the first passive aggressive surgeon I'd run across. Who knew they existed?

USC memory: Betsy coming out—it scared me—I loved her for showing up but Betsy had never been to LA then two weeks after the CVA she comes out for the weekend. She's an RN; I thought she knew something they weren't telling me. I thought I was dying.

Rancho Memories: Speaking of test monkeys; Physical Therapist took me upstairs to a classroom setting. She was nervous and told me I'd have to pay attention. Whatever, this was the same woman who told me to stop working out altogether a week earlier. Doctor Polanski was a stern white haired woman that took herself seriously and everyone else had better too!

The Polanski would tell PT '…have the patient do this…have the patient do that…' PT would then repeat what she said to me, as if The Patient couldn't hear The Polanski. Surreal / Absurd. The Polanski never looked at me, her severe face cowing all therapists (with patients in tow) assembled. One young man courageously asked me how I got burned / relieved there was a human in the room / I started to tell him. The Polanski cut me off mid sentence. 'Have the patient walk without her cane.' I was wheeled in, was she kidding? I could barely stand, knew I would fall and refused. PT was pissed for days. She didn't care if The Patient fell; it was ordered by The Polanski.

Surreal test monkey.

Size 10 clown shoes. My feet are 5 ½, had swelled to 7 and I was wearing huge men's tennis shoes from Lost & Found.

Surreal circus side show freak.

My right foot was pointing; common in stroke and called 'drop foot.' They put a cast on to flex it / scared me to death / crying no no no / irrational fear caused by brain damage / *no one tried to calm me or told me it was a symptom.* They simply ignored me. I thought I was losing my mind.

Surreal scaredy cat.

A doctor I had never seen before stalked into my room, haughty, angry! I should be massaging the stump of finger I had! Toes too! Didn't I know anything about being an amputee?!?

Surreal...was he real?

Prison break with Kevin (like Jerry the orderly) he told the nurses he was going to push me around the campus and then we went to his rental. He showed me the hut everyone was staying at. USC's Social Worker found it—housing for families of patients. It was cute, clean and only three hundred a month. When parents weren't in town, Tony was staying there. He'd made a collage from his visitor's badges. It looked like a cave painting—it softened me.

Surreal Tony.

Therapist showing me how to bathe myself sitting on a shower seat. How strange it is letting people touch you, help you to do anything, while you're nude. How long before you get used to it? I never did.

Naked Frankenstein, yuk.

I started to tip over in my room / strangest feeling / no control / I was unable to move and going down. Husband and Friend were watching me go, frozen, slow motion. My heavy set, older nurse *zoomed into action* and saved me! She was farther away than the two of them. We all were amazed by her quick reaction, even her.

Surreal Super Hero.

Being lonely for Wayne loving Wayne missing Wayne and having deal with Tony glomming into my life. A horror show of constant bickering; giving me ridiculous self help books and sniveling when I didn't read them, I didn't want to think about him just escape him somehow.

Surreal lost time warp.

Friend came from out of town for a weekend and parents were there so she couldn't stay in the little hut. She spent Saturday night at Catherine's, who talked her into drinking until 2 then had a pet drive them all over town looking for blow. Friend was in so much pain I could see it rolling off her when she showed up late Sunday afternoon. It was Bizarre Self Involved Behavior, why did Cat wipe out my friend for a whole day when she was only there for two? I was just as hurt as Friend was. In hindsight, duh.

All too real drug problem.

And finally, my inscrutable mother: Sitting in the cafeteria one afternoon she said, 'do you remember when I had Martha make you that Renaissance gown?' Shooom—Shields Up! Why talk about an ancient horror show? I was 19 and lived in Minneapolis. I was doing the Renaissance Festival and was going to be in the Royal Court. Mom had a friend who made costumes for a theatre company. 'I've bartered with Martha, she wants some of my Teddy Bears for X-mass presents and you need a Renaissance gown...'

I remember thinking, No Thanks, not again. One of Mom's passive aggressive behaviors was to promise a prize, then snatch it away. It had been happening from my earliest memories; offer something, a dress, Halloween costume, jacket: what was presented was irrelevant, the outcome was the same. 'I don't know why I do anything for you! You don't appreciate me!' and snatch away the 'gift' at the last second, acting out subconscious issues, I was (she was) The Bad Daughter who had to be Punished.

I was seeing a psychology intern on campus, she offered coping skills; 'No Martha's work is too expensive. No I don't want you to pay for it...' I went through my No collection, it didn't faze. I acquiesced, maybe things were different, I'd been on my own for a few years and maybe we were past the drama.

I went to Smallville and met Martha for a fitting. We picked material, burgundy for the bodice and skirt, dark blue and amber for the underskirt. It was beautiful. A few weeks later, when the pattern had been made, the material cut, Mom called me up. I was ungrateful! She went to all the trouble and what did I do? Breath wrong? Whatever it was, I could pay for the dress myself! Click. I fell for it again!? Again!? What the hell was wrong with me!? Humiliated, I drove to Smallville and tried to explain to Martha. I had let my mother down she wasn't going to do their Trade Deal anymore. Could I pay for the dress myself? 'Those bears were going to be Christmas presents. Is she still going to make them?' Martha looked like she was going to cry. 'I don't know. I'm sorry.' I meant it; Mom's need to punish knew no social boundaries.

Cut to 19 years later: Mom sat across from me happily reminiscing. She'd rewritten the story, now it had a happy ending. She made the bears, Martha delivered the dress and I was ecstatic to be given such a lavish gift. I struggled to speak (hatchling vultures releasing from eggshells) 'I was paying her installments for months!' 'Didn't I make the bears...?' She was remembering something—she looked at me with a just woke up face. That's when Pop snapped, 'I can't believe you're arguing about this, it happened twenty years ago!' He stalked out. 'I better go with him,' she left too. The realization that Mom redesign's the past was disconcerting, disconnecting from reality and all that but it explained a lot.

SAG Residual Checks—Winter 2004

Simone / Feature Motion Picture	Total Gross	1818.12
Scorcher / Feature Motion Picture	Total Gross	125.55
Storm Trooper / Feature Motion Picture	Total Gross	33.54
Time Lapse / Feature Motion Picture	Total Gross	376.40
Project V.I.P.E.R. / Feature Motion Picture	Total Gross	121.52
Simone / Feature Motion Picture	Total Gross	432.03
Shockwave / Feature Motion Picture	Total Gross	39.59
Wishmaster 2: Evil Never Dies / Feature	Total Gross	16.56
Man on the Moon / Feature Motion Picture	Total Gross	31.01
Man on the Moon / Feature Motion Picture	Total Gross	.70
Angel, Fredless / Video, Basic Cable	Total Gross	13.97

I was pleasantly surprised at the Simone checks. It was a film starring Al Pacino; I worked a couple days on the Stampede. A pack of well dressed event guests think they spot Simone and run over each other trying to reach her. It was fun, everyone in evening gowns and tuxedos getting pushed and thrown into the fountain pool.

Damien said, 'you have tons of money! Why should I pay for groceries?' He meant it. I explained, like talking to a tween, how little a few grand is in the real world. With no new jobs coming in, residuals will get smaller and smaller, I can't live off them forever.

Damien never felt guilty about sponging off me; his sense of entitlement was shameful. He had to go to MN for face time with his lawyer. I left with him by default. If Alex hadn't invited Tweak back, I would have stayed in LA. Pre-injury, if a relationship became problematic, waivers, but I needed him. I straddled his lap and stared directly into his eyes. 'It's us against the world baby we have to be a team. I'm barely keeping it together, I can't fight you too.' I so wanted to be half of a team.

His truck broke down in Vegas; we found a garage and I paid for a hotel. Sad news in the morning, the truck had chronic cancer it's vulture was busted. It would be thousands to fix, the truck was old, it wasn't worth it. 'My truck would be fine if I hadn't driven out to see *you!*' He morphed into a spiteful man-child and stomped out of the room. I desperately wanted to get away but couldn't. Without a suicide ball, driving through mountains was impossible. Fuck. I was stuck. I went and found him playing slots. He apologized for his rant and I saw a slick teenager afraid of losing his meal ticket. I rented a van. We went back to LA, transferred our stuff to my van and dropped off the rental. The closer we got to Minneapolis the more hateful he became. The perfect travel companion five months earlier had become a little bitch it was hard not to slap.

> '…takin a slow ride in my soft top
> sippin my favorite drink and puffin a blunt
> laid back
> with my mind on money and money on my mind…

> paraphrasing Snoop Dogg

March 2004—Minneapolis, MN

Bone has been poking through the skin of above my middle metacarpal for 10 days now. It's disconcerting to be in the land of shitty doctors; definitely on my own, I wouldn't let a MN doctor pick my boogers.

2007

Stranded in Minnesota again, time to make the best of it. I'd spent a year talking about CafeDeb.com, Just Do It. Friend is a photographer in Minneapolis, he'd taken pictures of me twenty years earlier. (He nick-named me Dreamgirl and still calls me that, aww Dreamgirl, how could you not adore?) I enlisted him as CafeDeb's photographer, advertised for models in the City Pages and over the next few weeks shot several in his studio. Organizing a simple photo shoot was now complex, phone calls, wardrobe, releases… Making myself work helped CVA recovery and being around young women who weren't jaded and bitter helped me reorganize my priorities. Photo shoots are fun, work was good for me.

I'd finally taken Goodfella's advice and hired a shrink in Pasadena. It took a month to find her, she went to a good school, was about my age and said she had experience with brain damage—which was what I needed help with—I called her from Minneapolis and spent the next six weeks talking about the Damien Horror Show. I was paying $140 a week to survive his negative onslaught; I felt like an abuse victim. I'd only had one abusive lover (Tony) and was fighting back. Couple of times I lost in and hit him (nailed him too) to his credit, he didn't do anything but block my next punch but he was insufferable. This was a typical entry:

April 2004—Minneapolis

We'd been ignoring each other all week then yesterday he asks me if I want to get something to eat. (What are you up to now?) I say yes. He's driving my van, going on and on about Melody (his ex) and the kid (who may or may not be his) and how his mother wants to spend time with the baby. I think he's blowing steam. I'm Switzerland lookin' out the window. Suddenly he lights into me. 'You're too negative to have around! I want Melody and the baby back in my life!' Melody hates him even more than I do, he's delusional.

We ended up at The Uptown. I ordered a tuna melt but couldn't eat. Damien was relentless, I'm awful, I'm horrible, bark bark bark. He'd lived like Pasha the Prince in California, turnabout and I'm the Matchstick Girl. I started crying. Of course our relationship is over, didn't he realize I couldn't leave by myself? Three days on my own was too much for me to drive? I'm trying to keep my sanity and work on CafeDeb. Stop treating me like a whipping boy. 'Then get out! If I'm so terrible! Get out of my house!' Loud wackadoo idiot. Everyone caught a furtive look at Mr Abusive and his pathetic for taking it girlfriend. It's his *parent's house*, I get along fine *with them* and I'm not going anywhere. He finally apologized, tired of seeing me cry, he's going to jail for a year, he wants my forgiveness.

'...take care of yourself
be in charge of your own shit
I don't sympathize
anymore...'

paraphrasing Bjork

2007

He a court appearance in Topeka mid April, another continuance. We agreed on driving to court then on to LA. Ross would give him another pass back to Minneapolis. Tax Return Companies around town had been paying him to give work massages, a treat for their employees during the busy season. He had worked the last 6 weeks. After We'd had been on the road few hours, he asked me to buy him a cup of coffee. He hadn't *brought a penny*. 'I'm *saving* up for a car; I have to *save my money*.' Belligerent, confrontational. Shock / Vultures. Bought him a tie for court, bought his lunch, his dinner, paid for gas and a room at The Radisson (he refused to stay at a motel and bullied until I gave in.) I took two sleeping pills after check in; he was leaving for court when I woke.

Sitting in the bath tub, did I have a horrid nightmare? Was he real? Who acts like that!? His behavior was so Looney it couldn't be true but I looked at the previous day's credit card receipts, I had proof. I must escape. I would do the rest of the drive myself. If it takes a week, so be it.

Damien appeared as I was out front tipping the bell hop for bringing down my suitcases. He realized how close he'd come to being stranded in Kansas. Suddenly contrite and sorry he'd been such an asshole! Let me make it up to you! You are over reacting! He worked me through Okalahoma, Texas, New Mexico... he didn't know how to handle stress he was sorry he thought he was losing his mind prison prison please forgive me forgive me. I did. Given enough time, I'll forgive anybody anything and I couldn't listen to any more self flagellation. Truce.

We stopped at the Grand Canyon, it was warm storm cloudy, expressionist cotton ball snow flakes floating dramatic and extraordinary. We hung out in and around the lodge all day and I think it helped us both. The farther we got from MN the more normal Damien became. OR: I'd become a doormat. Hideous Frankenstein doesn't date real men; the best she can hope for is a pretty gigolo. Still not sure about that one.

'…sink or swim, baby
I don't care anymore
and if you keep acting like a sniveling little bitch
I will kick your ass…'

paraphrasing Bjork

Today I feel hopeful. We arrived at Tweak House late Sunday afternoon. They'd had an acid party all weekend, just the stragglers left. Cat's car was in the lot. I was pleasantly surprised, thought she had waited to talk to me. I went downstairs, picked up Precious Homescrub and looked for Catherine. 'She was *just* here' said Alexander. The three of us looked around. *She had run away like a child,* probably when I was downstairs. We all laughed. This is the woman who'd hurt me so badly last summer / why did I care about her?

Once again Alexander kicked Tweak out but he was 'living there until the end of the month…' Whatever Mr Denial, I am not falling for it twice and have resumed my search for an apartment at the beach.

Damien's sense of privilege is out of control. He knows he is my guard dog and puppy wants kibble. It's a gorgeous am, spring in LA is the best and those idiots want to keep drinking, doing drugs and bitching about each other. Alexander is a Victim with a capital VICTIM, Tweak a Golem with a brain of black slimy ooze and Damien off to prison. See ya boys, my plans include a happy life.

2007

Damien flew home. I moved in with Friend and his lover. My therapist said, 'Oh no, more gay guys.' She meant it too, silly bitch. They both have careers and are a functioning, loving couple. Their house, a 1930's dream in the

Hollywood Hills; I could detox from the bad boyfriend, the meth addict and the enabling sniveler.

Friend had three cats and one was a Bobcat, I asked the only sober person left at Tweak House if he could watch Homescrub for the rest of the month. He said yes and I gave him $50. Reprieve, thank God.

May 2004—Tom & Bruce's, Hollywood Hills

I love it here. Got up this am and drove to Pasadena. I have a new personal trainer, Lizel. I love her too; she specializes in Neuro injuries and uses Pilates.

Went to Goodfella to get the prescription for physical therapy; he said 'you have to ask yourself if it's worth it, you *might* see a 20% difference.' I remember looking at his pudgy body and thinking, why try to explain that working out feels good and that's why I do it. Dot.

Friend worrying about his cat made me worry about mine; I stopped by Tweak House to visit. Gave her a brush and lay around with her for a couple hours watching TV. She purred the whole time, little kitty bear. There was a nail in my tire when I left (thanks Tweak.) I stopped by the tire place I go to in Pasadena and they fixed it free. Sweethearts.

Almost rented a place in Studio City, even filled out an application but at the last second (thank you Shiva) I found a bachelor hut walking distance to the ocean. I could move in the last week of May if I wanted. I did.

> 'I write only for myself and I wish to declare once and for
> all that if I write as though I were addressing readers, that it
> is simply easier for me to write in that form.'

—Dostoevsky

Fired my shrink today. I was talking about my injury and was about to say my arm was 'bad'—but because of wise advice from a therapist (my arm isn't bad, it's hurt)—I caught myself in time. Then humped and poked for another way to say it. Couldn't come up with 'hurt, damaged or even affected.' I'm so tired of not being able to think of *simple words*. Aphasia. Time was ticking by. 'My arm is…compromised.' Compromised! She loved the word! Weee compromised! Perhaps PTSD compromised me because I was compromised by my compromise! She killed me. Compromise! Caw! Caw! I spend all this time and cash and the best she can do is parrot the interesting words I use back at me? Does it show you're listening? Learn that in Therapy 101 did we? I got up and walked out, vultures in tow.

Skull farm, Homescrub, RIP.

I called Alex last Friday and told him I would pick up the cat on Monday. Monday am I showed up at 9:30 and she was gone. Chandelier—living in a tent village in their back yard—told me she heard meowing Sunday night. Monday am gone without a trace. Both doors to the downstairs were closed. Tweak hates me with the sizzle that comes with a brain tumor-ish intensity; the pop comes from too many days awake from sniffing and smoking the shit you keep under your sink.

Poor scrub. Little scrub. I was so naive about Alex and his codependence. Of course, he told Tweak, 'Alisa found an impossible to get apartment! She's moving to the beach! You lose!' It is as much their fault as the addict; the junkie will eventually crumble under the weight of their addiction but with a codependent partner to prop them up, their downward spiral goes hellishly on.

There's a camp of crackho's living in Alex's back yard. Alison and I spent hours looking for Homescrub and I walked through their encampment many times searching for her. A tent village haphazardly put together with picnic lawn awnings connecting them all. Christmas lights, light ropes and stereo equipment hooked up snake like to power cords coming from the house. And just to make sure it was a complete fire hazard, candles and kerosene lanterns everywhere. (The thought of all those people using the one bathroom, yuk disgusting.)

How could I leave my little lamb in the lair of a meth addicted Golem? Both Damien and Kevin say 'no honey, you were doing the best you could. It seemed like a good solution to a bad situation.' Poor Scrub. She had waited patiently while I mended. Two and a half years moving from house to house, state to state, she was blind but every time I relocated, she adapted better than I did. As long as she was with me, she was fine. She would have loved this small light box. She should have died here.

Alison confronted Tweak as his entourage watched. His shriek fest didn't work on her and she grilled him all afternoon. He's so guilty it sweats off him like spit. Alexander, head down and wearing a hoodie, hid out side of the sliding glass door, afraid to speak or even look at any of us, scared shitless of confrontation. The bastard sniveled up to me when I was alone, 'I'm disappointed in you! And very disappointed in Alison! You know Tweak has a martyr complex! How could you talk to him like that?' I was rendered speechless by this pathetic version of reality. He wouldn't stand up to his drug addicted boyfriend but was fine with hiding in the bushes to attack his grieving friend? I screamed Fuck You and he slinked off a cowering clown.

There's another loser living on their couch. Far too sleepy and fat to be a speed freak, he seems another lazy boy looking for a free place to stay in exchange for sucked dick. 'Cats go outside when they're going to die,' the freak mumbled, determined to stick up for his meal ticket. Alison called her vet and asked 'would she suddenly go outside if she had been scared of the outdoors her whole life?' 'No, cats will usually go someplace where they feel comfortable.' Definitely not outside. It's the reason she lived so long, I'm sure of it.

None of my other cats had made old age. Coyotes, cars and the quake of '94 got them all. My first cat was Thrbt (he had no vowels). Hit by a car. Mickey (kitty #2) and I missed Thrbt so much; I went to the pound to get him a friend. I was heading for the 'Cat Room' where socialized cats frolicked. Cats that didn't play well with others were in individual cages against the wall; I was ignoring them. I heard Howling Meowling! La la la, I'm not listening—but I was Lot's wife—I turned. I opened her cage and she leaped onto me, wrapped back legs around my tummy front legs shoulders and buried her face in my neck, still crying. What could I do, peel her off and stuff her back in the cage? I was salt. I took her to the desk and said, 'I'll wear this home…' Four years later Mickey slipped out of my apartment during the Hollywood Christmas Parade. Ten thousand people pack the streets and it disoriented him. I found his little body later that week on the corner of Yucca and Vine. I was crushed.

Homescrub my Boa Constrictor, Bat Face and I lived in happy pet harmony. Boas won't try to eat anything that's too big and Homescrub regarded Bat Face with detached amusement. I was at the pet shop picking up rats for the snakes dinner when I saw the dearest kitten sitting in a cage. She had a harlequin face. Perfect squares of orange and black. Couldn't resist her and broke my rule of pound only pets. Nirvana, Stigmata, Euthanasia, no name seemed to stick. I ended up calling her Kitty Come Here. She was a tiny elf with huge eyes.

Kitty Come Here would sit up on my shoes and play with my laces as I lay on the floor, feet in the air. She would chase the plastic jingle balls I bought at Ralph's and lay them at my feet. She also ran out into the courtyard whenever she could and once got stuck in the abandoned muscle car in the back alley. (Mr Right Now jimmied the hood with a crow bar to get her out.)

The day I realized she was pregnant was a shocker. At eight months old, I'd never even realized she was in heat. She had two kittens Icky Groucho and Lupo the Butcher. They were so wee, so adorable. Icky Groucho died ten days later. Distraught, I took Kitty Come Here and little Lupo to the vet. 'This cat is too little to have kittens, he told me, and she's not producing milk.' Icky Groucho had starved to death! He sent me home with a teensy bottle and formula for Lupo the Butcher. I had to feed her every couple of hours so took her to work with me.

I was doing extra work on Ed Wood. Technically, I'd said goodbye extra work years earlier but would make an exception for great directors. (Like Postcards From the Edge, directed by Mike Nichols.) Ed Wood was directed by Tim Burton whom I admired for his individuality and it starred Johnny Dep who is just yummy. I spent a week watching Dep do a strip tease to a leopard spotted bikini in a meat locker. In between set ups I would slip away to fall deeper and deeper in love with Lupo the Butcher; a calico ball mewling for formula, then falling asleep in the palm of my hand when satiated. Kitty Come Here was would move her to a different spot each night, trying to keep me from taking her in the morning.

It shocked us both when she died. Dressed like a harem girl, I held her in my hands on Warner's back as she breathed her last. Three tentative, fragile weeks here and then back to the abyss. Long enough to fall completely and hopelessly in love. I didn't know how I was going to break it to Kitty Come Here. She ran across the room to meet me as I walked in and looked up expectantly / happily. I started crying as I set down the carrying cage and opened the door. 'I'm so sorry, baby.' She didn't pick her up like I was expecting her to, she lay down by the open door and put her head on her paws. It broke my heart.

She sat by my side as I buried Lupo the Butcher next to Icky Groucho under the rose bushes in front of the building. We were sitting there quietly in the moonlight and were joined by another cat, a black Tom. The three of us made an odd, sad tableau. We sat there for what in retrospect seems like hours but in reality, maybe twenty or thirty minutes. The Tom was their father I have no doubt. I finally picked up Kitty Come Here and took her inside. She never reverted to her wacky former self she was always subdued.

A bit later, the Northridge quake hit. (On January 17th, Dad's birthday.) Homescrub, always the scaredy cat, hid under the fallen clothes rack in the closet but Kitty Come Here disappeared into the morning mist. I like to think that she found someone else to take her in, that she didn't get stuck in another car or get hit by one; it was just too sad a place for her to stay.

I'm such an idiot.

I finally stopped crying about Home Scrub and now I'm crying about Kitty Come Here. Home Scrub was my success story. Her refusal to go more than a few steps from the door kept her safe. More and more these last years she slept her days away, dreaming kitty dreams. She should have dreamed her way into Kitty Heaven comfortable in my company. I knew she was going soon and wanted to hold her in my arms when she left. My cat was my Achilles heel, that's why Golem tossed her outside the fence. She was my Sweet Kitty Bear for seventeen years. She deserved a better end than being ripped apart by coyotes.

June 5, 2004—Venice Beach

Enter the Skull Farm, Ronald Regan.

Sunday June 6

Skull Farm—Ray Charles. Saw him at the Bowl in 2001. Rest in Peace, gentlemen. (Deaths come in 3's)

Finally moved my bedroom in, I've been sleeping on the floor for the past two weeks. I only saved bedroom furniture. Bed, dresser, bookshelf, vanity— Gram's furniture. As I watched Nancy standing over Ronnie's coffin / frail and sad, I thought of Gram sitting in the hospital as grandfather lay dying. He was asleep. 'How can you leave me?' She spoke so softly I could barely hear. Crushed. Fifty plus years of marriage. My poor poor granny. I was 16 when my grandfather died and was self involved the way sixteen year olds are. I wish I would have gone to her, put my arms around her and told her I loved her. Not knowing what to do or say, I did nothing and said nothing. Grandpa slept, Granny was locked in grief and I looked out the window at falling snow, waiting for Mom.

Cut to a year later: I would go out to Granny's and clean, she would give me a few bucks, we would chit chat. My jeans zipper was broken / don't remember how it came up / she was almost blind, had been for years. 'I can fix that for you,' she said happily. I wasn't sure she could do it and said so. 'I can change a zipper, I've done it a hundred times,' she chided. The next day or following week, she gave me the jeans back and the zipper was replaced clumsily—I got *angry* about it. 'They look horrible,' I said or something just as mean. The sands of time have etched away the actual dialogue but I remember the exchange hurt her. Sweet lonely Gram. She was looking for things to fill her day she was still grieving. Who gives a shit about a pair of jeans? How hard would have it been to just take them from her and say thanks honey, they look great. Watching Nancy Regan this afternoon brought those memories back and I've been crying all day. Not just a tear either, hopelessly sobbing. My face is too puffed to go out.

Gram lived another ten years. I saw her a lot before I moved to LA and every summer after. My first year of college she had to spend a few weeks in a nursing home from some ailment that left her temporarily wheelchair bound. I was driving her car, a big beautiful '72 Buick Le Saber. (Super fun at eighteen) and I visited daily. She didn't like the nursing home, bright, clean and well staffed it was hospital-ish. I knew the thought of spending the rest of her life in one was horrifying. I'd help her to the wheelchair and put my leather motorcycle jacket on her tiny shoulders. 'Let's see how fast this baby goes!' 'Don't be silly,' she'd say smiling and we were off. I would get a running start then lean fore ward on my arms and lift my feet. Back and forth past the nurses station, past the television room and the other residents who would stare, surprised at first, then wistfully as the days went by. Of course she knew I loved her. She raised four kids, I'm sure she remembered how surly and appalling teenagers could be still, Granny Gram forgive me.

2007

My depression would last. Homescrub's death started it and being alone exacerbated it. I wrote pages and pages of all the shit I was sorry about or wished I'd done differently but aside from being mean to Gram, finishing college and smoking cigarettes are the only two that stick. I wish I'd finished school because I flailed around for years doing nothing. I wanted to move to LA but was fearful about going alone. (Didn't recognize it as fear until years later.) I was aimless and spent a lot of time in the Caribbean, Miami, Tampa. Cohoon was my friend and he had a fun crew. And fuck Cigarettes, it was horrid being addicted.

Those few weeks I spent at Bruce and Tom's I was happy for the first time in a long time. I needed peace or I wasn't going to make it. I had to let

Homescrub's murder go. After spending thousands on Shrink, I couldn't stand the thought of searching for another one.

Shrink had called to ask why I had walked out; I told her that thinking and thinking and then coming up with a strange word like 'compromised' didn't have hidden meaning. Aphasia is a CVA symptom, dip shit. She admitted that she *didn't have experience with stroke survivors* but insisted it didn't matter. (She's telling someone suffering from brain damage that her BD doesn't matter.) She was a good therapist for functioning minds—dealing with emergency Damien trauma for example—but Shrink lied to me about her experience and I felt used.

'Ultimately, no one can extract from things,
books included, more than he already knows.
What one has no access to through experience one has no ear for.'

—Nietzsche

I was lonely but romantically uninterested in the men I'd been meeting in Venice. You congregate most with the people you work with. Not working? Neither are the majority of people you meet. Before the CVA, the type of man I liked was same age as me or older, accomplished, fun and funny and usually a workaholic doing something he loved. (Tony was an anomaly, it was unusual to let beauty trump substance. I think women in the entertainment industry have our midlife crises' at thirty, not forty like everyone else and Tony was the product of mine.) I never found the perfect match and never got Baby-Fever. I always told myself if I Suddenly Must Reproduce, I gave myself permission but it never came up. If I'd met Mr Right and he'd wanted children, I would have had one and adopted one but I had no interest in dealing with a baby alone.

I always blamed the business. LA has an overabundance of smart beautiful women but the men are just, ehh. Not everyone, I dated fun men but no love connection. He proposed to me a couple times but I couldn't marry a man if we didn't both feel it, I couldn't do that to a friend. (I may have been more mercenary if I'd caught Baby-Fever but I didn't have to find out.) When

Right Now loved me when I really liked him, when I loved him, he really liked me.

The LA basin is full of wanna bee's, shysters, carnival barkers and delusional freaks, ranging from mildly annoying to Dangerous; being a smart female is to be aware of your status as prey to these jerks and not fall victim to a predator. My girlfriends and I would travel as an entourage for whomever in the pack needed it that minute, party hopping Cast & Crew shin-digs, screenings. Mr Right Now is still busy being productive. Me? I'm alone most of the time.

2007

I *finally* told Coolchick about my night pain in July of 2004. She said, 'I thought so, it always seemed too soon,' and started a low dose of maintenance Oxycodone. To the brain, pain becomes 'normal' after a year and harder to eradicate. Once again, balking hurt me.

I saw Litzel (Goodfella's prescription for Pilates) twice a week for a couple months. She was great, pushed me, helped me to fine tune the workout prosthetics Robin the hand guy had been making for me. I told her I missed flying trapeze, for a warm up swing I used to hang by my knees and let my back stretch, Litzel helped me hang upside down. Pilates is fun—I love being upside down—and love the wacky S&M look of the machines and the dimly lit room. Working out made me feel better but often it was just for that hour. I would wake in stroke pain between five and seven, watch TV and wait for my medication to work. Hit the beach eight-ish, have coffee and watch the boardwalk come to life. Things could have been worse, I was aware and thankful but *so lonely*.

My neighbors were inhuman yuppie nightmares that absolutely ignored me. If I was dragging groceries or dragging laundry, they let me drag. Except for Simpering Neighbor who whined at me Once, I was invisible. It added to the surrealism.

Aside: There were three parking spots for my building and three storage spaces but they weren't vulture'd together. Life would have been a bit easier if My Storage was in front of My Van. Simpering Neighbor told me, 'you shouldn't even have that parking space that should be ours! And—my husband has to have easy access to his surfboards!' Another snail on the camel. I started weeping and I turned my back to SN. 'That's all I have to say, I'm leaving now.' She sniveled away and left me standing there, a crying gimp being a Pain In Her Ass!

July 2004—Venice, CA

Monday at Walgreen's pharmacy: The woman behind the counter asked when I was injured then couldn't believe the answer. 'Two years? TWO YEARS…!? She kept screeching louder and louder until everyone was staring at The Gimp. 'Well <u>try to have</u> a good day! As good as you can!!!' Shrill and invasive, she chicken clucked and pursed her lips, first the sad hang dog face then a You'll NEVER have a good life, I PITY YOU, combo. Yet another thing I have to look forward to forever and ever and ever. (Channeling the twins from The Shining.)

Addicted to The BBC World News, Charlie Rose and The News Hour with Jim Lear all on PBS; the only news that's propaganda free is public broadcast. US and UK soldiers have been abusing Arab prisoners in a freakish sadomasochist gay sex way, yet the White House wonders why the Abu Garab scandal won't disappear. The Corporate Administration 'winning hearts and minds.' Idiots.

Friday: Hit the Teriyaki shop on the boardwalk for am coffee. They have tables outside under umbrellas and I'm trying to read again, short stuff, Dad sent some Orwell, a collection of his essays—he is a great great writer but so *easily* racist it astounds—Africans and Indians are inferior. Dot. Circa 1930. It made me feel a little better about the species, we are moving forward, just too slow to see, generation by generation not decade by decade.

Allritini successfully removed a neuroma from my right kneecap this week. When I wiped out at Melinda's in the winter of '03 it had never healed. I thought it was a bone chip but it was a nerve. I got two cortisone shots in June but it only stopped the pain for a minute.

'Fame is like a river, that bereth up things light and swollen
and drowns things weighty and solid.'

—Francis Bacon (1561–1626)

2007

I was in Playboy March '95. They were doing a pictorial of stuntwomen; there was grumbling from some females in the community about Playboy Vultures making women Objects but I love that silly old magazine (the 1st Playmate was MM) and was flattered to be asked. They made me look great of course. I remember thinking; years from now I'll look back on The Babe I Used to Be, but it was only seven. (For the 'stunt' shot we lit my arms on fire! Skin-mag Ouiji?)

I wanted Café Deb to be Playboy-ish fun. Tame no porn (porn, yuk.) I found local kids on Craig's list to tutor me and Husband gave me the programs. Dreamweaver for web design and Photoshop for pictures. Learning with tutors was a victory, I could learn and retain. I was baby-stepping CafeDeb. com but moving forward. It would have eight different pages to peruse. Front page, gallery, movies, cafedub (music) deblog (I shot graffiti for a couple years, that went in the blog) contact, links and Debbie Likes 2 Read, which was my favorite; I could finally do something with all those old short stories. Damien (using hilarious pseudonym's) Monk and MySpace Friends contributed stories.

Before my injury, I was happy with occasional bouts of depression. Post: Opposite. I was so tired of being so sad. CafeDeb was lighthearted fun and I needed it. I'd eventually have male models too but wanted to start female.

July 2004—Venice Beach

Saw Ramayana again last night. They've been on tour for a year. Went with Calvin and a couple of his buddies, stayed out late having dinner with Dez and Rich and laughing with acquaintance friends I haven't seen since before my injury.

Got home and the back gate was locked! My gate key was inside. I didn't know what to do it was after one. I went and found a shelf someone had thrown out by the dumpster and dragged it up the back stairs to the gate. Small gate, not too imposing, comes up to my neck. I climbed up the rickety shelf then swung my left leg (the un-compromised one) over the spiky rails. Stay calm you can do this. I was scared but determined. I reached my left toe through the bars ½ way down and got a little hold. I swung my right leg up BUT—pants cuff was hooked on top. Fortunately, I slowly reached the ground with my left leg and then was able to use my left arm to lift my right pants leg off the spike. Shaking when finished, I was proud of my accomplishment (that was a 'split' thank you Pilates) and sad to think of how completely fucked I am. Capable woman to shaking cripple (she's live and on the inside…if she's not real…) Barely able to make it over a five foot fence. Small physical steps forward, big mental leaps back.

'…it was almost perfect a good omen
The Princess listened to confessions
of an actor on a lifeboat to Ararat
he talked about making a good script great
she ruminated on Chico, Harpo, Groucho and sometimes Zeppo
starting from scratch in the age of reason…'

~Al Christ

Haven't eaten today, did I eat yesterday? Must have. I know I had a power bar / not enough. I'm not taking care of myself, not taking vitamins. And I'm *not strong*. I hate it when people say that to me; Allritini the other day, '…you're so strong; a lot of people would have given up.' I have given up; you just don't want to acknowledge it. I'm not strong I'm falling apart. I barely function; spend most of my time inside, hiding from experience. The attention attracting three fingered troll gimping along. The sorry looks, the pitying or grossed out stares and that quick look away before eye contact. It's better if you're with someone but I'm always alone. I go for days without speaking except to order smoothies at the coffee shop. That sounds like giving up. I'm so sorry for myself it's pathetic. Didn't bother enlightening, why wake up the birds?

End of July 2004—4:46 am—Boston MA

Decided to change scenery, I've been suicidal so long I'm boring myself to death.

Georgene is custody battling with The Cretin. My problems are on a slo-mo train to The Island of Misfit Toys. Her nightmare should be over next week. The Cretin has the kid this week so we decided to go to Plymouth a small beach town a couple hours away. Took photos all afternoon the pier, the statues, the old sailing ships, the freakin' rock. Then, somehow lost them downloading and cried. (Inappropriate CVA response.) Funny thing though, that rock.

'…The pilgrims landed at Plymouth Rock…'

—all my grade school teachers

Whenever I'd heard about Plymouth Rock—usually Thanksgiving—I assumed it was big enough for boats to land and Pilgrims to trample. Surrounded by gaudy, Romanesque pillars, there's a board walk along the shore like a crescent moon. We parked a quarter of a mile away and were meandering along, looking at kitsch and trinkets, buying postcards and refrigerator magnets.

'We must be over the top of it…' I said as we closed in on the tourist entanglement; I imagined a tremendous stone jutting out of the surf. We walked up and looked down. We both started laughing. It was simply any old rock, the size of a big television, sitting on the sand. Someone had carved

1620 in it. A ship full of people couldn't 'land' on it. The vulture next to it said the rock had been 'found' again 75 years after the pilgrims arrived and brought here to this spot. The first American Tourist Trap. Sublime.

People in The News are Lance Armstrong and Christopher Reeve. Armstrong's now divorced and dating Cheryl Crow and Reeve is always the tireless advocate. Last summer I thought of them constantly. I read my babble from last summer and it breaks my heart. I've accomplished nothing and my cat's dead. Smoking more pot though, that's something.

> '...four five six c'mon and get your kicks
> you don't need money
> when you look like that, honey...'

> paraphrasing Jet & Morgan Stanley

A Morgan Stanley broker said that to me mid 90's. I called the office to complain about by my investment monkey, he was ignoring my meager IRA investments. The manager said he'd replace him. The next morning a cocky young man called. 'Hi Babe! Monkey has your Xmas cards in your file! (I used to send foto holiday cards.) You're HOT! You don't have to worry about money when you look like that! I handle all these millionaire guys, ugly as shit! You're incredible!' I asked to talk with the manager again. 'So... I shouldn't feel bad when I'm when I'm 70 eating cat food in a freezing apartment because I was HOT when I was 30? This is what you thought I wanted?'

If you're a rich prick, invest with Morgan Stanley but if you're an attractive woman, ignore the future because you're HOT NOW!

2007

Georgene prevailed in court and could move The Cretin's daughter back to Phoenix; I left her packing with her family and stopped by my family compound on the way back to LA. Cousins were visiting and everyone was cabin bound. It was a mistake. I didn't talk about my problems with George and Co—until the crisis was over, focus was on beating The Cretin—rightly so.

But there would be no 'unpleasant talk' at the cabin either. Mom took me aside and told me to cheer up. I don't think Mom's insistence on a brave face and no talk of injury was intentionally cruel; my parents grew up in a different world. Born in the 30's, little kids during The Great Depression, no money, prohibition, everyone's father drank, you didn't talk about it. Teenagers in the 40's, Pearl Harbor, the horror of war, the men that returned weren't the same. You didn't talk about that either.

'…kill yourself when you get home
kill yourself when you get home…'

—August's Mantra

I couldn't leave a body behind for my relatives to throw off the island. That would eff a vacation.

August 2004—Smallville

Clinging to a sponge. Rag coming over later, we'll see how that goes.

August a week later—Smallville

Rag snubbed me *again.* He called to cancel last Monday, asked if I wanted to get together Tuesday. I said sure—the prick never came—never called. I've been friends with this man for 25 years. It's unsettling, like the furniture's suddenly been rearranged.

Damien drove up to Smallville to apologize (again) and drive me back to Minneapolis. Seems like years since he left LA. He's still in limbo, waiting for the gray bar hotel. Good to see him, forgive him and have a few laughs. He took responsibility for his bullshit, (it's probably what's kept him alive this long.)

2007

I was losing it in Smallville, hitting myself in the head with my cane hard enough to form lumps. I would be floating above watching, looked painful.

'Up to a certain point in my life I have known more ups and downs,
I do believe, than fall to the lot of the ordinary man.'

—Henry Miller, Big Sur

Back in LA. Quit weed for a minute. Helped with droning pain but was making me paranoid to go out. Still daydreaming about suicide; current favorite: Driving a convertible out to a point in Malibu as the sun is setting and having a cocktail of sleeping pills, pain killers and a slushy mocha thingy from Starbucks. Then some unlucky jogger finds the body, your family has to deal with the body… ah, fantasy wrecked.

Andy Warhol wished we would just disappear when we died. That would be Perfect. I'm not going to kill myself but a girl can day dream.

September 2004—Venice Beach

Sent Victoria Burroughs an email, told her what had happened to me and she left a sweet message on my voice mail. 'I wish I had known I wish I'd been in the loop!' Tony and Kevin had a lot on their minds; they compiled a huge list of people, most of whom I didn't know, for website updates but they didn't think to access the address book in my laptop. People disappear, it happens all the time in big cities, unless you know them well, you let them go.

2007

I hung out with Victoria's crew for a few Saturday's. They find homes for hard to place rescue dogs, Pit Bulls, Staffordshire Terriers, Rottweilers… Victoria and Co hit the shelters in depressed neighborhoods and save sweethearts from unfair death sentences—the dogs don't know they're supposed to be vicious—they love everyone desperately. I would take the young rammy ones for runs / throw sticks / have fun. But it wasn't anymore and wasn't self pity for a change; (having a run with a big happy dog is fun but I was realistic and could still enjoy walking calmer animals) I was volunteering with right wing actors. (Who knew they existed? I thought Alison was a glitch.)

A 19 yr old man: 'I won't audition for anything unpatriotic!' Angry about an anti-war audition he'd just picked up 'sides' for (the scene or scenes from the script the actors are auditioning for.) I told him if he was serious about acting he shouldn't be a diva at the outset of his career, he'd kill it before it had a chance. 'It's a small town honey, news travels.' 'Those people won't be in business for long!' Cocky and delusional, he's talking about a studio. Blue eyes, blonde cropped hair, healthy, tall, athletic, Aryan, creepy. I couldn't understand young men being brainwashed into fascism by the Bumbling Bush Co. Mussolini, Eva Peron, Hugo Chavez—I can see—but *Bush*?

Nothing pisses off war mongers like someone telling them war is wrong. I'm a pacifist, diplomacy seems obvious and this illegal war is all about the Benjamin's. Duh. But saying Saudi's flying into US buildings for Allah had nothing to do with secular Saddam in Iraq was met with angry disbelief. I'd have a pack of them barking at me. They believe every lie they're told. They live with and (try to) work in this industry and they still *blindly believe the media*? Absurd. If I brought up something that couldn't be argued away, the prison scandal for example, they changed the subject.

Idiotic blood lust took the fun out of volunteering. I can't remember what BS excuse I gave Victoria, I think just told her I was leaving town. I didn't want to diss the dip shits because they're volunteering for a worthwhile organization.

Labor Day, September 2004—Venice Beach, late afternoon

Coolchick wanted to try a different drug for stroke symptoms—I love that she doesn't give up. First I had to get off Baclofen jesuschrist my stroke symptoms seem as bad as 2002! Depressing.

I creaked through a couple days of electrocution Baclofen free then had a bad reaction to the new stuff. Zanafex's generic, Tizandine. (I wonder if they're different, always suspicious of generic, a lot don't work for me.) Heart pounding in chest all day; I can still hear it in my ears. Couldn't eat anything, stroke symptoms all down my right side (pointing toe, curling arm) can't stop yawning, jaw clenching, horrid taste of metal. Strong effing drug. Thank Shiva Law & Order SVU is having a labor day marathon, been watching all day waiting for this drug to wear off.

2007

Goodfella kept pushing for more surgery. Sand the thin skin off the back of my hand, put Integra over it and then cover that in a month with a skin graft from my leg. I weirdly started thinking seriously about it. Still cant explain why I was still listening to the idiot, something about the difficulty involved in finding another surgeon.

Robin talked to Bio Concepts (the company that makes pressure garments) and sent them exact measurements of my hand. Two and a ½ years after the fire, my wounds were finally closed. No more bandages! I presumably would have to wear a pressure glove forever. My fingers don't bend, so they swell. (Edema) I was hoping to get a few colors.

Dr Carol was in town for a wedding weekend. We went to the beach for dinner; she was surprised that I never hear from the trapeze gang. 'Well, I don't keep in touch with them,' I excused; they were the first to go. 'They should keep in touch with you!' She was surprised and (like Kev) didn't quite believe me. I was obviously depressed and depression makes you hide in a hole. Right on cue: Trapeze Friend called Dr Carol—chatter chat, chatter chat, hey I'm at the beach with Alisa, want to say hi? Long pause. 'OK, bye.' She hung up. 'Something was burning on the stove?' I guessed. 'He was late picking up his son.' We looked at each other. The reality of my loneliness took a minute to sink. She told me it was eerie, she always assumed we were good friends. 'We were.' That's the first thing healthy people say about Friend Drop Phenomena: 'They weren't REAL friends!' But with the few notable exceptions, they were.

The entertainment industry is a huge ocean liner going full speed ahead. It takes a speed boat and a bit of luck to catch it but once you embark it envelopes you. It's lavish, ridiculously so, but satisfying after that bumpy ride; you get accustomed to cosseting remarkably fast. The big suites house the stars (and they change a lot) but the boat holds thousands and everyone's comfortable. A lot of people are born at sea, not just actors but stunt people, camera men, the crafts unions, writers. Everyone on board is Cocooned from the outside world. It's Exclusive, which makes it Desirable. A lot of folks want on and some want off but the ship never stops and never slows down.

> '...I'm ignoring all the dumb stuff
> cause nothing good ever comes from it...'
>
> paraphrasing Cypress Hill

Allritini removed a hornet's nest of neuromas in my left ankle the day before I left for my brothers in the South Pacific. It'd been annoying for years but it didn't occur to me to eliminate it until I had the neuroma removed from my knee. Unfortunately it backfired.

October 2004—Guam, South Pacific

Sitting at the kitchen table with a kitten on my lap. I'm lonely. The family is in the Philippines shopping. The kitten is six weeks old and like most babies, hollers half the day, sleeps half the day. Made me miss Homescrub, which made me think of Alexander. I wanted closure / apology. Embarrassed or ashamed—probably both—enough time had passed for him to pull a Catherine. I knew I'd never hear from him again. I called him at work. 'This is Alexander the Great,' he answered, business like. 'Hey, it's Alisa.' He switched to his informal sad voice. 'Oh hi...what have you been up to?' 'I'm visiting my brother in Guam. Something made me think of you, I was wondering if I was ever going to hear from you again.'

'I've been super busy...' He launched into work tirade. He's there all the time, practically sleeps there. Work, work, work, they have him enslaved, new projects, old projects, he can barely keep up, he can hardly find time to eat. '…not that I'm complaining,' he added when it became ridiculous. 'I left a television stand over there. Black iron with turquoise pottery, Calvin can pick it up; he lives in Highland Park now.' 'Does he? I haven't seen him. I haven't seen anybody.' Why wonder why—Calvin doesn't do meth, has a kid, has a job. Calm down, bitch. You're not going to get steamed; I changed the subject. 'How was Burning Man?' 'Not fun, not at all. Not like past years, I didn't enjoy myself. I think everyone was saying that, did anyone else tell you they didn't have a good time?' Nope. Alex perked up; 'how's Damien?' he had a crush on the tall straight man. 'Is he in LA?' 'No, Minnesota.' 'Say hello for me.' Damien said he'd like to beat the shit out of him. 'Alex, you don't have a friend in Damien any more.' 'Why?' I couldn't believe his denial. 'Remember Homescrub? My cat?'

Long, long, long, pause. I didn't say anything. Now would be the time to express regret, you emotionally anemic putty man. I waited. 'Have you noticed how, I don't know, people are flaky? They say that community is everything but you can't count on them. They talk a good game but…' he trailed off. 'Honey, you are forty six and hanging with beautiful twenty-something party people. You're the old man with the big house, what do you expect?' 'I don't know…' 'Was there *anything* you wanted to say to me?' 'You know, I just work, I don't call anybody.' I had to laugh. 'That's your story and you're sticking to it?' No response, I hung up.

'…you'll have to shoot me like rabid dog
better not miss
because I'm not going to lay down and die easily
some say life is a bitch
ask that last little sniveler
he dug his own ditch…'

paraphrasing Cypress Hill

Skull Farm: Christopher Reeve, Rest in Peace brother. Thank you.

I had a bad fall in the kitchen the other day. A few nephews and I were weighing ourselves. My turn, I don't use a cane indoors, I got on fine but stepping off the scale sideways I started to tip. The babysitter (a 25 yr old man) and three boys watched me go, it was in slow motion. Just like that time in Rancho only no big nurse zooming to my rescue. WHAM! Left hip / hurt so bad that I thought it had broken. The weirdest is how *none of us* could talk or move—like that time in Rancho—the babysitter was so close all he had to do was stick out his arm but he was frozen too. Crazee.

2007

I might have fractured it but didn't get an X-ray from Guam's cartoon ER. I was creaking like a ninety year old for three weeks—the neuoroma's on My Left Foot were constant electric shocks, I couldn't wear socks, just a big lose slipper. Thank You Allah for poppies! I doubled my pain meds, I couldn't decide which pain was more hideous, they were so different.

Gimp Ville / Stroke Land / Scar Town and Mismatched Shoes on the Falling Clown. I was a scary freak to my nephews. We politely talked about school at dinner and then they avoided me. Broke my heart but I couldn't think of a way to show them Alisa was still there. My brother and his wife were always working and they had no television! Good idea if you're raising a pack of wolves but I had constant TV when I was home; white noise, I was going through withdrawals.

Ross had a Koran in his library and I read it. Expecting to find (actively looking for) negativity and condescension about women but couldn't find any, it was a normal religious read. Lead a good life, love Allah, be compassionate, give to the poor, love each other. That cheered me.

But Guam is a sad little rock. Ross and Wife live on a hill in absolute silence. The birds are dead, killed by Brown snakes. (Not indigenous, brought in accidentally on airfreight.) Black butterflies flitter noiselessly like daylight bats and huge spider webs are everywhere and need to be swept regularly. I would float in their pool in the mornings. It's circular and above ground; four feet deep so I didn't have to worry about drowning. I would try and swim for a minute then spend an hour laying on a floatie and watching dragon flies mate. With my wrist fused, my right arm was clumsy and felt frail; my right leg couldn't kick coordinated. I knew I should be taking advantage of the warm private pool, the fact that I didn't reinforced my gloom. I was a loser. I was ridiculously sorry for myself and tried to get a grip. Spent a lot of time on the net Googling: Stages of Grief—Five, seven, nine? Lots of theory's and so much disagreement I eventually concluded it was all bullshit. Everyone handles grief in his or her own way, there's no formula. Broken and fractured hips / it was most likely badly bruised. Paranoia, hypochondria, depression, insanity, burns, brain injuries, neuromas and sinks.

I called Allritini's office and emailed a few times—no response—which pissed me off. I began obsessing on the procedure; he was an hour late, I'd almost left. He was cocky, overly confident and I'd made an observation at the time of the change a few short years had made in him. I began to hate, hate is a lot like love, if you think you hate someone you do. Irrational and CVA related but a real emotion.

After three weeks my hip felt walk able. I decided to try Bali. A test, I would do four days.

November, 2004—Guam

Back from Bali. Over populated, skyscraper unemployment, rice fields being replaced with condos and if a crippled woman is considered a mark, your nation is a mess. They became self governing 1965. Forty years is long enough to completely eff a country.

2007

Depression is malevolent. I did have fun in Bali; yes it's over populated and bla bla but gimp or not I was still from the US and therefore wealthy. Reality is different in Indonesia. I met a sweet kid when I got off the plane. Kertut was a baggage cat for Continental and he took a shine to me. He picked me up from my hotels in the mornings (I stayed in three different places) and drove me around on his motorcycle. The Monkey Forrest had us laughing our heads off. He lived with his brothers' family and they were great. Can't beat a $5 massage, I had eight in four days. I adored the temples, thousands of them, ornate and inviting. However, I answered my test, traveling alone was a lot harder. I could still travel but I had to come to terms with 'permanent physical disabilities.' Still balking.

November 2004—Venice Beach

> '....I'm a dogmatic punch in your face
> ruining your prospectus
> don't fall for spin anytime from anybody
> I'm a brilliant machiavellian and a threat to your cocoon
> now you want to incarcerate me
> because a sniveling little bitch tried to shoot me
> self-preservation is instinctual
> I killed him in self defense...'

> paraphrasing Cypress Hill

I love CH especially their old stuff. This is from 1990, I would rhyme along, knew every word. Post CVA no way. I can't rap, can't think that fast anymore, can't remember lyrics I've known for fourteen years.

I switched insurance to Husband's without incident, thank Allah. Goodfella is still peddling surgery, he asked me to go see Doctor Hacksaw. Did I really remember him Snidely Wiplashing around? He seemed more like Doctor Droopy Dog. (Morphine mystery.) He said he could cut off a few inches of ulna and make the bone blunt. Didn't have an answer as to how it would look.

2007

When I returned from Guam I had gained twenty pounds. 135! That's fatter than my We Ho meltdown. I got serious about my diet and joined a new gym in Santa Monica. Everything New, no man sweat all over the machines yet. Nice staff and nobody went in the afternoons but the regulars. (Everyone can get the staring out of the way. Yes I walk with a cane, no you're not seeing things I am missing a finger, yes I'm human.)

More stroke insight: I realized my right side limbs weren't controlled by gravity. (Betsy told me the name of the nerve damaged, it affect's a lot of stroke survivors.) I would see my arm rising above my waist *without feeling it*. Usually when walking. I would push it down with my left hand. I still *think* about pushing it back down when it starts to float (usually in the am) but I can do it with my mind now. My elbow won't hang straight unless I think it down. Same thing with my right leg, I walked with my right knee bent for two years. I couldn't get it to straighten.

> Aside: Rancho memory, Physical Therapist laughing at me, 'you look like Groucho Marx.' Both knees were bent when I tried to walk. She didn't tell me the name of the nerve that was damaged or how to deal with it, just a nasty laugh. It was after The Polanski incident and she was still angry at The Patient.

I put a five pound weight on my compromised ankle and left it on for the next year. My right hip was always sore but it helped get gravity back in my leg. I still wear it occasionally. I had the hand surgery scheduled for Jan 10th but felt uneasy and put it off.

December 2004 / Venice

One evening on the phone with Dad, he was giving me a pep talk, you're doing well, you're smart, you should get a job or something that gets you out with people, you love being social, you have so many friends. Grrr! Bark Bark! I told him those friends had melted away—I was mean to my father, broke a freakin' commandment.

> 'I am too inquisitive; to questionable too high spirited to rest content with a crude answer. God is a crude answer, a piece of indelicacy against us thinkers—fundamentally even a crude prohibition to us: you shall not think!'

—Nietzsche

The Stuntwoman's Foundation gave me $3000. It was welcome! $900 a month rent was steep; I'd been living frugally and was spending roughly two grand a month. With $430 from SSDI and wilting residuals I was in the red; living off of the money raised by Tony and Kevin in 2002.

A woman from their board befriended me. Mrs X came to help me fill out their application—a formality for their files—then took me to lunch. There was something off about her and I wasn't immune to the grapevine. Fifteen years ago Friend told me horrific stories of a Monster Boyfriend, crazee beatings, midnight police intervention, restraining order; Friend had to move to a gated community. That boyfriend was Mr X—Mrs X said she was happy they had a nice life but I was suspicious; of men in general and evil ones in particular. Evil never really disappears, it hides.

She asked me if I needed any help and I did. My attorneys had been asking for back taxes, ten years if I had them—I did but they were boxed up in the storage space. Mrs X came down and helped and we found them. We had boxes of stuff in the carport, books and toys I wanted to give to her kids, stuff to go in my hut and some back in storage. Mrs X helped me with a genuine smile and happy chatter and I was glad to be done with The Chore. I found my jewelry. I keep it in a crystal egg, it was just sitting in a box of books. I meant to bring it in but forgot about it for a couple days. When I did remember, I started obsessing. Did it get left out? Did it get put in a bag and tossed, mistaken for garbage? We tossed so many empty bags and boxes, or maybe she took it with the stuff for the kids? I didn't think she was a thief but she was a little spacey.

Nervously I called and told her I was obsessing. 'I'll come and help you look, it's probably in the storage space.' I went to sleep feeling relief. My phone rang early, five am. 'Are you Accusing Me!' A deep voice, I didn't recognize it for a minute. *'Are you accusing me!?'* It was Mrs X low and snarling, she was *pissed*. I scrambled for words vultures vultures 'I don't think you stole anything I think you may have spaced it...' 'I'm not coming down! I was trying to give you love! And you Won't Accept Love! You have never accepted love from anyone! Even before your accident!!!' ohmygodshesanutbag 'You don't know me,' I said. 'Well I know people who know you!' I wanted to laugh at that but I tasted metal. 'Who, Mrs X? Who do you know that knows me?' Click. Wow. That was scary / mean and freakish.

2007

Shaken, what a way to wake up. I have never accepted love from Mr X, perhaps? He had to know what I thought of him. It was 7 am in MN, I called and talked to Betsy (I knew she'd be up with the kids.) Doth Mrs X protest too much? I never accused her of anything. Betsy thought Mrs X could be borderline considering she picked Mr X to have children with. She might be a klepto but you should get together with a third party after you've both cooled off. I called Kevin around nine he said I should fill out a police report. Good advice from both but, why bother? I could hardly move.

The missing jewelry was another snail. I stopped eating, stopped showering, it was a sign, I was being stripped of everything sentimental, if I didn't give it away (boxes at Moe's) it would be taken. Madness. And Mrs X's nasty gossip hurt. 'I know people that know you!' Means, she knows other women that gossip about me. I very intentionally kept work and play separate. I didn't date stunt men and didn't hang out with stunt people, I saw them at work. Dot. Stunt men gossip like tweens and I didn't want to be on the grapevine. It also was rare to work with stuntwomen. Action films usually were over a hundred men, then me and my actor. I saw stuntwomen at commercial auditions and in the occasional crowd scene.

I ruminated for a few pages on Volunteers. Most people volunteer to someway-somehow help themselves, whether they admit it or even know it. From actors volunteering for a busy casting director, hoping for an audition, to a gimp giving wine to Homelet; I always got a smile and a kind word, I got what I needed. Many volunteers are freaks. It fills a void and gives needed validation for whatever hidden subliminal childhood Thing they refuse to deal with. *They* are doing you a *favor* and you had better *show* the proper *vulture*! Narcolepsy doesn't happen instantly, you feel it coming for a few hours, once it starts it cant be shut off. Everything starts to get dark around the edges and you move slower and slower until you have to lay down. (I hadn't been this overwhelmed since Homescrub's disappearance six months earlier.) A few days later, I finally got up, took a shower, hit the gym and grocery store; I was getting too skinny. I took Betsy's advice and called mutual Friend; asked her out for coffee and a talk about Ms X. The first thing she said was 'You look great!' (Too skinny is hot.) The second, 'I had a miscarriage so I know exactly how you feel!' Vulture change subject. I asked her if she thought Ms X was a kleptomaniac and WOOF! She protected her with such ferocity I had to put my hand up. 'You can't be mean to me I said quietly, I am recovering from a serious brain injury.' She settled down immediately. (Mental note: save that sentence.) She defended Ms X, she wasn't a thief. (I knew that.) Friend said something about Mr X being behind her wackadoo switcheraroo, I'd thought the same thing but was too hurt to admit it.

We started talking about other things. She insisted her sad miscarriage was the same as my injury. 'Look at my back…' I pulled up my shirt to show her the Frankenstein scar from the back flap. She ooo'd and ahhh'd that my ribs were showing. 'You think we're the same, don't you?' She kept asking, I finally said, 'no honey, I don't.'

Her miscarriage was the *worst thing* that had happened to her; Friend was looking for someone empathetic and was clumsily stumbling over words. How many times has my injury been compared to—fill in the blank?— *Hundreds* of things, everyone does it. (I had a Friend compare my injury to her abortion.) I could have should have shown compassion and listened to her but I was a self-involved mean girl. Didn't realize it, couldn't see it.

December 2004, Lake Oswego, Oregon

In Oregon, The Kettles are here for a week, having an early Christmas, they flew out on a 'parents pass' and it's easier to travel earlier in the month. Saw Dr Beijing today; he hasn't seen me since before the elbow surgery; he was amazed at Specialisto's work. Wishing again that I was here permanently.

December 2004—Venice Beach, CA

Giovanna (Goodfella's assistant) asked me to come in so she could take pictures of my arm; my new insurance company needed them. Goodfella stopped in for

253

a minute, harried, said the burn unit had recently lost a couple docs. 'Keep working out, I notice a change.' I looked at him like he was stupid. 'I've had a gym membership since I was seventeen.' 'I know…but…' he wanted to give himself credit. The last time I saw him was before Guam and he was *still* dissuading Pilates. I wonder if he's aware he waffles. Fat people refuse to consider that working out is fun and eating healthy is tasty. They tell themselves they cant lose weight and they're right. You tell your body what you want it to do.

We put the surgery off for awhile and Giovanna made me an appointment at Hanger Orthodics. Surgery concerns: What will my wrist look like? A skeleton arm? What about putting something like silicone in there to keep its shape? How many times has Goodfella done a surgery like this? How long will the skin grafts take? How will I keep my hand sterile while Integra is growing? How long will it take to heal?

'They're pretty determined and a respectable enemy.'

—US Soldier in a German hospital, groggy from meds
missing fingers and talking about the insurgents in Iraq.

Watching BBC of course, CNN would never air that particular opinion. The vile War Corporation stupidly chugs along destroying our economy, white washed for viewing pleasure; every once in awhile a lackey from the Whitehouse gets on a podium and says, 'It's goin' great!' There's nothing about The Horror Show that hasn't been written thousands of times but this is simple beautiful sad…

Anthem for Doomed Youth
by Wilfred Owen

What passing-bells for these who die as cattle?
    Only the monstrous anger of the guns.
    Only the stuttering rifles' rapid rattle
can patter out their hasty orisons.
No mockeries for them; no prayers nor bells,

nor any voice of mourning save the choirs,
the shrill, demented choirs of wailing shells;
and bugles calling for them from sad shires.
What candles may be held to speed them all?
     Not in the hands of boys, but in their eyes
          shall shine the holy glimmers of goodbyes.
The pallor of girls' brows shall be their pall;
their flowers the tenderness of patient minds,
and each slow dusk a drawing-down of blinds.

He was a US soldier who died overseas. He was twenty five in WW1 or was
it today in Baghdad? Time flows in circular waves.

Residual Payment's received by SAG: 4th quarter, 2004

Mouse Hunt / Feature	20.94
Simone / Feature	111.20
Man on the Moon / Feature	30.72
Angel / Fredless / Series	4.18
Candyman: Day of the Dead	37.52
Wild Bill / Feature	20.71
Mulholland Falls / Feature	.53
Deep Cover / Feature	28.20
Destiny Turns on the Radio / Feature	12.98
The Replacements / Feature	480.00
The Replacements / Feature	72.06
The Replacement Killers / Feature	44.54

A package from Disney—Face Off / Snake Eyes / Coyote Ugly	410.40
From Paramount—Another 48 Hrs / Jade / Face Off / Snake Eyes	276.23
Metro Goldwyn Mayer—Candyman II,	
Farewell to the Flesh, Wild Bill	100.10

Stuff gets traded around—SAG keeps track of it all—one more reason to have a strong union. They're all good memories (even Jade) but 'Man on the Moon' is kinky sweet.

I always found Jim Carrey attractive, good looking and funny works for me (and he has Dad's birthday, January 17th.) Our director was Milos Foreman, a cool gentle polar bear with a thick Czech accent. We were shooting a montage of Andy Kaufman wrestling women. It was a late summer afternoon with downtown stifle; everyone hot and crankish. Jim Carry and I were standing in the boxing ring waiting for the next set up. All of the short vignettes had been rehearsed and he'd already wrestled several of us. 'I wish I could fight for real…' he said to no one in particular. 'I'll fight you for real!' I showed him how I could easily flip someone bigger than me by sticking my hip bone just behind theirs. Didn't let him fall (duh) and he lit up. 'Let's do it!' 'I'll wrestle as hard as I can but you're bigger so let me wiggle away when you pin me.' Jim was happy, Milos was happy and I was over the moon. 'No No No! Stick to what we rehearsed our stunt coordinator ordered, that's how people get hurt.' 'Ahh, he's not gonna hurt me,' I said. 'I'm not worried about you, Alisa! Don't hurt the $20 million dollar actor!' Everyone laughed. 'We'll put four cameras on the ring and you can call your own 'Cut,' said Milos. That word is not coming out of my mouth, I thought.

Action!

We were rolling all over each other, hilarious, swearing, spanking, biting; I shamelessly molested him (was I ever getting another opportunity?) He did let me wiggle away when he pinned me and we didn't stop. Cameras have eleven minutes of film, one by one they all rolled out. We lay on the mat panting, the crew laughing. Jim gave me a hand up and we rushed to watch the playback monitor. He lit us cigarettes, we were giggling like teenagers who had just finished enthusiastic sex.

> '…if you involve yourself in constant drama
> you're praying to devils
> I say no—oooo—oooo

help each other love each other
makes it easier so much easier…

paraphrasing Bob Marley

Christmas eve with Cheryl's family and Xmas dinner with Velvet's / nice to be invited.

Went to the California Vocational Rehab in Westchester (near LAX) this am. They were nice but weren't for brain injuries / sad / back to the hut and smoked weed then wasted the rest of my day on the net. A tsunami took out Sri Lanka, still counting the dead. A cease fire was called among local hooligans. That's what the world needs unfortunately. The 1994 Northridge quake left twenty thousand people camping in LA's parks. No robbery, rape, looting or other assorted horror shows. When a natural disaster hits, nice lights turn on automatically. Everyone in shock, their first reaction is empathy.

'…oh lets all go for a swim in the sea
and play with the friendly manatee
oh lets all get scratched and bitten
frolicking with a puma kitten
oh lets all go for a ride on the tail
of a giant man-eating killer whale…'

~Al Christ

Trying to understand the new crazee brain terrain has been bizarre with only hindsight for insight. Keeping this journal has helped—I know I'm getting better, too slowly to notice. Still forcing myself to read, not really sure about that one. Reading a few lines would put me to sleep a couple years ago so it's much improved but I still can't make myself read much at a time. Oddly I have no trouble writing, it must access a different region.

I go walk on the beach when I get up (6–7) and read in the am with coffee and a smoothie. My brain seems to work best early. Reading a couple books this minute, I can only read one thing about a half an hour then have to switch or stop. I like the LA Times and I like reading classics because you know they're good. It's annoying to get ½ way through something and put it down from lack of interest. Many classics are short which is great for brain damage. The Prince by Niccolo Machiavelli, (1469–1527) is excellent and only 78 pages. He clearly shows how this kingdom has done *everything wrong*. Starting with the preemptive strike, then click click click all the way down.

January 2005—Venice Beach

Went to Hanger Orthodics today to look at prosthetic hands, the guy there reminded me of Will Ferrell, whack and irreverent but kind. Silicone hands are horrid looking, heavy and don't work any better than what I've got, they just pinch and no sense of touch. Hooks are horrid, strap it on and make it work by moving your shoulder. Will thought I should keep my paw. (He's right, I want to keep.) I have one pesky itsy spot on the top of my wrist a tiny blow hole, I dig out flakes of chalky bone every month or so. I cover it with antibiotic and gauze but it can't go forever.

Went to Dr Secondopinion in Long Beach. (Will Ferrell recommended.) He was a hand specialist but didn't have experience with burns. He took new X-rays and surprised me with Good News! None of the holes Cookieboots drilled show anymore! Little hand, healing itself. Dr Secondopinion made me a report; it disagrees with everything Goodfella wants to do. My wrist circumference is diminutive but looks normal as long as the rest of my body stays small. Don't take out a chunk of ulnar, it wont make the arm more stable, could easily backfire and *it will* turn it into a skeleton arm. Debriede my hand and cover with Integra? Unnecessary surgery with a ton of recuperation, don't do it. Dr Secondopinion's conclusions echo mine. He wouldn't have kept my paw and said so but after finally getting close and ugly with prosthetic arms I'm glad I have it.

'...oh lets all go up to a grizzly bear
and dye pink patches in his hair
oh lets all make a giant noose
and snare the tail of a moose
oh lets all go to Timbuktu

and bring along a kangaroo
just for fun we'll paint a possum
roll him in a ball and toss him…'

—Al Christ

Back from a weekend retreat, a burn survivor thing in San Diego; torn between loving my new friends and hating the beastly nut job running it. Six women drove down in my van, it was fun. I needed to lighten up and laugh with other survivors. Met a couple of boys from Phoenix (late teens) whom I instantly adored. They'd been burned in a car crash seven months ago. They were obviously still hurting, open wounds, all of it. Beastly Nut Job was a drill sergeant, the first thing she said was, 'If anyone thinks they're on vacation you're in the wrong place! You're here to work!' Yolanda and I made eye contact but didn't laugh out loud. Au contraire salope, we're here for a vacation. One of the things we did was an above ground obstacle course. We were in safety lines held by firefighters (adorable firefighters) and climbed up a telephone pole then walked down a series of wires and ropes culminating in a 'slide for life.' The idea being, doing something difficult that tackled your natural fear of heights would make you proud of yourself. I'm not afraid of heights and pre-injury I could have run the silly course easily, no safety lines required. It backfired, depressing me. I hate being hobbled and don't want my nose rubbed in it.

Beastly Nut Job had our weekend activities planned to the minute. The girls and I didn't let it bother us and ignored whatever we didn't feel like doing but Beastly was torturing The Boys from Phoenix, running them around like P.A's. They were in obvious distress and needed down time but found it hard to stand up to the formidable ogre. Beastly was a *burn survivor and an RN in a burn unit*. Her behavior was Unforgivable. She was another Fat Disability Nurse poking her patient's with a needle. She said to the group: 'You burn patients don't realize how mean you can be!' As if she expected manners from people in Excruciating Pain. Stupid bitch.

The last night we were having yet another meeting. Beastly expected attendance, dammit! 'Where are The Boy's from Phoenix?' 'I think they're asleep…' 'OH NO THEY DON'T!' She charged—*into their bedroom*—and forced them out! I wanted to kill but kept calm. I told The Boys From Phoenix not to be shy; 'you're eighteen, adult men. Tell people, I'm still recovering and can't do—whatever it is—because people that aren't burn survivors don't realize <u>how long it takes</u> to heal and will be sympathetic once aware. And go ahead and ignore this monster, she should know better.'

I remember Betsy smiling at me when I poked You're A Bitch Lady in the butt. I felt just as proud when they told Beastly they were tired and left the room. She is a perfect example of a wackadoo volunteer. She was harmful. Her needs should have been met by a psychiatrist not a group of innocent survivors looking for friendship and community.

February 05—Venice Beach

Goodfella was visibly annoyed by Dr Secondopinion's report. As for making my already altered paw into a skeleton arm he said, 'Your arm already looks so bad, I can't believe you care.' Of course I care, reckless fool! He was Dr Idioto at Rancho all over again, he wanted a test monkey; there was no reason for surgery, it would just be interesting to see what happened.

2007

Archetypal villains were everywhere; I withdrew further into a weed coma. I would walk via the beach to the coffee shop in the am, go to the gym around noon and be flopped in front of the TV by three smoking myself stupid.

March 05, Venice Beach

Payment received by SAG 1 / 25 / 2005
They Crawl / Feature Motion Picture
Legal Department, SAG

Re: 'Crawlers' Case No. 2004-0179

Dear Performer:

As you are aware, SAG pursued a residuals claim against the producer for payment of monies due on the above-referenced picture. Enclosed is a check for monies owed to you. A corollary contribution will be made directly to the SAG Producer Pension and Health Fund on your behalf

Sincerely, Champion for the Workers

I thank my Angry God for SAG again. Crawlers was a hard movie to shoot (endless foot chasing through empty warehouses, running down fire escapes, jumping off balconies…) and the low budget kept stunt adjustments to a minimum. My unions are damaged; 30 years of anti-union politics taking their toll. Actors are vulnerable to every kind of nightmare, I can't think of a group of people that need a strong union more.

'…ride a rhino, pinch an ape
cover a bear with surgical tape
oh lets all feed a hungry skunk
lets throw a lemur at a monk
let's wash a wombat in the tub
give a giraffe an alcohol rub
shave a zebra, cradle a stork
tease a lion with a fork…'

—Al Christ

Settlement conference all day. I sat in a closet in a high rise in Long Beach while the lawyers behaved like beautifully dressed wolves. No resolution. A weird high stakes game, I can't let myself get too involved I get too angry. I've made up my mind about giving trial a miss. The bristling posturing is too much and I don't blame Sleeping Bag Co 100% anymore. (I blame them 90%) I was high and share the fault. I thanked them all for trying though, thought it might throw them. I want Sleeping Bag's sharks to think of me in front of a jury. I'm sympathetic. (Thank you peaceful Buddha for reminding me to take a Valium.) I don't think I'll get a resolution in the Year of the Cock. Next year is mine, the year of the Bitch (Dog). The Chinese horoscope works better for me, my life is rolling in big waves year by year, not little ripples month by month.

That maybe wrong, I just remembered this lil' buddy who was a skilled astrologist; at a Friend's Xmas party he was reading chart's for the coming year. He had a website, put the date and time to the minute, latitude and longitude of your birth and it would make a pie chart, which Friend then interpreted. My info didn't make a pie—it was a bunch of horizontal lines crushed together at the top—Friend was colorless and gave me some excuse but I didn't buy it.

That was in the middle of my We Ho meltdown. One evening I knew I was too drunk to drive, took a cab home then fell down an unlit staircase, knocked myself out and almost knocked my teeth out (I had to wear braces for a couple months.) I remembered the busted pie chart a month earlier. 'This is what he saw,' I thought. But maybe it was THIS. I felt doomed for awhile, it was a long dark night. (I wrote a one act play called Super Nova. Four women hanging out after they've died. Harlow, Peron, Monroe and Princess Di. To keep the status quo patriarchal, women at their height of power and fame are sacrificed.)

March, 2005—Venice

The ousted president of Kazakhstan is on BBC wearing an ill fitted suit and mopping his brow. No Mongol Warrior, he was a whimpering mongrel, speaking to the press with a worried look. A sad fall from Kahn; I just watched a History Channel program on Genghis Kahn and his descendant Timor. Khan believed he was blessed by God and couldn't be defeated. He never was. He headed east and killed everyone in his path. He died in a freak riding accident on his way back to conquer China. His descendant Timor was many years later / bloodier / richer / also blessed by God and never defeated and he too died on his way to conquer China. (China has crazee voodoo.) Timor died of cancer; since he knew it was coming he had time to build a grave site temple. Timor promised he would bring death upon its disturbance More Fearsome than when he was alive. He was buried in the dark ages and dug up June 22nd 1941, the day Hitler sent his army into Russia.

Chance coincidence? Or amusement for the War God? Nothing seems arbitrary anymore.

> '…You will do me the justice to remember, that I have always strenuously supported the right of every Man to his own opinion, however different that opinion might be to mine. He who denies to another this right, makes a slave of himself to his present opinion, because he precludes himself the right of changing it. The most formidable weapon against errors of every kind is Reason. I have never used any other, and I trust I never shall.
>
> Your affectionate friend and fellow-citizen,
>
> —Thomas Paine'

April 2005—Venice

American Idol night. I still watch but it's lost it's cute new puppy smell. I try to act normally, don't always succeed. I had road rage today at a guy in a black SUV, I changed lanes in front of him; I was exiting the 10 on my way to the gym. I didn't use my blinker because he was *20 car lengths behind me.* He started honking from way back there and *sped up*, leaning on his horn until he was sniffing my exhaust. Instant insanity! I slammed on my brakes and slid twenty feet to a full stop, how dare that mutherphucker try to Bully me!

Idiot miracle, there were no collisions but a lot of near misses. Looking through the rear view I saw at least 10 cars in 'almost crashed' positions. Instantly MORTIFIED. Jeopardizing innocent people? What the hell is wrong with me! I never used to get road rage and would lecture friends who caught it; childish and dangerous. Now it was hijacking me nearly every day. I drove to the red light at the end of the exit. And here comes Jerk: 55–60, fat, long greasy gray hair with a salt & pepper beard. I was going one way, him the other. We sat at the light looking at each other. My windows were up with air con on so I couldn't hear him, but he's screaming at me so hard his face his red and veiny. He looks like huge mutated squirrel. I started laughing. I turned up Baby Fox and opened the window so Mr Aneurysm could enjoy the dub too. Reggae made him rage harder—the sublime Absurdist Theater of it all—I had tears in my eyes I was laughing so hard. Light change, wackadoo minute over. Off to the Stairmaster and afternoon soaps.

'…if you can't except my apology
then it's you who needs forgiving…'

—Rainbow Kittens with Wings

The Social Security Disability Insurance Story: $430 a month from SSDI is directly deposited into my checking account. Never seemed right. CA State Disability paid $1400 a month for a year (their maximum.) That ran out February '03 then SSDI started. I worked for twenty years, why so low? Been to the Social Security office three times, standard response, 'I don't know, its not my department…' They're in Westwood; I was there for <u>four hours</u> yesterday. Round and round the habit trail, take another number, catch the rubber ball with your nose. Round and round. Round and round. 'Eliza Christian? Eliza….Eliza Christian…?' 'You're not eligible for SSI. You must have less than $2000. You're not impoverished enough…soon though, you seem to be inching closer to homelessness…' Breathing heavy his eyes glaze over. 'I've heard this before; I want to know why my SSDI is so low.' He looked through miles of paperwork. 'Oh here, see?' He pointed to gibberish. 'It's not my department you understand—not my fault—but it looks like you should be getting another $600 a month.'

2007

It was welcome. I thought of the people that couldn't spend days in the SS office and wondered if it was intentional—think of the money saved by shorting $600 a month from a million people—but concluded it was bureaucracy. Horrid, sluggish, wasteful bureaucracy.

The owner of my building owned the whole block and we all shared one laundry room a couple buildings away. It was an arm buster dragging laundry back and forth. I befriended a homeless woman named Rain and had her help me when she was around. The manager gave her a handful of beans to pick up garbage around our buildings and she was keeping her belongings in the laundry room. I asked her about the streets / how long? Five months. (She said 5 months for the next 5 months so I never really knew.) What happened? Common law husband died and she couldn't pay the rent. She was sixty two. She had difficulty trusting people, when asked about anything upsetting she could get frantic, speaking fast, not always sensible. I'd give her a Valium and it would calm her down. If she could get a prescription, I knew it would make her daily grind a little bit easier.

I tuned Rain into a pet project. I paid her $40 a week to do my laundry and basic cleaning in my bachelor box. I walked her through the cities homeless habitrails. (Speaking of surreal bureaucracy, miles of red tape, monstrous forms to fill and hours and hours of sitting in crowded waiting rooms; we were together, so could laugh at it all, but there's no way she could have done it by herself.) I started looking for a Woman Only shelter. She was afraid of men / who could blame her. After weeks of Endless Bullshit I got her admitted into a haven run by nuns! Rain was Catholic! Perfect, I thought. It was in Echo Park, fifteen miles from the beach. Rain became a bit frantic 'so far from home.' I took the bus with her to and from Venice, she could come easily. It calmed her and she seemed to settle in. She Loved the food (I had lunch with her once, it was homemade and tasty.) Sister Paul gave her a job keeping their small garden in order. Rain loved working with her hands in the earth.

About a month later her schizophrenia (or whatever her particular demon is called) started to wake up and with no lithium (or whatever medication is used to control it) she was looking haggard and wild eyed. 'Try and talk to someone, maybe the nuns know a therapist, a doctor, don't run away baby, you're safe where you are…' She looked at me with sad, scared little girl eyes. 'I'll try.'

May 2005—Venice Beach

The Rain experiment ended badly. She's back on the street; the bus was 'making her old' (dim yellowish light in the thin mirror above the windows would make a supermodel look old) and everyone was suspect. It was her illness—and it was the sin of pride to think I could magically help—I was following my 'I can fix it' pathology. I yelled at her once, out of frustration and instantly became one of THEM; the nameless, faceless THEM trying to hurt her. Sister Paul called me a couple days later, asking if I'd seen her. I confessed my sins, I had blown it with Rain the minute I lost my temper, I was so sorry. Sister was kind and told me she had also seen it coming. 'It's very hard to get them off the street, if you see her, remind her that she always has a home here.' I learned something about Homelet (at poor Rain's expense) I think I understand some mental illness issues. It's a wave, Rain could feel coming, she could feel normal for a long time between episodes. The normal times were the worst / being so aware of feeling sad and scared.

2007

I always had a difficult friend or two. Some super high maintenance bitch that no one wanted around, that everyone warned me about. I always thought—oh she wont do whatever horrid thing she always does to everyone else—to me. It was psychology 101 but I'd never put them all in a row before and really looked at my pattern. Starting way back with Dominique, I always had one.

My favorite Crazee Lady was Lana, she was up for anything and fun for a long time until she snapped. We went to NYC for a week to work on Terror Firmer. After Lloyd played the nun in We Ho Stories his office called a few months later to see if I wanted a cameo in his next film. Yes, can I bring a friend? Yes. OK! I taught Lana a nasty brawl—45 seconds of knock your shit out—we were going to be 'The Cat Fighting Bitches' two crew members having a girl fight in sexy wardrobe. I choreographed it so it could be done in two set ups and cut together easily.

They were shooting at Green Point in Brooklyn. I had a Friend we could stay with in Brooklyn, we just needed to be picked up in the am. We asked our 19 yr old driver how the shoot was going the day we arrived, 'yesterday all I said was 'that's so fucked up' he deadpanned.

NYC is naughty, the city that never sleeps. We'd instantly hooked up with a couple of beautiful Wall Street boys (NYC men are much more desirable than LA's. Focused, hard working.) They took us to dinner / clubs / cocktail parties (mine confided, LA women are so much nicer than NYC's. Ice princesses.) The last am we woke up LATE in Manhattan and ran for a cab. It was 8 am—The Kid was waiting outside of Friends apartment in Brooklyn—that's so fucked up. We were wearing traditional nightclub uniforms: jeans, boots, black jackets. The cab driver taking us to Brooklyn started regretting it the minute we saw the bridge. Lana took pride in her easy and total control over men. She reached through the window and massaged his shoulder, speaking softly. I dozed, if memory serves it took an hour and Lana and Cabby were friends by the time we arrived, he would wait for us.

We changed into The Cat Fighting Bitches and came back to Cabby looking like pole dancers; carrying makeup bags, clothing bags, electric curlers and a coffee pot. Cabby was 21, he was amused. Waiting on a light, a transit worker got out of his truck and started rolling a big orange barrel in front of our freeway entrance ramp. 'Shit!' said Cabby. 'Leave it to me...' Lana got out and jogged across the street, shoulder length blonde, tall and fit; wearing thigh high boots, hooker shorts and a leopard print, push up bra. The street noticed.

She was talking to Trans Guy, pointing at us and petting his arm. He was shaking his head and mouthing No. 'What should I do?' asked Cabby, the light was about to change 'Go through, she'll get him to move it.' He did and she did. As Trans Guy started moving the orange barrel, everyone else at the intersection saw what was happening and were positioning for a rush. A cop rounded the corner—took it in—turned on his siren.

'Get in!' Cabby yelled! Lana jumped and Cabby floored it. Our stuff went flying, 'don't lift your heads!' He drove like a stunt man and hid among the other cabs on the freeway. The three of us were dying with laughter, we peeked up and a guy driving next to us was smiling and giving a Thumbs Up, one of the cars that chased us through. 'You girls must be from Los Angeles,' Cabby said. Is it that obvious? We got to the set two hours late and found Lloyd to apologize. 'You're still here?' He thought we'd left *days earlier*. We never did shoot The Cat Fighting Bitches. (But that was my favorite trip to NYC.)

June 2005—Venice

I weigh 111, Thank God. Working out hasn't fixed my temper but it is helping Hideous Frankenstein Syndrome. Saw Coolchick today, love her. Goodfella accused me of disliking all Dr's but I only dislike Doctors that behave like arrogant a-holes. He's *still* defending Girlinaboysclub, he makes me sick. I woke up a little more and realized *that* is a lot of the anger I've been feeling. Fucking bitch that let interns stick a catheter in my neck, the Moron that gave me a five-inch scar across my stomach, fucking Mr Roger Insipid, Agh! There's too many, it's stepping through a cow field blindfolded.

Specialisto looked me in the eye and told me I wouldn't have a CVA in his OR. He knew (like everyone involved in the OR knows) that a simple dressing change shouldn't cause a stroke. When I told Goodfella, I could see he was annoyed at Specialisto but what he thinks was a break in the 'Doctors Code' cooled my debilitating fear. I gave Goodfella waivers and it feels right, however I need this blowhole on my wrist dealt with. Fellow burn survivor Nancy is my new housekeeper (she's in school so can use the cash and isn't schizophrenic.) She recommended Dr Torrance. I went down there and got a pie in the face when I saw the vulture on the door. Dr Torrance and John Allritini! I can't escape USC—Plastic's all know each other—I have to laugh.

Doctor Torrance remembered working on me (who didn't?) He was filling in for someone when I was there. Torrance told me about his County snail. One of the nurses was leaving and the rest were throwing a going away party. Torrance had a surgery scheduled so some of them wouldn't be able to go. The day of the party there was a leak in the ceiling of the OR, it couldn't be used. Next day, maintenance figured out what was wrong, the air-condition unit upstairs had been mysteriously turned off, causing condensation. Dr

Torrance said they all got their cake and ice cream and his sick patient had to wait. That sounds like the County Hospital I know and loathe.

Dr Torrance sent me to 'Wound Care' one building over. I appreciated his attention to detail in getting a second opinion. (Opposite of Goodfella.) I was sitting in the examining room with my hand undressed. Nurse comes in makes eye contact and smiles, I smile back. Then she looks down and is startled by my paw. I see it clearly, the smile fades, eyes widen. It's happened hundreds of times, never gets boring. Instead of acknowledging the severity of my burn, she 'hides' her reaction and mindlessly starts chit chattering an octave above her regular voice; 'Oooo! How <u>Good Your Hand Looks!</u> I'm so Impressed with your Hand! It looks So Good! Oooo! Ahh!' Stupidly on and on, of course I'm speechless. I was absently picking my thumbnail and she latched onto that. 'Your Cuticles look so Great!' As if I'm getting manicures.

I am tired of making strangers feel OK about my injuries; I'll do it for friends but I don't give a rat if she's uncomfortable, she's a wound care nurse for Christ sake. 'I'm not here about my hand; I'm here about my wrist. See this little spot? It's been open for three and a half years. I don't think it will heal without surgery. Do you?' Yes, it needs surgery.

'A dream itself is but a shadow.'

—Shakespeare

An old director Friend emailed, he found me through CafeDeb, nice surprise. We met on a film called Madam. He was a spiritual lapsed Catholic, we had fun metaphysical debates about where's it going and what do you think has been, I sent my cell, he calls, chatter chat, what's he been up to? Tons! Me too! Let's lunch! I should have picked a spot and told / shown him my injury in person. (Duh.) But Friend is fun to talk with and I miss talking. SO I'm honest; I've been seriously injured, I'm still recovering. But you're fine now, right? You sound great! You're fine right? He sounded broken hearted. Boom! Change the subject. He reminisced about a big steak I ate, thought it was sexy / cool, most thin women in LA eat salads or fish. I've been off meat for many years. The film was in either '93 or '94. Never heard another peep from him, the one two punch—injured and vegan—was too much. My feelings are stupidly hurt, of course, since I knew what would happen if I talked.

I had one recently do it to my face. Alison hangs with this art crew, a bunch of warehouses good for sculpting painting or partying, it's in Santa Monica close to the 10. The crowd is exceedingly shallow but they have some interesting events. We were there at a party, counterfeit as ever, I was listening to the yakking of a self-confident guy, he asked if I'd like to go to LACMA. Almost said no, then reminded myself I need to get out even if it's just museum browsing with a boring blow hard. So I say yes. We're sitting around a coffee table with ten other people and he asks for pen and paper to get my number—they're produced—he hands them to me. 'Please write for me,' I ask, holding my right hand with my left. He had been so busy talking about himself he didn't realize he'd been sitting with a gimp. Eyes widen, stare stare, time ticks, stammer stammering something about HIS hand was hurt once and HE had to learn how to write with HIS left. He demanded I write lefty, 'I want to see you do it.' Why why why do I bother to try? 'No' I said. 'You're not going to give me your number because I wanted to see you write left handed? Pompous petulant, self-righteous. (I was going to take that gimp's phone number and she blew it.)

'Obscenity is a cleansing process,
whereas pornography only adds to the murk...'

—Henry Miller

Velvet, her son Bobby, his Girlfriend and I went to the San Diego fair. Tried to rent a cart but there weren't any left; figured I might as well try walking it. I harkened back to August of '03. I did MN state fair with a cart, no way I could have walked. (Physical recovery.) I freaked on the chair lift over the park though; the long chairs held all four of us. The operator at the front stopped the ride so I could slowly cane over. We asked them to stop on the way down, 'just get up...get up and walk...' they couldn't see my cane and we all look fit. Agh! The ground! Fear! 'STOP! Mutherphucker!' EMBARRASSING out burst, the guy I yelled at just walked away (nice of him) or I would have apologized. Bobby thought it was hilarious though, 'stop mutherphucker,' he kept saying in a high squeaky voice. 'Stopstopstopmutherphucker…' We laughed our heads off, rode rides and tasted ridiculous fair food. (Deep-fried pickle chips?) Walked all day—feet sore but OK.

Georgene invited me to Phoenix before summer got too hot, I went out for a week. Dr Torrance and I had planned surgery the first week of August. He had told me that even though it was a fast simple procedure (use a tiny drill / when the little hole fills with blood, the necrotic bone is excised) anything to do with bones hurt and he wanted me out. I have to get every procedure pre-approved by Husbands Insurance. They'd been approving every big whack surgery Goodfella wanted to do since January; I had cancelled every one, my subconscious yelling No! Don't make it worse! But I felt great about this one. Dr Torrance was also going to shave a bone spur from my index finger. (It hurt!) I gave my insurance info to The Dee, Doctor Torrance's personal assistant, before I left town.

July 2005—Phoenix, AZ Georgene & Co's

The Story of The Dee: She called me a few days later. 'Your insurance was cancelled in Oct 2004.' 'That was Producers Health Plan, I tell her, Husbands insurance started when Sag's ran out.' Annoying, I had given her that information before I left. 'No you have to call Blue Cross, it's cancelled…' she was a skipping CD. The Dee wouldn't consider the possibility that she might be wrong. Vultures circling, I had Georgene talk to her but she couldn't get The Dee to join us in reality either and hung up frustrated. 'Let's double check,' George called MPI and Blue Cross, 'yes Alisa is covered, she can have the surgery, have The Dee call, here is a direct line.' George called The Dee back and gave her directions a four year old could follow. Hours Later: 'No, you're not covered. Your insurance was cancelled.' I thought I was going to lose it. 'I had this same surgery scheduled last month. How do you suppose that happened?' 'I'm not trying to fight with you—I'm just telling you that you aren't covered.' She called voice mail a couple days later, 'Please call me to schedule surgery.' Thank Dog! She finally figured it out. 'I'm going to schedule you but just to let you know, you're not covered. You're going to be responsible for payment.' It's like running up against a big rubber wall. Boing! Ta Da! The Dee has spoken.

July 2005—Venice Beach, CA

I still haven't dealt with it—it's been a couple weeks—I can't stand talking to her AGAIN. God I miss Giovanna (Goodfella's assistant) or Jane (Allritini's).

I am also anemic, I've been taking ferrous sulfate (iron) for months with no improvement. My periods are under control so there's only one other place I could be bleeding from. I (of course) am convinced it's colon cancer and I'll be dead by Tuesday. Rational Coolchick thinks it could be a number of things so lets do more testing and figure it out. I love her. She likes the puzzles; she sent me to a GI, Dr Nice.

Couldn't have been nicer; made me feel at ease, felt around my belly, told me about the procedures, there would be two. Endoscopy is a tiny camera snaking down your throat to peer at the stomach and small intestine. Colonoscopy goes up the butt. If there are any bumps, polyps or freakish cancer activity, it gets a biopsy immediately. That sounded good although the procedure scared me. I'd be put to sleep with an IV of Demerol and Valium. The dressing change where I was awake and screaming still haunts. I told him about the fire, the stroke, years of valium and opiates. 'I have a high tolerance for pain medication,' I warned him. He looked in my eyes while I was talking; I thought he was listening to me.

I was sent to the lab where they sucked my vein. Tube after tube, the nurse must have filled 10 of them. No pain. No bleeding when she removed the needle and no mark. Nothing. (The only other nurse I remember doing that was at Rancho.) They gave me poo collecting utensils, 9 vials filled with different colored liquids and plastic collecting cups. I took the stuff but would never do it. Sorry, I don't dig through poo. It's unthinkable.

'…oh little man
you're just like the Titanic, sunk

but somehow you float
you're mentally frail
but still you keep talking
and talking…'

paraphrasing Baby Fox

The day before the procedure, no eating, liquids only; Fleet Phospho-Soda at night and again 3 hours before. Uncomfortable. When I woke up in St Joe's and was told they didn't do the procedures, I didn't believe them. Surely I was still groggy from the IV. But it was true. Dr Nice told me I had sat up and pulled the scope from my throat and I wouldn't let them near my ass. I sounded like '…a Haight Ashbury hippie chick. You had a lot to say!' A real quote from Dr Nice.

He told me I'd been given the minimum dose. He couldn't understand why it didn't work. 'One in forty people have that reaction!' Not, I'm Sorry I didn't listen as you explained your high tolerance for medication. 'There's stronger anesthesia we can give you. I'm really disappointed.' Poor Doctor Nice was disappointed, how sad for him! I was humiliated mortified furious embarrassed depressed, if my vultures would stop, I'd have better words. I came home and slept—narcolepsy for 24 hours—woke the next afternoon with grisly depression setting in. My attorney was coming by for lunch. Dr Nice called and told me all about the anesthesia they *should* have used. Told be how disappointed he was *again*. 'What do you mean *you're disappointed*? I have to figure out why I'm anemic before my surgery! I was supposed to the have the results this week! I have to go through that three day hell again, not you!' Since he's Dr Nice, he apologized, maybe he meant it but all I could think of was the looks I got as I was waking up, nasty hippie chick and I hate hippies! Smelly lazy holier than thou hypocrites is how I saw them. Now I'd become one? What did I say? I've been hating myself, Freddy Kruger legs, hideous Frankenstein nude, it's too awful.

My attorney arrived in the middle of this conversation. She commiserated and innocently asked why didn't I change Doctors? I snapped, a BD bitch 'I can't explain it!' I couldn't even talk about it. Later, on the phone with

Coolchick, I broke down sobbing like a child. I had to do the humiliating procedure AGAIN! I had to find someone else, I hated Dr Nice. She was 'disappointed' as well but at Dr Nice not me. I went to St John's website and picked a GI at random. I called and explained my situation. The earliest they can see me is next Thursday.

Yesterday I managed to do laundry and grocery shop but I was symptom-ish / the disjointed disconnect / happening to someone else / suicidal / hitting myself you loser / stupid loser. Talked to Kevin. We used to be friends but he's sick of me too, doesn't know what to say to the wackadoo.

2007

Dr Nice set a creaking clopping wheel in motion that would spin me around crazee lane for the rest of the year. My new GI Doctor Davidson was sympathetic and ordered the MAC anesthesia that Dr Nice had decreed unnecessary. He fit me in as soon as he could, a couple weeks later.

The nurses at St Johns were abysmal. When I arrived at 6 am, exhausted from being on the toilet all night, they told me that Doctor Davidson didn't order MAC anesthesia. There wasn't an anesthesiologist there, I could come back tomorrow. Rude, dismissive. The thought of doing the horrid preparation for the third time was too much. I started crying and had them call Davidson—who bitch slapped them and told them to get an anesthesiologist—they woke one up—he'd be a half hour. They let a fledgling practice putting an IV in me. She was getting ready to stick me painfully for the third time when I figured out what they were up to. 'Why are you torturing me?' I yelled at the pack of them. Fucking bitches. The oldest of the group came over and slipped the IV in easily.

Procedures done. Everything normal. What now? The middle of July, we had to cancel the August 4 operation date, no elective surgery when you're anemic. Dr Davidson recommended I go to a hematologist friend of his and get IV iron. I started seeing Doc Century City weekly. Their nurse was good at finding a vein and I loved the office manager, Friend. Iron is black and you can taste it as it goes in your arm. I called it reverse vampire treatment; RVT.

Aug 2005—Venice Beach

Depression. Endless doctors appointments, driving and waiting, lonely and waiting, 'obsession with self...' I'm tired of myself. The Leher News Hour, BBC World News and The Daily Show are my news trifecta. How *crooked* politics have become, we're under the thumb of a dimwit mafia boss, non-stop bullshit about this illegal corporate war. I can't believe how many people still believe it. (Alison believes every bit of nonsense that spews from the Whitehouse, how is that possible?) I'm on the outside looking in—in a rut going to the gym.

> 'There are all kinds of experimental methods of determining how men and women behave under various circumstances. You can put rats in mazes and men in barbed wire cages and observe their methods of escape. You can administer drugs and observe their effect. There is real hope that by getting to understand the science of human behavior, governments may be even more able than they are at present to turn mankind into rabbles of mutually ferocious lunatics.'

> —Bertrand Russell

20 / 20 was doing a fluff piece on modern art. Interesting enough to watch, most of it was cute; they put kid's paintings next to Pollock and de Kooning and the public liked the children's work just as much.

Fluffy until the end—then it became ominous—maybe only to me. The reporter starts going off; 'Well I don't see it, it's ridiculous! Art is for the rich, for people that think they're better than us! Politicians spend YOUR MONEY on this! They give grants to museums that buy this!' With close ups of the most *abstract / minimalist* art.

Uhwhathafuck? It was an Aldous Huxley minute. He wrote Brave New World in 1931, I read it in 1984. A totalitarian future, test tube babies genetically engineered and molded to specific social statuses. The government controls people with happy pills called Soma and sexual activity is encouraged. In one scene, labor babies are being brainwashed. They were nine months, pre-walking. A teacher in the nursery puts out paintings of flowers, rainbows, brightly colored happy baby stuff and they start crawling towards the paintings. ZAP! An electric shock from the floor, they all start crying. The teacher takes the pictures away. When they've calmed down, she puts out the pictures again—some babies are already wary but others head for the pretty colors—ZAP!

Politicians spend your money on this crap! ZAP! Art is for the rich! ZAP!

Drugs I'm on: Baclofen, 20 mgs 3 X a day / Ambien 10 mgs every night / Oxycontin 20 mgs twice daily and birth control. Took myself off Wellbutrin, so far no suicidal thoughts. Still wake pre-dawn with right side electroshock therapy. Take Baclofen and wait for it to work. Depressing. Switch between Howard Stern and Good Day LA and try to find a reason to get out of the hut. Usually go to the corner coffee shop and read the paper. Watch Italian tourists clash with the local crackho's. Gym at one, RVT at three.

Went to The World Burn Congress in Baltimore this month. (I don't know why I skipped it last year.) Firefighter's Quest paid again. Nice week. Met a woman who'd had a similar experience with a Rancho psychologist, a woman fixated on drugs. What kind of drugs did you do in high school? What did you do in college? Drugs, drugs, obsession, obsession. Friend told me how violated she felt; still pisses her off years later. She lost her arms, her nose and an eye in an explosion. Hey Idiot, think THAT might be bothering her? Monsters. Mr Roger Insipid still makes my head explode three years later. (It was nice to be validated. Did he really behave that badly? Yes.)

Met a guy I liked, great attitude, funny. But he was burned in the Great White / Rhode Island fire. In some complicated intricate self-involved way I still felt responsible ...madness... the seduction of madness.

'The one thing we can never get enough of is love.
And the one thing we never give enough of is love.'

—Henry Miller

I just published Volume 12 of CafeDeb.com. I'm getting good at airbrushing, takes time but what the hell else do I have to do. I've been thinking it might be a way to make a little cash, People, Entertainment Weekly, everyone Photoshop's, not just skin mags.

Finally talked with Allritini, I've been angry at him all year about the neuroma disaster, seeing his name on Dr Torrance's door made me realize I had to talk to him. He didn't get any of my email, didn't know the procedure hadn't worked. He agreed with me about Goodfella and LAC / USC. He'd started to break ties with them as well. When I apologized for blowing steam he said he understood (and meant it.) Allritini and Coolchick have been steady in a sea of dangerous incompetence.

September 13, 2005 Venice

did my surgery yesterday / finger bone spur / hole in wrist / ulcer in heel / scar revision down lost dorsi

October, 2005—Venice

This is the 1st time I've been able to write. Too much pain. Torrance asked what I wanted for pain after surgery, 'Vicodin?' I was too scared to laugh but I smiled. 'I need something STRONG, percocet, percodan…' 'I'll have John write it, I don't have the right prescription pad with me.' Effing drug war.

Was picked up at five am by Nations Transportation (arranged by Elaine from Firefighters Quest, then she flew to France, she's a superhero.) We drove down to Torrance Hospital in the dark and checked in no problem. I'm paranoid of mean people unable to do their jobs and scared of another stroke but they were nice. I had prepared well pre-op, I've had over a year of anxiety over this surgery. I had gone to the gym six days in a row and did six cardiac hours; made different nibbles, sweet potato curry, pea soup, stocked up on sparkling water, tea, power bars, soy milk, popcorn, bananas. Did laundry, cleaned the kitchen and last not least, 'Hindu Dozer'. No kidding, that's what it was called (and lived up to it's name.)

I told friends I would be needing help but not for a few days. And I told The Dee over and over I would need home care—I need an RN for dressing changes and my insurance does pay—I had it pre-approved. I knew the dip shit would forget. Four months of endless issues with The Dee / nothing is my fault / your insurance is cancelled / your Dr didn't send your blood test results / you did this the hospital did that / she made me physically ill. Kevin tried to help. He called Torrance Hosp. They told him that I could set up home care the morning I checked in. In retrospect it's a silly thing to believe. I checked in and I told them I would need home care then was passed along assembly line style...the admitting nurse has that paperwork...the recovery room nurses do it...Torrance's office should have arranged it. Duh, The Dee.

The Nasty Anesthetist was sharp with me, I wasn't responding fast enough. I told him not to be mean to me, that I'd had a stroke. 'You don't think that's worth mentioning?' He snorted. I shut down, didn't tell him about the horror shows I'd recently had with back-to-back GI's. They were definitely on my mind. I was freaked that they only had me down for two of the four procedures. Dr Torrance was *hiding behind his hand* at the foot of my bed, whispering the other two procedures to a surgical nurse. I heard someone say they didn't get my blood work. After 20 reverse vampire treatments and a pre-op, that's a lot of punctures to blow off—The Dee at work.

Allritini showed up late. Nasty Anesthetist didn't tell me I was going under. I was waking up / surrounded by faces / yammering jammering, mad at me? I did something wrong / they couldn't do the operations / I had an uncomfortable bedpan under my ass, was I pissing myself? What kind of freakish nightmare was this? Please do the operation please do the operation / I was crying / I had been trying to have this surgery since last December.

I finally came out of the anesthesia. I'd had a reaction. I could barely speak my lips were swollen. They were all around my bed from worry; I mixed all the recent hellish procedures into a big sloppy gruel-ish horror show. All four procedures WERE done and surgery went fine except for…well uh, your face is a balloon…other wise, perfect. I had asked for a catheter so they thought I needed to pee, that's why the bedpan. (Who knows what subconscious yukedy yuk that was about, something to do with Dr Nice.) Nasty Anesthetist told me I should see an allergist 'or the next time you have surgery you could die! Do you understand? You could DIE!' Over and over. My reaction was from something he administered and he was scared shitless. Jerk.

I spent the rest of the afternoon in the recovery room as my face slowly came back down to a more reasonable puff. They were sweet, encouraged graham crackers and apologized for my having to hang around all day. No problem, I was way to effed up for the long drive home and it took awhile to get my foot cover. Dirk was their PT guy. Dirk Diggler I told him. Yea, yea he heard that one a lot and some country singer I didn't recognize. None of the adult splints worked, feet too small, he ended up giving me a large child's cast shoe. It was temporary, I needed a plastic boot cast. I felt pain coming, asked for medication and was given a percocet and a prescription. Drove to the toilet in a wheel chair and got a look at my face; a boxer that lost. I turned around to look at my back. The monstrosity from armpit to waist was gone. Allritini had cut the entire retarded simian scar out—eighteen inches of inside stitches—and a drainage tube coming out of my side. That's where THE PAIN was coming from but I was SO HAPPY!

Doctor Torrance had told me he'd do a Z plasty. An incision that looks like a Z used to break up scar tissue. That's what I was expecting. Having the grotesque mistake removed was fantastic. Hideous Frankenstein be gone. When it heals it will be a long white line. No more RR tracks and hideous franken-pulling the skin parallel to my left breast down and the skin on my back in, turning me into an antique carnival freak. Nice thing about small breasts is they're still perky at forty. To have some half-asleep intern's pathetic attempt at stitching wreck my rack added to self-loathing. Allritini was happy Puffy was almost gone, said it was scary, they started with me face down and did my back 1st when they turned me over they saw Puff looking rough up but did the other three procedures because my vitals were good.

Nations Transportation drove to a prosthetics place and got me a mini walker. I was too unsteady for my regular cane. The mini walker looks like a stepladder, light weight, made of aluminum and has four sturdy rubber feet. Nations T drove me back and forth for ten days. Every one of those drivers was a sweet heart and always on time. Cabs would have cost a fortune and I was dreaming sweet dreams about driving myself anywhere. Thank You Thank You Elaine at Firefighters Quest. I don't know what I was thinking. I have to laugh. I ALWAYS DO THIS. Think it will be easier than it is. No thoughts of post op. Took the 405 back and forth to Torrance Hospital. Taking pain meds and taking pictures of the graffiti on the construction sites. I'd wanted to do it all year (take fotos of the 405) but I'm always alone.

Dr Torrance was happy my face was almost normal. He was happy about everything and his happiness was infectious. He wanted to keep my foot bandaged the rest of the week but we looked at wrist, finger and scar revision, all fine. I asked him again about a home care nurse, 'I'll need one tomorrow, I need one every day I'm not coming in.' I have a tube coming out of my back, the thingy needs to be emptied of blood, the dressings need changing. Hello? Anyone home? The Dee tells me she's on it, I'm horrified. I turn an accusing eye on Torrance. THIS is when your assistant decides to arrange a nurse? Vultures everywhere / couldn't speak. I got home and the plumber had stopped by, cut the carpet out of my closet and left everything that was in there out against my bed.

Another brick of sanity chipping snails circling.

The Dee called and asked if I knew any home care nurses. I remembered the nurse that came to The Oakwood's two years ago and I could find her file, I keep all medical files together. I gave her the number. Three in the afternoon The Dee calls back, 'it's been disconnected.' She was perturbed. 'Do you know of anyone else?' I snapped at her, 'No! I'm tired, do your own job! I need someone here TOMORROW!' I get the usual rant—not my fault—this time it was Dr Torrance. He didn't write a Dr's order for home care and she can't do anything about that, so Ha! She kept calling back, would have been funny if I wasn't in so much pain. She's so proud of herself! She figured out what to do! Well kind of, she called Jane who gave her a couple numbers. She told me about each call and how hard it was to find someone who could go to Venice on such short notice! Blabitty blabitty on and on... The Dee has to explain herself three or four times, finally 'they will call early this evening to set up the time.' Thank you!' Click. Long winded empty headed grumbly grumble grump...she made my pain worse.

I napped. Seven pm I get a call from Sun Plus Home Care checking my address, 11288 Ventura Blvd, Studio City? My mailbox. 'Oh, that could be a problem, I'll call you back in the morning.'

Pain really dug in the 2nd night / fitful nightmares / woke crying / called Dr Torrance's office at nine am crying to the girl who answered / talking to a refugee / I cant help you, I'm hanging onto this plank of rotten wood...there's nothing I can do. Called Kev again, 'please help me; I can't do this alone...' Ate more percocet, slept fitfully. Sun Plus called me back 'we're coming this afternoon.' Dozing, the phone rings, its The Dee and she is pissed! 'YOU gave us the WRONG ADDRESS!' 'I can't take your incompetence any more!' I hung up on her. Got an email from Kev later that afternoon, he'd been trying to figure out my wound care schedule with The Dee. Took hours and he was sick of her too. Every other day, ten am.

The week goes by, time to have my foot dressing changed. I'm in an examining room; a nurse has the dressings off, it's cool. A rubber looking sheet stapled to my Achilles tendon and covered with a silver strip of bandage, giving my hoof a metallic hue.

Torrance comes in to see how it looks; all good. I tell him that I cannot take The Dee anymore, it's not just her incompetence, it's her nasty disposition, her insistence that every time she screws something up it's anyone's fault but her own. That was Kev's idea. Face the problem head on instead of blowing up at someone who doesn't deserve it. (Like Kevin.)

Torrance looked like he got caught with his dick in a hooker. 'The Dee loves you!' (He *really* said that, like Alexander last year, Tweak loves you!) 'No one has ever complained about her! I'm not in love with her!' he strangely added. Oh yes you are, stupid old man. I clam up as soon as I need a voice but I was armed with Kevin's letter. 'My brother wrote this, he agrees.' 'He's a relative of course he's going to agree with you!' I told him Georgene had to deal with The Dee last spring, she'd write him too. He was POKING me HARD in the right arm with his finger over and over. 'You can find another doctor if you're not happy with The Dee!' POKE POKE 'Stop Touching Me!' He made a run for the door. 'Take this letter from my brother!' He took it but I was certain it was trash.

Stunned, followed quickly by anger and then finally laughing at how stupid men can be when the penis is involved. Thank God the nurse was there to witness his melt down or I'd be wondering if he was REAL. How was I supposed to find another doctor? I asked Century City the next day, he said he'd look but couldn't think of one off hand. Friday back at wound care: Torrance and Allritini show up together. Oh No Ambush! I thought, but Torrance said he read my brothers letter and Kevin was right, The Dee is incompetent and will be replaced. Like an errant schoolboy that's been given a speech to recite. I've lost respect and it's not coming back, he was bat shit Looney tunes and didn't apologize. Not even a Damien apology.

Weekend had some mix up—no nurse Saturday—residual's from TD. Week 2 repeat, without nasty The Dee stuff. I was in so much pain it was debilitating. Friend took me out to dinner, Nancy did my laundry, cousins Lance and Kathy came down and took me to dinner and Alison brought me groceries but terrible loneliness is still eating my organs. Always the dark side, run to the light, Carol Anne! I don't want to die but I don't wanna feel like shit every day either. What 2 do what 2 do?

2007

Duh. Get back on the happy pills, silly! I didn't make that connection for another month.

October 2005, Venice Beach

Coolchick was happy my globulin was back up to 12. It had been 2. Harder than normal dealing with bureaucratic nonsense; Torrance Hospital wouldn't give me a proper walking cast. I had one, they insisted. I was still seeing Doc Century City twice a week. He wrote a prescription for a plastic walking cast and sent me to Doc Culver City.

Pakistan quake / floods in Guatemala / hurricane's Katrina, Rita, Stan / the Amazon river is flooding the clear cut land / AIDS has made 20 million orphans in Africa. Earth is scratching—people B gone people B gone—I hate this rash. I tunes is popular / hundreds of songs you can listen to as you go to your job like Metropolis / ignore ignore / the government cuts more rights / patriotic patriotic / listen to your favorite music / don't interact you might form some nasty revolt.

> 'Those things which mankind has hitherto pondered seriously are not even realities, merely imaginings, more strictly speaking *lies* from the bad instincts of sick, in the profoundest sense injurious natures—all the concepts of 'God' 'soul' 'virtue' 'sin' 'the Beyond' 'truth' 'eternal life…' But the greatness of human nature, it's 'divinity' has been sought in them… all questions of politics, the ordering of society, education, have been falsified down to their foundations because the most injurious men have been taken for great men—because contempt has been taught for the 'little things', which is to say for the fundamental affairs of life. I do not count these supposed 'pre-eminent men' as belonging to mankind at all—to me they are the refuse of man kind—abortive offspring of sickness and vengeful instincts: they are nothing but pernicious fundamentally incurable monsters who take revenge on life. I want to be the antithesis of this.'

—Nietzsche

Watching the BBC, they had a group of scientists showing photos of the polar ice caps melting—but honestly dude, people in their 40's and 50's are supposed to be in charge and we all knew about 'Climate Change' thirty years ago. (Didn't I learn about it in grade school? Maybe I learned from Pop.) Academia has been aware of the greenhouse affect since the '50's but our government—except for that pesky Carter—has refused to deal with it. Democ-rats and Republic-rats, scurrying around the same rotting tree.

> 'For some, life turns out badly. A poisonous worm eats its way into their heart. Let them see to it that their dying turns out that much better. Some never become sweet they rot already in the summer. It is cowardice that keeps them on their branch. Would that a storm came to shake all this worm eaten rot from the tree!'

—Nietzsche

Cheryl and I were having lunch with Ex-friend about a week after Katrina. I said something like, 'those poor people …' and Ex-friend went into a tirade against THEM, those Black People! I changed the subject. Talked instead about the cause of all the hurricanes. Ex-friend started POKING ME IN THE ARM! (like Dr Torrance) 'There's no such thing! The earth is going through a normal cycle!' When I told him my father was a scientist for the EPA he said, 'Your Father is an Idiot!' Calling a white woman's Daddy an idiot is like saying something bad about a black mans Mom. Waivers, asshole.

November 2005, Venice

Coolchick didn't know an allergist on the West Side but a nurse in her office used to work for Dr Eyesclosed in Santa Monica and gave me his number. Dr Eyesclosed was unavailable, I talked to Rita Kachru by default, she was free that minute. She was too young and cocky to tolerate. After a negative conversation, I swore at her and hung up fuming. She freely acknowledged she had <u>no experience with anesthesia</u> yet kept loudly insisting, 'you have to wait two months! You can't have surgery until I test the anesthesia! You have to come over here right now!' Surreal bitch.

What if I was 9 months pregnant and needed a C section? What if my appendix burst? If I were in a car accident? There are ways to handle allergies when time is a factor; I thought as much and it was confirmed by the other allergists I spoke with. I also learned the drugs used for my anesthesia can't be skin tested. (What Kachru was insisting upon.) To avoid a repeat of the reaction, I could have a shot of steroids or Benadryl, I could take Hydrox, Decadron or a combination. I discussed options with Dr Coolchick, we agreed I should get anesthesia tested before I was intubated, fortunately skin grafts aren't that invasive, I only needed MAC.

Couple days before surgery, Dr Allritini called. 'I just got off the phone with your allergist, she said bla bla…' My response: 'I haven't hired an allergist!' I'd talked to several but only phone conversations. Rita Kachru had *sent Dr Torrance a letter* that gave the impression she had been retained by me! ('Thank you for the reference' means exactly that.) Allritini was concerned and had called her. S*he led him to believe she knew me; I* <u>*had been to her office*</u> *and hired her! I'd had blood tests, I'd made another appointment!*

When Allritini heard the truth he was speechless. He had cancelled my October 12 surgery. 'Maybe we should get an opinion from a real allergist…' She had scared him, I couldn't talk him out of it. Dr Coolchick was taken aback, she signed off on MAC and she was my primary physician. She called Allritini to see where his head was at. Doc Century City asked if I wanted help finding another surgeon, he'd been picking up the pieces around me for the past three months.

But I don't blame Dr Allritini for being duped by a liar. He had never heard of a doctor *lying* about being retained—WHO HAS? A New Fresh Hell of malpractice. I called Dr Eyesclosed to complain and *he refused to believe me!* 'Are you sure you didn't forget coming in? He stupidly asked and, do you have any proof?' I hung up. I do have proof, her fucking letter. I wrote to California's Medical Board, it was a 1st for them, they'd never heard of bullshit like this either. (I had a long chatty conversation with Med Board guy. He said since I'd never hired her, their hands were tied. He told me about the shit they dealt with, like removed the wrong: foot / kidney / lung etc.) I talked to the allergist Coolchick recommended, he said to get a vulture blood test, it was fine and the fastest I could get booked for surgery <u>again</u> was Thursday October 27.

When Allritini removed the dressing 10 days later, half the skin was pink and healthy the other half was soggy and starting to stink, like rotting flesh. Integra sat for two extra weeks on fragile granulation tissue, causing bacteria to build up under it, thanks to Rita's inaccurate, unasked for diagnosis. Unforgivable. I'm not sure what I'm going to do next. I'm so angry that I have to have ANOTHER operation. (If you have another surgery you could die! So I'm going to make sure you have TWO MORE!)

CVA symptoms make it nearly impossible to deal with stress; it took ten days to write about the RK Horror Show.

I just got off the phone with Kev telling him not to give in to pessimism, I have to laugh, look who's talking. Ayn Rand was right, Orwell, Miller, Huxley, Sinclair, Steinbeck, they all were, the evil needs to be deleted. (Shrug off the fungus.) Water is being depleted by keeping hundred acre green moats around multi million dollar castles in the California desert / waterfalls in Vegas / pea green golf courses in the brown-beige landscape of Arizona.

Ignore ignore, turn on I Tunes and dance. And some kind of nuke is going off in the middle east, I can feel it. (Madness makes you think you know the future.) They've been at war for sixty years, it's become chronic pain. Africa is folding in on itself / crumpling like a leaf / blowing away. I think of Africa as a pack of souls / born / die / born / die of poverty war genocide aids malaria / ignore ignore. A handful of people care desperately, everyone says fuck Africa, fuck those starving children!' (An ex-Friend really yelled that at me in a crowded restaurant, 'I don't give a fuck about Africa! Fuck them! *Fuck those starving children!'*)

2007

Anger at The Bitch RK was unmanageable. I was supposed to be free of the plastic walking cast. Supposed be back in the gym, taking fotos of graffiti and organizing shoots for CafeDeb. It wazz the snail that broke a camel back.

If you ever ask yourself, 'what else can possibly go wrong?' Having a doctor you do not know and did not hire, torturing you, lying to your real doctor, canceling your surgery and keeping you in a walking cast for another month, is it.

I could and did meander my way to the hoops. It'd taken a year and a half but I'd made friends at the beach, nearly everyone a black male. We'd smoke a spleef then sit in front of the Teriyaki Shop and watch the show. They'd make funny comments about the women walking by and I'd point out the six packs on surfer boys I was fond of. Killed hours, weeks, laughing at and taking fotos of tourists. They were big brother-ish protective and made me feel part of the pack. One afternoon a fat black dude was wandering by and made a slur 'why is that white bitch always sitting with you?' 'Keep walking, you don't have anything else to say...'

> '...Shannon disappeared
> she was swimming in the ocean
> maybe she'll find a desert island
> with a stand of palm trees
> like the shady one in our back yard...
>
> paraphrasing Henry Gross

Looking back, it's not just anger and depression that astonish me, it's any emotion at any given time. Crazee strong and backwards whacked. Summer of '02 Friend and I found ourselves in a laughing vortex. I was crying at the Shannon song and laughing about crying so hard I got Friend laughing and crying too. We were sitting in her car in front of the liquor store by Rags house howling out of control. The clerk smiled at us when we finally calmed down enough to walk in. 'I don't know what you were laughing about but you got me laughing at you.' 'Shannon, she's gone I heard...' giggle snort.

I used to use that song as a trigger to cry. I had a theatre professor that hated fake crying on the stage. He wanted real tears in under a minute and made it part of our grade. 'You need a trigger you can tap into when needed. Using something real, like the death of a loved one, isn't good, you need to turn it off just as fast.' That was a good advice and I always used it. A melodrama like Shannon was perfect. I visualized a boy ten-ish and a big dumb Irish Setter, his best friend. They live in Key West, he's looking at the ocean thinking, 'maybe she'll find an island with a shady tree…' He knows on some level that Shannon drowned but can't admit it yet. It worked like a charm, turn on the tears, turn them off.

I remember using it for Another 48 Hours. Andrew has me hostage and I am screaming, crying. All afternoon we were working on this one sequence and thanks to Shannon I was water works whenever the AD yelled 'Roll Sound!' At one point he said, 'are you OK? I mean, I know you're acting but…' it seemed real. 'I'm fine, I use a breathing technique to cry.' Another tip from that old professor, 'don't dilute its power by discussing it and change your trigger whenever it gets stale.' I hadn't thought of Shannon for years. I was always crying for the camera and changed my trigger a lot. Sometimes a movie minute, a book I'd just read, if I still had difficulty making tears I'd think, 'if you don't cry, you're fired,' that worked but only as a last resort because it was too Real. (Made me feel bad.) How can you feel bad with Shannon? Impossible. What a surprise to have it come back so strong and out of control that summer afternoon. Another clue to stroke shenanigans but only clues.

'…bong bong diddley
diddley bong bong
diddley diddley bong…'

paraphrasing Rankin Joe

Surgery was scheduled again for Dec 1. A week before I got a creepy foreboding. It got worse and worse until the day before the procedure I called it off! I'd been seeing Allritini twice a week since September, he asked why, he knew my situation was arduous. Told him I felt negativity, couldn't place it but it was fierce and getting worse, too much to ignore. 'I'm superstitious too! We'll reschedule.' Crazee that we both felt it. I'm not getting my heel refitted until the 22nd of December.

Jane has the patience of Mother Theresa. Elective surgery is hard to schedule *anytime* but there's an end of the year rush for space in every decent operating room before everyone's insurance vulture rolls over. Trying not to be depressed, I miss my work out / I do crunches by the hundreds.

X-mass week, 2005 Venice

Cohoon called me out of the blue and came out for the holiday. I met him over 20 years ago in Jamaica. He and his ex-wife used to be friends of mine. He worked for the Feds / Pablo Escobar / Iran Contra / Miami Vice all blend together over time; he was in the thick of it. We lost touch in the early 90's when they started having kids. (He found me on the net.) Two years ago his wife tried to kill him with strychnine in his coffee—it gave him a stroke—not as bad as mine but newer. He's still in the lost in space phase, trying to get through the day. I was able to validate his atmosphere, 'you're not going nuts, it will pass.' I picked him up at LAX and said, 'Baby, you look so old!' 'So do you!' We laughed, like we've never been apart. Spent Christmas at the beach. He drove me too and from St John's on the 22nd for the last graft on my ankle. I sit with a lump of sticky yellow Xeroform stitched into my skin, covered by more dressing (and walking cast) for another week. I hope.

Cohoon helped me get all the way through the storage space and we found the box of jewelry! Called Ms. X right away, she was still a wackadoo and had already rewritten the past (I had *called her* growling at 5 am) but at least that chapter has a happy ending.

2007

Another friend from the past Magically appears when I needed help. I believe the universe, the never ending mystery, was sending me what I needed and him what he needed, he's in a small town, no stroke rehab. Thanx Shiva Allah Buddha God and Yahweh we cheered each other. Christmas alone with that walking cast could have been bad. Everything about it was horrid. Hurt my hip, showering had to be done sitting sideways on a director's chair and once a week I'd go to the salon to have my hair washed. I'd been doing it since September and felt grubby. Walking was difficult, talking was difficult, crazee vultures. I felt like I was going backwards; I always wrote that suicide wasn't an option but it wasn't exactly true. I would write things to try and make them true.

Jan 06—The Year of the Bitch—Venice Beach

The Stunt Women's Foundation gave me $10,000! That's serious cash. The first thing I did was get shiatsu from the Asian guy down the street. 'Work on my scars,' I told him. Relief! My ankles are the worst. Sad that I have to pay someone to touch me but thank you thank you Stunt Women! I can pay Nancy to clean again.

Felt like writing erotica (that's got to be good.) I wrote some stuff for Debbie Likes 2 Read. It's relieving to disappear into virtual reality, CafeDeb got 260,000 hits last month. I either work on my web site or sit at the beach and watch baskets, life floating by. Foot is still playing the waiting game.

My SSDI checks stopped paying in November but I didn't notice until now. Had RVT with Doc Century City then went to the Social Security office in Westwood and waited two hours. Some mix up, they say, promised to 'release the funds.' Once again I think of all the people that can't sit for hours in the SS office.

> '…your mind is a paper back novel
> and the hero is heartbroken
> it's me isn't it?
> isn't it me?
> what *are* you thinking?'

> paraphrasing Gordon Lightfoot

The Weed Guy wants me to get a medical marijuana prescription. I've been reticent but he almost had me. I've always thought marijuana should be legal like alcohol; the government wants to keep its 'narcotic' status because millions of pot heads make good slaves. Prisons make Fortunes selling slave labor. Victoria's Secret is that the people stitching her bras are non-violent drug offenders making .13 an hour.

Weed Guy has a Doctor friend, Pussy. I could call and make an appointment with his receptionist, Deak. Deak was a freak! He behaved like Tweak! I could practically see his crack pipe. They get $150 for every 'prescription.' I told Deak I really was hurt and was just getting a prescription as a favor to Weed Guy. 'I don't give a fart about your problems; I have another call from a PAYING CUSTOMER!' Click. *Paying customer.* Creepy. I called Weed Guy, 'what the hell just happened?' 'He yells at everyone,' he said, as if that excused it. Weed Guy made Deak call me back and apologize. It was funny, it sounded like a Damien apology. 'I'm sorry Weed Guy didn't tell me you were calling.' Very funny but not good enough. 'You raised your voice, were rude and hung up on me. That's what I want you to apologize for.' I pictured steam coming out of his ears. 'I'm sorry you think I was rude. Do you want the appointment or not?' I laughed, 'sure.'

What kind of Alexander fool is Pussy? I wasn't getting a prescription from that dysfunctional duo but I thought I'd tell Pussy about Deak. Like telling Doctor Torrance about The Dee / someone should do it. Besides he only lived ten blocks away.

I went to the little beach hut and knocked; Pussy stuck his head out the door, he looked like a surfer. (His med school was in the Caribbean.) 'Can you wait for a minute?' Before I could say No he closed the door. I did wait, more than a minute, then left. I felt transported through time, I was 15 buying a ½ ounce of homegrown for $20. I had to laugh. The Weed Guy called me 20 min later but I let it go to voice mail. Sorry I'm being wimpy; can't do it for many reasons, the biggest being the meth factor.

I am fascinated by the trickery though. I Google'd 'medical marijuana doctors Los Angeles' and called 10 of them. They ranged from $100 to $300 per prescription and they all wanted *cash only*. There was one guy was willing charge a stipend because I was SSDI. One in ten. Hippocratic Oath? Me no think so. I asked Coolchick about it, she prescribes Marinol to cancer patients (THC in pill form.) She doesn't know any one who writes prescriptions for smoke-able weed. California vote's medical marijuana legal every election but the feds say no. Feds trump States. Weed Guy cares about seeing schnizz legalized, I don't. And—not interested in being a martyr to medical marijuana—typical pot smoker's hypocrisy.

February 2006—Venice

My heel is healed! Allritini was right and redeemed in my critical eye. He gave me an injection of cortisone in the neuroma nest on my foot. Yieeeyieeeyoowww! Put me in orbit with a hideously interesting new pain. The nest was numbed for a day but feels the same now.

I've had physical therapy for the last six weeks at Cedars-Sinai. Therapist was nice, taught me how to walk without a limp. New idea, instead of trying to lift toes up, think of pushing the heel back. It works and I can do it walking slowly with a cane. He told silly kids jokes and massaged my left arm, it does all the work and never gets attention. He also got me a new AFO (the plastic brace in my shoe to keep my big toe from tripping me) Therapist thinks the one I've been using the past two years is too stiff and not long enough. The AFO is from Beverly Hills Prosthetics Orthodics. We tried different ones for a couple weeks and decided on a custom made.

> Aside: Beverly Hills is fun and takes his job seriously, we talked freely. On Strokes: The maddening way they train wreck your auto pilot. If I don't want a limp, I must *think* of walking. It wont become automatic if I'd only work out harder. He got that. I told him about the new backward thought process, successful for me. He didn't believe me while I was *showing him*. 'This is thinking nothing (my gimpy scuffle) this is thinking 'toe fore ward' (toe chips in first) this is thinking 'heel back' (walking correctly.) Walking back and forth, BevH would say, That! The way you just walked was correct. Me: It was heel back. No! That doesn't work, show me toe forward again. He *would not believe it*. Both laughing but definitely one of those, is He REAL, episodes.

The lawsuit against Sleeping Bag Co is still chugging along. I'm convinced the reason it takes so long is so everyone can play reindeer games. Each side gets a specialist to test the bag, both sides pay vulture fee's to everyone they can think of. Milk milk heifers. I pray for it to be over this summer, I want to move to Portland and have been looking at real estate on the net and day dreaming.

Solitary; I go for days where the only people I talk to are in Doctor Century City's office, hello girl at the pharmacy, hello kids at the coffee shop, hello worker bee's at my gym. Simulated conversation's that mean nothing.

My residuals are tiny now, I don't open them. CafeDeb.com has paid another peanut, its been good to do, I've learned 2 new programs and it gets me out of the neighborhood. It's fun to arrange shoots, scout locations, garment district wardrobe gather and meeting new people is always good. Failure as a moneymaker, though. I have no interest in marketing, that's a problem and it always has been. If you don't like to sell your wares yourself—and who toots an annoying Me My & I horn? Creeps freaks and wannabe's—you need a mouthpiece. Agent, manager, attorney all three if you can afford it but you need at least one and proper protection is hard to come by.

I shot 2 models myself this past month. Jessica at Birgit's house and Mark 'The Naked Man' all over downtown. I'd put an ad on Craig's list for male models with sculpted bodies. I want CafeDeb to have a few nude men but don't want them shot like the women. (Boys trying to be sexy look gay, gay men don't mind looking at straight guys, but not vice versa. Friend and I shot another male model at Matador Beach in December with a background female as a prop.) Mark was a personal trainer, his body was outrageous. 'You'll have to be nonchalant about nudity,' I said. 'I'm Hawaiian, I love to be naked.' Perfect. We met at MOCA early Sunday am and shot guerrilla until noon. Cheryl came and chauffeured us around in my van, we'd hop out and shoot until we got kicked out (or just got great shots, a lot of places didn't notice us) I'd get myself set, then give a nod to Mark, he'd slip off his T-shirt and shorts and climb the art. We hit MOCA's fountains, various banks, the Ghery, the main Library; Mark was great, a fearless model, Cheryl and I were giggling like teenagers. Nice Man distraction. Cool fotos and it felt good to control all aspects of the creative process, 1st time I've wanted to.

2007

I'd had a relationship with Bio Concepts (pressure garments) for years. They're in Phoenix, when visiting Georgene I'd gone to Bio Concepts and let them measure my hand Themselves. They sent gloves that were too small, I sent them back, this went on for awhile and they were perturbed. When the woman who'd taken my measurements called to bitch, I should have remained calm, *after all, I was in the right.* Instead I fought back as crazee as she was. All out war!

Bio C has made over 10 G from my insurance but she sent a $350 bill to collection's because she was pissed. I called collections and said 'if the gloves don't fit, you must acquit.' Then sent an e. 'Sorry you're in the middle of this, you seem like a nice guy.' He was a nice guy and it didn't go any further but that was the end of my relationship with Bio Concepts. I didn't stop to think of the consequences. More than a *year later* I found a local designer (she specializes in ice skating outfits) I was wearing ratty old gloves forever because I couldn't control my self. Lose your temper, lose the fight. Even if you're right.

March—Venice 06

I woke up yesterday, depressed and crying by nine. Smoked weed and laid in bed all day. At 3:30 I went to the Westwood courthouse and filed a small claim against The Bitch Kachew for $7500, the maximum. Good Decision. Woke up today, walked to the beach, coffee and a blueberry smoothie, worked out, felt great. Court date April 10. Time to take control and discontinue doormat status.

Sat at the ball court talking to Betsy; I've been calling her 2 or 3 mornings a week for the past year; she stops me from eating breakfast alone and helps me distinguish fact from smoke and mirrors.

Stopped seeing doctors after my foot healed; a needed break. I want my lawsuit to settle / get a cozy house in Portland and adopt. I've thought about it for years. Finally am done with surgery's, finally in shape. There are adoption sites on the net, so many girls want to be the only child of a single mom.

April 10, 2006—Venice Beach

Alison came with me for support. The Judge was careful, asked me if I wanted to sit down, paid close attention and asked questions. I read from a script to keep myself from stammering. He listened to RK; she lied like a rug. He busted her chops about me never being to her office, and what did she mean by her letter? 'Thank you for the reference...' doesn't it mean exactly that? In the end he apologized to me and said 'unfortunately the burden of proof is on you, she just has to raise a reasonable doubt.'

I had a chance to refute her bullshit but my brain doesn't work quickly enough. She PERJURED HERSELF! A felony! I could prove it and did nothing! Vultures eating my brain cells.

'...I may have problems but a woman isn't one of them...'

paraphrasing Jay Z

Double jeopardy? There's a way around it. Sue for perjury. Ahhhh. Happy again. Even if I don't win I'm dragging her sorry ass back to court.

2007

The second time I had her in front of the judge got her attention. 'I can't keep coming to court, she's making me take time off of work! I'm sorry she's so angry! I'm scared of her!' Glad to hear it. I'd written a scathing letter to her boss Doctor Eyesclosed and pictured him berating her. The judge dismissed my case again, saying 'if only you had brought your doctor in' but I wasn't going to subpoena Allritini. In California you have a year to file a proper lawsuit, 'I'll see you in Superior Court,' I said to her as we were leaving, let her worry about that next. Her husband was a little puppy, staring at me stupidly. 'Come here!' She yelled at him. Funny. Relief, you got revenge but why did that wicked freak have such a hard on to hurt you? I think it was an arrogance evil idiocy revenge cocktail. I was rude to The Bitch RK and she thought 'Fuck You Too lady, I'm going to *hurt you*.' Hippocratic oath? Me no think so.

'…let animals live all over your house
give your cupboard to a grouse
give your oven to a ferret
give your chandelier to a parrot
let a baboon have your skirt
let a dolphin have your shirt…'

~Al Christ

I stopped by SAG, deposited some checks at the Versetel and got an honorable discharge; I've been paying dues since '02 for nothing. Producers Health Plan wants their money back once I have a settlement. If Sleeping Bag Co's insurance policy is two million, my attorneys take a third and PHP wants $800,000 back that doesn't leave me much to live on.

Walking back to the van, what's this? A tear? I got in and started crying. Caught me by surprise. Goodbye SAG after all these years. I loved doing stunts. I loved the countdown when 'Pictures Up.' Get on your mark and it begins…The 1st AD calls Roll Sound, sound man yells Rolling, A Camera Mark, (clap board) A Marker, B Camera (could be a bunch depends on the stunt and how much money the company has) waiting on Action / adrenaline pumping / everything slows down / super aware and in the moment / that beautiful adrenaline rush. I miss that. Called Alison and she made me feel better.

May 2006—Venice Beach

Settled my Sleeping Bag lawsuit. My lawyers were bad. (I don't feel like making a list but they were embarrassing. I'll write a short story and post it on Debbie Likes 2 Read.) When I visited Georgene during her custody battle,

The Cretin's lawyer was ineffectual. George said, 'I keep thinking he's going to pull a 'Colombo' and suddenly be smart.' I told her, 'no, he's Dulumbo.' That's what my attorney were, a couple of Dulumbo's. When you have more common sense than the 'experts' working for you, you're effed. Sleeping Bag Co's sharks swam in from NYC and saw the flounders from San Diego dulumbo-ing around, they had them for breakfast. I got a <u>shit settlement</u> but took it anyway, it pays for life and I have to get on with mine, it's been in a holding pattern for four ½ years. My surgeries are over, I can finally leave LA.

It doesn't pay until August but I bought a new box spring and mattress, I've been sagging myself to sleep on sprung springs. The delivery company called me early and said they'd come after noon. Eleven am I am wakened by knocking on my window. I stick my head out the door and tell them to wait. Throw on baggy jeans and a bathrobe over my baby T. Went to unlock to gate and one guy says '…let me help you…' rushes over and brushed his hand against my left nipple when grabbing the key. I thought it was an accident (gullible and still sleepy.) They set my new bed up. Luscious, huge oversized fluffy goodness, I couldn't wait to get back in. I had let the sales woman talk me into a $70 special mattress pad. I asked them to put it on for me. Boob Grabber walked by and *patted my belly.* I was shocked SPEECHLESS! 'You have a new bed are you gonna try it out?' Leering, he patted my belly again! I backed up into the kitchenette—lecherous Latin, long haired and fat—between me and escape. There was a rack of weed cookies next to me on the counter, I held them between us. 'Do you want some cookies? They're for after work…' I was babbling scared. 'Yea! I'll be by after work!' I finally found my voice. 'NO! You're not coming back here!' 'Let's go,' said the younger one, who seemed embarrassed by Boob Grabber's lewd show. They left. Three hours later I was still thinking about it; my reaction, my slow response, my 'duh…do you want some cookies?' idiocy. I finally called and had Boob Grabber fired and even *that* was wimpy. I felt guilty for having a *predator* fired? That is not me, so although I see physical improvement my vulture brain is still broken.

June 2006—Venice Beach

Good work out late afternoon, did an hour of stair master, a few right arm weights and 50 sit ups on the chairs highest level, almost straight up and down. (I love the looks I get, the crippled chick pulling a GI Jane, I don't even see the guys doing it.) Felt great, I thought I was in a good mood.

Waiting for the elevator to the garage, a strange woman barged into my personal space, she looked high and was blabbing in a foreign accent. 'I know you're sad but you will get better I know you will recover from this, it's so SAD you're SAD...' I should have ignored her but she was SO annoying I held up my compromised hand, 'I'm not going to grow another finger, I'm not a lizard, now fuck off.'

I walked away and she followed into my freakin' space *again.* 'No you will get better I know you will get better blah blahh.' I shoved the open palm of my left hand into her Face! Hard enough to push her away from me! The Terminator *she kept coming*, I couldn't believe it. 'I love you anyway, I love you anyway...' slurring her words. 'Lady if you don't get away from me, I'm whacking you in the head with my cane.' I held it right next to her face. She finally realized she was in imminent danger and left.

A girl to my right had witnessed to whole thing. We looked at each other, blank stares. The elevator came. Wonder what she thought. Was she as surprised as I was?

Drove out of the parking lot and called Cohoon. 'I scared myself, I was seconds away from committing a felony...' He's funny, listened and understood what made me mad. Told me he's never heard of me hitting a woman but he remembered me slapping quite a few guys. I calmed down a little. It's freakish when a stranger invades your personal space. (Only a foot wide.) It used to be men that did it, usually drunk wannabe Casanova's.

No matter how stupid, misguided and wasted she was (Zanax or Valium is my guess) it was still a positive action. My response? Negative. I have to stop.

Dream: Moving my fingers and wrist putting in ligaments and muscle myself.

'...stoop not down therefore
into the darkly splendid world
wherein continually lieth a faithless depth
and Hades wrapped up in clouds
delighting in unintelligible images
precipitous, winding, a black, ever rolling abyss...'

—The Chaldean Oracles of Zoroaster

Fury at The Bitch RK was sucking freaks to me, a black hole of hate.

Coming home from the gym Monday afternoon there was a white SUV in the neighbors spot parked at a sharp angle. I look over expecting to see Simpering Neighbor but it's a chick I don't recognize. She looks at me and smiles the crazee smile. Hard to explain but you definitely recognize it when you see it—madness close to the surface—plenty in Venice. Whatever. I turn away. I'm futzing around, it takes me a minute to get my gym bag together and put CD's back in their cases.

Feel something and look back. She's staring at me. I stare back. She keeps staring. I keep staring back. I can do this all day, I'm great at The Rock Star Game. (The Rock Star game is urban lore, friend of a friend thing. Its fun to play. The Tale: Rock was working in a LA recording studio and before she showed up everyone got a memo No Speaking Unless Spoken To. The usual but added was, No Eye Contact. Friend of Friend was annoyed. Early one am she pulled into her parking just spot as Rock pulled into hers. They made eye contact and Rock held it. F of F held it. They got out of their convertibles and were walking into the studio staring at each other and Rock walked into a poster of herself and broke eye contact, F of F won the game! I thought that diversion was fun, whenever I accidentally make eye contact, I try to hold it.

Stare, stare, stare, stare. I'm starting to get bored, I have things to do. I was just about to smile in defeat when BOOM! Crackadoo explodes! She's screaming in her car, I can clearly read her lips. 'Do you want a piece of me? Do you want a fucking piece of me!? Thinks she's De Niro? It was too much, I laughed, which of course sent her into a red faced frenzy. When Kevin and I talked about it later he said, 'it's like you had a stare down with a baboon, they think it's threatening.'

She rolled down her window and kept swearing. I rolled down mine—completely involved—told her to Fuck Off, she didn't live here! I'd call the cops if she didn't leave! I opened my door and here comes Crackadoo running around the back of her SUV. I jabbed her with my cane as hard as I could in the solar plexus and she doubled over gasping for air. *Then she came at me again.* She grabbed my cane with both of her hands and ripped it away from me. I went auto-pilot and instantly closed the gap to prevent her from swinging. I grabbed her collar, pulling her in and down, shaking her like a rag doll screaming, 'WHAT THE FUCK IS WRONG WITH YOU? I'M A FUCKING CRIPPLE! YOU ARE ATTACKING A FUCKING CRIPPLE! YOU'RE GOING TO JAIL BITCH!' She dropped my cane. I let her go and slowly backed away. Her shirt was ripped, her neck scratched. 'You're lucky I'm a gimp, bitch.' She reached out snake like and grabbed the sun glasses off my face, threw them on the ground and stomped up and down on them like a five year old throwing a tantrum.

Handyman was working on the apartment next door. Girl fight! He came running with the plumber to see. Crackadoo backed off with men there. (Chicken shit junkie.) She pulled up her shirt 'look what she did to my stomach!' There's a bulls eye on the bottom of my cane right and beneath her skinny ribcage, an exact replica in red. As scary as the situation had become, I had to smile at that. My reactions are getting faster.

Trying to call the police, I lost my Blue Tooth, found it on the ground, called 911 then hit end instead of send, freaking out; I finally get through, give my name and address and describe my attacker. 'Her license plate is xxx she's still in our parking lot!' Crackadoo is yelling crack speak. 'Nobody cares about your injuries! You don't love God! You're hurt because you don't love Jesus! Bitch! You don't love God!'

I left the guys to watch her and went to my apartment to wait for the cops. I had to calm down. Hard to think when I'm so stressed. What just happened? I don't love Jesus so he sent a scabby crackho to beat me up? I can't see God being that petty. The cops arrived a few minutes later. 'Slow day,' they answered when I asked about it. One stays with me, the other goes to the alley to speak with Crackadoo. I told mine what happened, the stare down, the attack thwarted by a hard poke. He chuckled at shaking like a rag doll.

The other cop came back. She had left, he'd talked to the neighbors, Handyman, Plumber, no one knew who she was. 'Want to press charges? I have to tell you that if she says you attacked her, you'll both be arrested. Well? Are you gonna press charges or not?' They looked bored. (Stupid girl fight.) I though of her ripped shirt and the bull's-eye on her stomach. Spend the night in the jail because Crackadoo attacked me? Wah. I let myself be intimidated by cops. I didn't have her arrested and have been skittish ever since. I bought two cans of tear gas, one for car, one for gym bag.

June 2006—still in Venice

PBS did a show about the filthiest river in the country. It's in Calexico, going into the Salton Sea. It was made accidentally when a levee broke. It's been ignored for a hundred years. California and Mexico pointed fingers at each other and both have been dumping sewage and chemicals ever since. When the Salton Sea dries up (within my life time) it will become a dust bin of cancerous toxins. The Crackadoo attack was a sign from the universe to leave So Cal.

I talked it over with Priest. He's become my best friend in Venice. A calm, seen it all Jamaican; fifty something. He agreed, negativity breeds negativity. Priest and I meet for coffee and watch the morning show. Joggers, surfers, back packers, busloads of huge fat American tourists and normal size foreigners interacting with the home team: homeless drunks, run-away teenagers and crackho's. (My name for all scrawny meth addicts, male and female.) There are more of them all than last summer.

2007

Also a sign to get my temper under control, I'd been having too many altercations with nut bags. My anger was drawing them to me; Ms Menopause at Bio Concepts, The Bitch RK, The Stoned Freak at the gym and now Crackadoo! Enough already! White flag.

Having a six pack was my goal, it took a long time but I finally did it and my abs are bigger on the left side. Even my ribcage is more filled out on the left. Breaks my heart that I had such horrible therapy at first, I'm sure would have recovered more with an expert like Litzel from the start. Even Smallville had Pilates but it was six months before I got there. The first few months after a stroke are the most important / I know I keep saying that but it's so significant / your brain tries to find ways around the carnage for awhile, not forever.

> I wrote: 'I have been working out like I'm getting ready for
> a job since returning from Guam 18 months ago. So. This is
> as good as it gets. At least I know.'

I could stop blaming myself for things beyond my control and I did stop. Went to a new pain management Doctor, referred by Coolchick. He seemed smart. He prescribed Lyrica, a new drug for neurological pain. Seems to be working, I feel better in the morning, easier to get up.

July 2006, Venice Beach

Alison and I got hugged by AmmA last night. She's Indian. I'd never heard of her. It was interesting, calming and lovely. She hugs 50,000 people at a time, takes over a day. She looked at my arm then quietly chanted something soothing and sweet into my ear. It's was a good hug too, firm, warm; she held me for eight or ten seconds and I hugged back. What a crazee cool way to raise money for her charities. The event is free but she had chachki for sale and a tasty dinner for six bucks.

The Airport Hilton (huge) was filled with a happy vibe; she had musicians playing, singing and drumming Indian music. We got special treatment for gimp status and because it was our first time getting a hug from AmmA; after we ate we were allowed straight into the main ballroom. (Fire marshals were keeping count of the masses; we would have waited our turn, snaking through the labyrinth downstairs with thousands of others, watching AmmA on closed circuit screens.) We waited for four hours, laughing and talking with the people around us. A positive way to spend Saturday night.

> '...the world is so fucked up
> crime corruption vice
> even grocery shopping
> you're buying chemicals additives poisons
> rape murder suicide
> everyone is evil
> and taking a bribe...'
>
> paraphrasing Third World

July 2006, Venice Beach

Woke up at six and walked to the beach it was a beautiful morning; empty except for Homelet and city workers cleaning. I am going to miss vanishing (gentrifying) Venice Beach but I'm finally Escaping LA.

2007—Portland, OR

I bought a ranch, no stairs, attached garage, in an old neighborhood between two parks. Perfect for me. Birgit drove us up here in my van, then Betsy flew out for a week and helped me get settled. However the past 18 months have been the loneliest. The only reason I'm able to go on is that dramatic pronouncements like, the only reason I'm able to go on, still crack me up. I thought I'd be happy leaving LA and location wise j'adore but what I was worried about has happened. I'm alone most of the time. No one in Portland knew me pre-injury except my brother and his wife and they don't talk to me.

I don't know what turned Kev frosty, he was normal until Betsy left August '06, then viciously attacked my fledgling self approval. Negative Nutty for months, he'll stop I thought, he's just blowing steam take it like a man— but come on, it's kicking a puppy and he knows it. Betrayal by my brother, heartbreaking Madness. A Doppelganger lives in his shell, my real brother wouldn't beat me up. I can't dis him more than this in print. I hope someday he tells me what his problem is.

2008

I wanted move up and out of depression and despair but couldn't do it alone. Bogged in a murky mire of dull loneliness I was willing to try anything. I went to the pound and found 15 lbs of heaven. Half Chihuahua, half Corgi, her happiness is transmittable, I take her everywhere. I tried all of my neighborhood churches. The Methodist had a bible study one night a week, we were a crazee crew of misfit toys, absurdly fun that only lasted a few months but I met Friend. We agree on most things, read the same books and he has Parkinson's, brain damage. (Brain Damage has a Secret Club like Life Altering Injury's but we can't quite remember, where is it? what time? what's the secret handshake?)

Made a new friend who was a bit of a skyscraper, she had been a friend of Latham's (my RN friend that mysteriously died.) She came to Kevin's to visit in the spring of '02. I really appreciated it and called once I moved here. We'd been hanging out a couple months, she was interesting and had a nice family but she was the center of the universe. She happened to call after an argument with Kevin and kept insisting I take unasked for advice (you have to call him, write him email...) getting angrier and meaner every time I disagreed with her (I don't talk well on phones, writing email to address a problem is wimpy...) It was weird. I told her I didn't want help solving problems with my brother. 'Well what then? What do you expect me to do?' Nothing. Just be sympathetic. Annoyed she said, 'I don't give sympathy to people that don't deserve it!' Waivers, baby. I recognized my negative blueprint and escaped unscathed. My friend protocol has changed, no more high maintenance women to fix, shop's closed.

'I have become a problem to myself, like land which a farmer works only with difficulty and at the cost of much sweat. For I am not investigating the tracts of the heavens, or measuring the distance of the stars, or trying to discover how the earth hangs in space. I am investigating myself, my memory, my mind.'

paraphrasing Camus

I've made Friends with the gang at my new coffee shop, Portland is dog friendly and Foxy's welcome but it's hard to get out of acquaintance mode and meet people I have anything in common with. Oregon is more like her sister Idaho than her downstairs neighbor CA.

I was getting a massage from a twenty something girl. She asked what I did before I retired and I told her. She asked for the Story of the Biggest Stunt I Ever Did and if I knew anyone 'famous.'(Questions #1 and #2) Then didn't know Glenn Plummer, Jeff Goldblume, Tom Sizemore—anyone from the 90's—amusing. I finally told her my Madonna story. When my massage was finished she went out to her waiting room and excitedly yelled, 'She's a Movie Star! She knows Madonna! Blabbity Blab!' Not even waiting until I'd left, I wanted to crawl out the window but she's on the second floor and no fire escape. Trapped. The two women waiting had blond mullets and glared daggers. I limped down, a freakish monkey in a surrealists' zoo.

I forget how wicky-wacky people can get over the entertainment industry. Once you're off the ship you're out the cocoon, it's isolating. I don't hate the business but I'm not in love with it either. (Neutral.) And I'm not up for storytelling. I don't want to dwell on the past like Lola in that Barry Manilow song. (Although I have a mannequin named Lola.) What to do what to do.

Took a French class, a finance class, all the Multnomah County Adoption classes and a couple on Home Schooling. Traveled to MN, NYC, Vancouver and LA. (With my little dog too.) Georgene visited the summer '07 and the Parents last fall. I tried volunteering at a couple places but couldn't find a good fit. (If you want people to volunteer for you, you have to be nice to them, duh.) January '08 I left Foxy in doggie day care for a month and went out to Guam then Ross, Nephew, Friend and I went to Palau. Beautiful but doomed, it's a poor country, their main source of income is fishing and oceans are depleting. Traded in the van. It was the perfect car for the time, all the cross country driving had amassed 150,000 miles, it was starting to go. I traded it for a Honda Hybrid that gets <u>horrible</u> mileage. My car gets 29 mpg, the sticker promised 49 to 51. (Why me? Why ask why.) Trying to settle amicably but it might end up in court. (Why me? Oh yea, I said that already…)

'The greatest saving one can make in the order of thought
is to accept the unintelligibility of the world—and pay attention to man.'

—Camus

On Adoption: Multnomah County gave me a 'Certificate of New Caregiver Training Completion' September '06. Every social worker I've met has been great but the Adoption Game is another book. One told me I'd have better luck if I went outside the country, the system is in such shambles. I read an essay by a Harvard professor online. According to his study, 90% of the people that consider adoption seriously enough to start the process decide against it. Ninety percent. Horrid bureaucratic nonsense, emotionally and financially draining and the people they have to deal with *are so negative* they give up.

The adoption powers in Oregon dislike separated un-Evangelical women and though discrimination against the handicapped is illegal (thank you Feds) many adoption agencies just don't care, they don't adopt to cripples. Adoption agency's are Private and get away with every type of horror show. One troglodyte actually said, 'Oh, we won't adopt to you,' when told of my disability. 'Do you realize it's against the law to discriminate against the handicapped?' I asked, stunned. 'We don't care about the law, we only care about the children.' I have 15 pages of gold in an Adoption file. To help with short term memory loss, I transcribe conversations as I have them and the Adoption file is filled with insane Hippochristian babble. (It would make a good book, Adoption Today in the USA, the rise of the Religious Reich. About a hundred pages.)

The money that changes hands is disgusting. People pay 25 / 50 G per child. That's 'normal.' It's been hard to get any real information about adopting from Africa. I was talking about safe travel on the continent, what countries to avoid, with an ADOPTION ATTORNEY. 'My husband and I just came back from Kenya, we were on safari and we loved it, why don't you adopt from there?' (This was before Kenya's election fiasco.) I knew Kenya didn't adopt to the US, but maybe she knows something I don't, after all, she's a specialist. I checked again with the state department—Kenya does not adopt to the US—Dot. It's amazing to me that *she doesn't get it, she was just there.* Yes Kenya is happy to make money off tourists but they don't give children away to the vile USA. Reminded me of the Third World song, '...don't you be the one to be caught red handed, don't you be the one who is offended...'

On Religion: There were many Homelet expeditions—Damien and I visited Calcutta a lot—only ten minutes from Montecito Heights. Making someone happy for a minute helped ease emotional pain. In addition to wine and cookies, we gave away stuffed animals, jackets, sweaters, blankets and sleeping bags. I told the staff at St Vincent De Paul's what I was doing and they let me purchase at .10 on the dollar.

Four years ago:

February 2004—Montecito Heights

...we were driving around looking for people on their own or in small groups as usual. Cold, cold night and we were enjoying ourselves, getting into a few whack conversations. Damien got caught in a God Bless You vortex with a Latin gentleman. 'God bless you!' Homelet said happily. 'God bless YOU...' Damien responded. No, God bless you...' 'No, God bless *you!* Volleying back and forth. It was sweet pure silliness but I found it annoying. 'Don't say god bless you, I said later, I don't want them to think I'm Christian. I can't stand hippochristians; my motivation is secular!' I'm giving alms to the poor to make *myself* feel better and thank Homelet for the privilege. The last thing they need is a warm dry freak preaching the Kingdom of God at them, hinting that maybe reason they're on skid row is because they don't love Jesus enough.

I've tried to lighten up, not all Christians are hippos. Even though I find the dogma ridiculous, it's no more so than any other organized religion. I pick bits of love and kindness and toss the whack proselytizing. I think reincarnation is a maybe, I feel part of a larger consciousness…bla bla. When you die and your energy goes back to the pack, do you make it better or worse? The Dalai Lama observes all religion is fairly similar and I agree, whatever your family is, your neighbors, countrymen, you may as well be too. You know when you are being good and when you're a naughty child in the wood.

I used to feel a connection with Kevin that spanned time. (Sadly gone now.) I had Real dreams as a child, we were adults on a big wooden ship at sea, it was snowing, I was wrapped in furs, Viking –ish. Real dreams. The Native Australian's think we slog through the day in order to return to reality. I used to believe that, I had fantastic dreams. Friend hypothesizes we live every life; mother, daughter, sister, brother, father, son, friend, enemy, black, white, brown, poor, wealthy, from every country, perhaps every age as well, time flows in circular waves. It's nice to think that I lived for a reason (though it's arrogant and unlikely, some things really are just luck) it might be adoption.

The reason I'm obsessed with dwarfs? I just was one. I don't feel like giving birth because I just had 10 kids in Guatemala. I'm comfortable with black males because I've been a black man. Could be true could be anything could be nothing, let your imagination loose.

I think that just like the ants I swept out of my kitchen this morning can't comprehend humans and human behavior, we don't see spirituality clearly.

Politics: Again the election game is trotted out, again I refuse to play. There isn't one human candidate, the lizard with the slickest team wins. Lets babble like freaks and try to get the wackadoo vote. Disgusting. You've read this far, I'm sure you've picked up my anarchist leanings. The system is based on cash, not human beings, it's corporate owned and too corrupt to save. I agree with Jefferson and Paine, scrape them off the bottom of our collective shoe and start fresh.

With the presidential election in '00 the United States was at the proverbial crossroads: Two paths diverged in a wood and long we stood wondering, which way will we go for the new millennium? Good vs. Evil. I believe the positive man was elected by a majority but it was so slim, the negative man was able to steal it. The Horror Show, USA Monsters, has been playing for over 7 years, ridding the world's youth of fond childhood memories like, I Love USA. We've taken the path less traveled by, preemptive strike on a poor nation run by an easily dispatched criminal with *the sole intent* of making money. (The immoral idiots can't even get that right.) My guess is we're going to pay for it, because Sadly, that has made all the difference.

Mental Health: I like to talk about and deal with life's never ending issues as they come up. It keeps them manageable, if you were a naughty child in the wood, you know it, so apologize. If you need an apology, ask for it neutrally, most people want calm resolutions. Maybe you'll have an uncomfortable minute then it's over. I like to think most people are like that.

But some wackadoo's are passive aggressive to the point of insanity. They *never* talk about issues so their shit pile grows mountainous. They become nasty because they won't apologize and evil, as they lie to protect their issues. There's a happy face for the world to see which protects the festering beleaguered ego behind the façade; fearful of people that recognize their brand of madness, they spit out quick-shot malevolence then hide behind the fake personality. I used *to laugh* at that disconnect but now, wackadoo's freak me. I can't take it, white flag, you are the meanest and craziest of all.

Most people find brain damage awkward (functioning minds have trouble comprehending, there's no point of reference) but are willing to work with you if you take time to explain your symptoms. But some clueless jerks are *afraid* of people that have been badly hurt, they're not only unsympathetic, they will actually attack to make sure you go away.

Example: My laptop was starting to die so I bought an Apple, my first. I thought I wanted to switch, believed the hype. Once home, I realized my mistake, it was too difficult (I can't *read* directions) and I'd have to buy all my programs again—another $1500—my Helpful Sales Boys didn't tell me that. Apple only allows two weeks to return but the Helpful Sales Boys told me that rule wasn't hard and was often stretched. I had Friend come over and load it back in the van. A pregnant Queezen Berry BURST from of her office and rushed me. 'You told me on the phone you had *Brain Damage*! I Don't Care!' She began <u>butting me</u> with her pregnant belly like an umpire, physically bumping me towards the door; 'you're on a fixed income? I DON'T CARE! You couldn't pack it up and put it in the car yourself? SO WHAT you're four days late!' She was horrifying, smiling a dog smile with crazee wide eyes. I was almost speechless but managed to eject 'Watch it Fatty!' the next time she touched me with her unborn spawn. 'That's it! You're Outahere!' Again, a freaking umpire. She called security and had the icky gimp was thrown out of the store *in minutes*. (Reminiscent of Bee Rainless, MD. Pregnant women equal hormonal Ogres.) Alone with no normal brain to help make sense of the bitch, I broke, narcolepsy and sucking rusty nails for a week. I called her superiors—repeatedly—wrote letters to everyone at Apple, from Steve Jobs on down, but got No Response. Apple's current campaign annoys; a slick cool young guy represents Apple, he dresses shabby chic, his tousled hair is splendid, his voice is warm—he uses his coolness to beat up a fat clueless dork that represents PC. If you're a fat dork or a crippled gimp, fuck off.

My reaction to appalling behavior is still smoky: 1st slow disbelief, then horribly hurt which is dreadful and meaningless. I can only control my reaction. Jerks are everywhere; I still need to toughen up. On the positive side, my injury has made me kinder my instinct to help is stronger my capacity for taking myself out of equations is clearer.

> 'Still today, I treat everyone with the same geniality, I am even full of consideration for the basest people: in all this there is not a grain of arrogance, of secret contempt. He whom I despise *divines* that I despise him: through my mere existence I enrage him...'

—Nietzsche

The Entertainment Industry: I put in war stories—I know they entertain but I have a pragmatic view of that reality. Every sleazy slippery tale you've ever heard about the felons, liars, child molesters, narcissistic bastards, plagiarist's, sycophants and professional grifters in the EI is TRUE; it's hard to envision the depths which some people descend to chase fame, as if they've changed species, it must be lived with until it spits up blood money and sweats on you before the lunacy sinks in. You're down the rabbit hole Dorothy and the ship has sailed, you're already on it—so pick your way through the predators and pretenders to find the humans—artists, friends and lovers.

Babylon was seductive, yet another secret club, it was fun being in on the joke of it all. Shakespeare said it best: 'All the worlds a stage and all the men and women merely players. They have their exits and their entrances and one man in his time plays many parts.' It was snarky fun to laugh at the people I'm hiding from now. Fun to make money doing shows I'd have done for free. And the folks you meet can be so adorably sweet.

I've reminisced mostly about movies but I loved working on television too. Melrose Place was about the only TV show I worked on that I watched regularly. I love the over the top wackiness of nighttime soaps, the crazier the better. I didn't write about shows that never pay residuals, shows that get cancelled, sometimes what gets cut is the funniest.

Titus was amusing, I worked on his show a couple times. Love & War was fun, it was a ½ hour sit com shot with an audience, we staged an enormous bar fight. Rehearsed for a week then performed it like a play. I thought The Jackie Tomas Show was hilarious but it was doomed. (Out side the stage in smoker's corner, Martin Mull remarked, 'sometimes you go through a script and put vertical lines through the S's.) I knew Tom Arnold from Minneapolis, he was a comedian with a good heart, a little much, he was super hyper but sweet. He had a silly act with goldfishes and would do it at the Comedy Club. I remember when he met Roseanne because the pack was all, 'poor Tom, it's just like him to fall for a fat, married woman…'

I worked on Days Of Our Lives here and there for years, acting and stunts. (I doubled Stephanie Cameron and was a secretary at the news paper) I love soap operas. It's the closest thing to theater on TV. Movies will shoot 1 to 3 pages a day, a one hour television show, 8 to 10; Soaps shoot 60 pages a day! 300 a week. If the actor is in a major story line, they work 12 hours, go home learn tomorrow's script and be back at 7 am. The crew does a technical rehearsal with the actors and then they shoot once, moving on. Rarely will there be a Take 2 and it has to from a real screw up.

Doubling Stephanie was fun she had a long ridiculous story line that went on and on: Once, running from her crazee ex husband (who had trapped her in the basement of a cabin in the grand canyon and she'd escaped by whacking him with a shovel) she'd fallen down a mineshaft. They had her down there hanging on a rope for a week, talking to herself, then time to climb out. The camera was above looking down; I had to climb 15 feet to reach the ledge. Shit, the rope was thin, I was afraid I wouldn't be able to do it. Taped shows don't call action, instead it's a countdown 5, 4, 3 and then you silently count 2, 1, action—adrenaline charged I scrambled up the rope—thank God I made it—and hear the directors disembodied voice from the control booth. 'That was good but you made it look too easy, do it again.' Doh! I BARELY made it the second time, had to walk up the wall with my feet while I pulled my body up.' That was great!' (Thank You Scuva.) I loved that crew—makeup and hair were outrageous, they won Emmy's and made me breathtaking exquisite—but I never saw any of it air. Once in the kitchen I heard my voice yelling from the television, I was saving my children from fire on Rescue 911. (Fire.)

Pacific Blue has disappeared but they had a good run. They were Baywatch on bikes. I'd read for a lead and didn't even get a call back. I would always tell myself, they're looking for a different 'type' couple months later I'm hired as Darlene Vogel's stunt double—she was playing the part I'd read for—we're exactly the same 'type' (height weight age hair color.) I had to laugh and admit to myself that my audition skills sucked. (Sadly true and there was no excuse; I'd done my own casting, helped Snyder and I'd watched casting with Ken. It's easy to get cast if you relax, production is rooting for you, they want strong choices, still I'd freeze and act stiffly.) It's one of the reasons I liked doing stunts, no auditioning. And there was much less 'who do you know' and more 'are you any good? can you do it?'

I had my acting need fulfilled by my weekly acting class (that's where I met Alison years ago, scene study). I had the occasional acting job, mostly low budget films directed by Friends. I booked a few through regular auditioning but not enough money to live on. Acting was a fun hobby and stunts were for money. It's strange to separate the two but most stunt people don't act.

'It is on this moment of balance I must end:
the strange moment when spirituality rejects ethics,
when happiness springs from the absence of hope,
when the mind finds it's justification in the body.'

—Camus

Coming back from the CVA has been tempestuous. I had to grow up again and learn many things twice. Strange how similar Damien and Tony seem, I didn't want either relationship after a couple months yet they both lasted eternities. Had to learn No Meth Addicts twice and Stop The Boob Grabber twice! I'd forgotten about a fat foul Santa in OZ, I sat on his lap and he did the same thing, 'accidentally' rubbed his paw against my nipple and I froze! Didn't have him fired. Wazzthatabout? I search my memory but don't come up with any childhood horror shows. Bad Men just freak me.

I can run a little—sloppy goofy—I run up and down my hall because it's safe, I can easily reach either wall when I start to fall, Foxy chasing makes me laugh. I've relaxed my work out. I walk the dog and do yoga (can't find a decent gym in Portland.) Symptoms I didn't mention, my taste buds were desensitized by the CVA, everything tasted like sand for a couple of years. I was eating left handed (surprisingly hard) scooping cardboard into a chipmunk mouth. And any loud noise is a shotgun blast behind me. I startle easily and often smack my compromised hand on whatever is near. Not held by gravity it goes off like a rocket.

'As nightfall does not come at once, neither does oppression. In both instances, there is a twilight when everything remains seemingly unchanged. And it is in such twilight that we all must be most aware of change in the air—however slight— lest we become unwitting victims of the darkness.

—Justice William O. Douglas

If all greenhouse emissions were stopped today, it's too late, it was too late years ago. We knew that as a country in the 80's. If I was born in the 80's I'd be pissed. Just because Carter was defeated doesn't make him wrong on science. Weather will get worse, millions will be displaced and we'll see the empire unravel. What will come from the chaos? I'm happy I'll be alive for it, feels preordained.

Journal November—98

Friday…what the fuck did I do Friday? My memory is GONE—I dreamt that my memory Really was gone—short term memory loss gone—dreaming that I had to leave some kind of passwords or codes to pick up a plane ticket.

Sounds familiar, that's what I have to do.

THANK YOU FAMILY & FRIENDS

I adore my parents, they're lovely and loveable and I did write about fun we've had but calm waters are boring. I kept a couple of arguments to show how stroke symptoms affected me emotionally, how freakish scary weird it was to revert back to childhood. (Backward circles of time.) I love you Mom, I'm sorry if this book hurt you. Thanks to my brothers, you took care me and my paper trails for years. Husband I love you, our relationship may seem odd to others but whatever.

Thank you Nancy, Yolanda and Elaine from Firefighters Quest, Sharon, USC-LAC's social worker, thank you Phoenix Society www.phoenix-society.org, you all caught me in the middle of a free fall.

Thank you Stuntwomen's Foundation for $13,500 that cash kept me going, I love you.

Thanx to CafeDeb's models—Marisa, Jennifer and Ménage from Minneapolis, Jessel, Jillian, Lux, Velvet Rose, Phillip, Adrienne, CC and Mark from the LA area, you helped me want to be creative and being sexy is silly naughty fun. CafeDeb's high mark was 290 thousand hits in July 2005 I stopped at volume 30 when I left Venice. Jennifer is the cover and the Nude Man is walking around Disney's Concert Hall. Thanx Conrad & Scott for the tutoring. The site's still up but I'm done with magazines, not sure what I'll do with it next but the name is great. CafeDeb's easy to remember and could be anything.

I *thought* gimp was finished in '07 but my life has a soundtrack I didn't want to delete the lyrics. Wow! It's hard to get copyright permission's. Thank you Joyce Miller at Integrated Writer Services www.writerservices.biz she tracked down copyright holders (a single song can have more than 10 and we were asking for everything gratis.) It took *months*. That job would have made my head explode. Every month that went by waiting for copyright releases was good for gimp. If I don't have a deadline, I pick and poke, shine and polish. Thank You Musicians and Authors I've quoted, (then paraphrased) I love you all. Even though, at the end of the day, I couldn't deal with all of the codas on my manuscript (we'll give you permission gratis if gimp is free / if gimp is fat / if gimp can balance the ball on it's nose) I don't love you any less.

Ken Russell, I have a lovely B & W portrait of us picking our noses at The Chiller Convention, its perfect and look at it whenever I need to lighten up. (Thanx Elise for sharing him.)

Thanx PaulDDB, Dr Carol, Fred, Lloyd, Alvin, Genevieve, Mikey C, Michael F, Terri A, Robin Anders, Jennifer C, Jenny S, Al Beaulieu, Laney Sayles, Big Johnny, even Damien & Tony—and all of my beautiful neighbors at We Ho Manor—meow meows to you all. You accepted the new me before I did, it helped the transition. Thanx for The Mexican, Hank.

Thank you Velvet, Birgit, Alison, Cheryl my LA women I could and did lean on. Thanx Betsy and Co for the love and sanity checks. Thanx Georgene, Jamie, Rowan and Ken Coffman, Thanx Charlene & Cherish, Teo, Mikkio (and wee little baby) Dez and Rich. I love you Mouse. To Melinda, Rebecca, Tom & Bruce, thank you for the warm and sane places to stay.

Friends I've made post injury: Jeff Lindsey, Priest, Maribel, Courtney and Bill Clawson, I love you. Thanx for seeing me not my injury.

Thank you Bill, Bennie B and Jerry for pushing through a 450 page 1st draft. I needed to hear I wasn't stupid and needed help editing it down. (Example: I had a lot of road rage stories, how to pick one? Thanks to Bennie, I chose funny.) Jerry told me not to pay a stranger 5G, to edit gimp myself. I'm glad I did. I'm sorry I'm forgetting You; I love You and think of You all the time. It's brain damage that makes me forget You. (My excuse for everything.)

Thanx to the doctors, nurses, therapists and anesthetists that didn't hurt me; the short list is troubling. If you are one of the dip-shits I trashed, remember I'm brain damaged, that couldn't be true! (And, phuk hew.)

'The world is beautiful and outside it there is no salvation'

—Camus

This book is vanity published as a gift for my family, friends and other survivors. I tried to find a literary agent and had one introduced by *two different* producer friends (the EI is a small bio coastal town.) While he generally liked my writing, he found gimp too rambling and thought it would only be of interest to family and friends. That was a nice pass from a sweet guy—and it killed me—that was my first and last attempt to sell gimp properly. I can't 'sell myself' I never could. (It's unseemly, smells desperate.) I wouldn't be adverse to another version being mass-produced but I'm not interested in pursuing it alone. I need an agent, manager or attorney to deal with the publishing reality; I need a wall against that beast.

Have I explained brain damage? Burns? E me if you need more. It took five years to feel more happy than sad but I do. I've accepted my limitations (somewhat mostly kinda) and that took five as well. Burn scars can be angry red for years before they subside, mine finally turned white a year ago, wear pressure garments, they work. Keep working out, its fun and good for you. Try to control depression don't let it keep you indoors. Maybe a Homelet activity, doesn't matter how or what it is. Be patient and seek other survivors.

If you've had a life altering injury it takes *years* to recover. The masses can't imagine the Clarity / Love combo that is part of the near death experience. They fear, so only see pain and loss. They will leave, it has nothing to you with You, it's their nature.

I'm still lonely but like my own company again. No dirt nap, I want to adopt a couple of sisters and watch the horror show. (The Weather Channel) The earth has become Crazee Land and I want to see it for as long as I can.

It's hard to wrap so here's my George Clooney story: I was doubling Sela Ward on Sisters. I was long blonde and she was short brunette but with her wig and wardrobe, I was a good replica. I had a scene with George; he was a ghost / she was blind / can't remember exactly. The stunt wasn't hard, being pushed to the ground by George with a crash pad to land on.

A year or few earlier I had worked on a pilot starring Pam Dauber and Clooney. They were private detectives who didn't get along (very original) Pam would start yammering and George would retreat to fantasy. Three (four?) sexy young blondes would appear kissing him, crawling onto his lap, massaging his shoulders, his chest—then Pam would snap him back to reality. I remembered that job fondly; I thought I'd play him. 'We've met before,' I said when we were introduced. He couldn't place me but he's friendly and was into the guessing game. No, it wasn't at a party, not mutual friends… 'Give me a hint.' 'The last time we were together you had your tongue in my mouth.' Caught by surprise! Oh no! Who is she! Did I *really* forget making out with her? I watched this amusing brain activity for a minute then told him it was work. We laughed about the pilot, it didn't sell. He was leaving Sisters for ER.

XOX alisa

alisa40@Gmail.com
alisachristensen.com
cafedeb.com
picasaweb.google.com / FoxyTheLittleDog

978-0-595-51065-8
0-595-51065-5